THE **MERCURY READER**
A CUSTOM PUBLICATION

**English Department
Hudson Valley Community College
Composition II
Volume One**

PEARSON

Custom
Publishing

Director of Database Publishing: Michael Payne
Sponsoring Editor: Natalie Danner
Development Editor: Katherine R. Gehan
Editorial Assistant: Abbey Briggs
Marketing Manager: Kerry Chapman
Operations Manager: Eric M. Kenney
Production Project Manager: Jennifer M. Berry
Rights Editor: Francesca Marcantonio
Cover Designers: Renée Sartell and Sharon Treacy

Cover Art: "Clouds," by Kathi Mirza and Scott Olsen; "Starry Night Sky," Copyright © Orion Press; "Sunset," by Darryl Torksler, and "Gigantia Mountains & Sea of Cortes," by R.G.K. Photography, Copyright © Tony Stone Images. "Dime," courtesy of the Shaw Collection.

Please visit our websites at *www.pearsoncustom.com* and *www.mercuryreader.com.*
Attention bookstores: For permission to return any unsold stock, contact us at *pe-uscustomreturns@pearsoncustom.com.*

ISBN: **0536691746**

PEARSON CUSTOM PUBLISHING
75 Arlington St., Suite 300
Boston, MA 02116

☙ General Editors ☙

Janice Neuleib
Illinois State University

Kathleen Shine Cain
Merrimack College

Stephen Ruffus
Salt Lake Community College

In Memoriam:
Maurice Scharton (†)
Illinois State University

☙ CONTENTS ☙

POETRY

	A	B	C	D	F
General	The A paper is generally excellent. It is characterized by maturity, insightfulness, originality, or creativity in developing the central idea. A strong sense of purpose, a keen awareness of audience, clear organization, effective language and full development are the hallmarks of the A paper.	The B paper organizes well thought-out material into coherent unified paragraphs that have clear topic sentences in support of a central idea. Overall, the B paper, while not as insightful as an A paper, is above average.	The C paper generally demonstrates satisfactory work and is not seriously deficient in any way. It may meet all of the requirements of the assignment, but it does not distinguish itself as having exceeded those requirements. Though adequacy in content, organization, style, and development may be evident, the C paper may lack the originality of ideas, fluency, and inventiveness of the A or B paper. In addition, the C paper may have mechanical errors.	The D paper is deficient in content, organization, style, and/or mechanics. Its sentences and ideas may be incoherent and/or loosely connected. The D paper's problems impair its overall effectiveness.	The F paper contains excessive weaknesses in content, organization, sentence structure, diction, and/or mechanics. It may contain numerous errors that impede comprehension and compromise clarity. A paper may also receive an F for failure to fulfill assignment requirements or for plagiarism.
	The instructor will apply the criteria below as appropriate within the context of the assignment.				
Content	The A paper develops an engaging, focused topic with thoroughness, clarity, and creativity. It exhibits interesting and well-developed examples, explanations, and supporting evidence.	The B paper develops a focused topic with strong development with evidence that is detailed and well supported, and an above average level of sophistication.	The C paper develops and supports ideas in a satisfactory manner. Ideas are convincing but may lack appropriate development and depth.	The D paper may have vague, unsophisticated, undeveloped, or inappropriate content.	The F paper may have insufficient development of topic and/or little or no specific detail.
Organi-zation	Beyond a well organized introduction, body, and conclusion in support of the central idea, the A paper is characterized by a logical sequence of ideas; graceful transitions; and balanced, thorough development.	The B paper is well organized; it contains an introduction, well-developed paragraphs, and a conclusion. A logical sequence and balance of ideas as well as appropriate transitions are evident.	The C paper evidences a recognizable pattern with a central idea: unified, coherent paragraphs; and transitions.	The D paper is often unclear, indirect, or illogical	The F paper lacks a central idea, a clear organizational plan, and development.
Style	The A paper exhibits a sophisticated use of sentence structure and language, including sentence variety as well as precise, appropriate diction, tone, and figures of speech.	The B paper demonstrates effective sentence variety, and tone.	The C paper may not be engaging, but the style is appropriate to the subject matter and audience. Inconsistent tone, and/or unsophisticated sentence structure may occasionally weaken the paper.	The D paper is characterized by simplistic, undeveloped, or inappropriate style.	The F paper has inconsistent, incoherent, monotonous or awkward sentence structure or diction that results in a loss of clarity.
Mechan-ics	The A paper is virtually free of mechanical problems, including sentencing, spelling, punctuation, and grammar errors. It demonstrates careful proofreading and adherence to format conventions.	The B paper does not contain serious or numerous mechanical errors. It demonstrates generally correct grammar, punctuation, spelling, and sentence structure.	The C paper demonstrates a basic knowledge and application of grammar, spelling, sentence structure, and punctuation. However, it may have errors that detract from the overall effectiveness of the paper.	The D paper may include significant problems in spelling, punctuation, sentence structure, and diction that interfere with communication.	The F paper contains many errors in sentencing, grammar, punctuation, and spelling that block communication.

ENGLISH DEPARTMENT GRADING GUIDELINES FOR USE IN EVALUATING STUDENT WRITING:

The English Department has prepared the following guidelines for use in evaluating student writing. It is assumed that before the following criteria are applied, the work has met the stated requirements of the assignment and is submitted in the appropriate format.

THE READING AND WRITING PROCESS

Perhaps it seems odd to write to a student about reading since you have been reading and writing most of your life and are no doubt quite an expert at it. Most of us are more confident about our reading skills than we are about our writing skills, though reading and writing are certainly connected. All our instincts tell us that the two activities come from the same skills, but those instincts may not tell us the whole story. Writing involves creating or composing meaning (although the section on writing that follows will complicate even this definition a bit), but reading can be even more complex than writing. Reading can mean different kinds of activities depending on how we define the word. For example, think of what we mean when we say that we "read" someone's meaning. We mean that we interpret what the person "really" means, sometimes even when he or she has meant something quite different from what apparently was said. This kind of reading, reading between the lines so to speak, is often what good reading of written texts demands as well. An essay or story can mean something quite different from what it first appears to mean, and it can mean different things to different readers at different times.

The Reading Process

Reading involves perceptual responses that work quite differently from those we use when we write. Readers *select* what they notice in order to be able to read at all. When we read, we notice certain information and ignore other information. So when you read a particular piece of writing, you do not notice everything. Instead, you notice what matters to you. You relate what you are reading to what you already know, and you make associations and connections to your own life as you read.

Reading should be an active process, a process like that described by Great Books advocate Mortimer Adler. In his essay "How to Mark a Book," he explains that good readers write in books, or at least they write on a note pad near the book. The notes that Adler refers to are indications of those associations and connections you make with the material, what you agree with and what you do not, what you are learning and what you already know. This essay is an argument to readers *to own* what they read—to consume it as they would a steak and to make it a part of themselves.

Take, for example, a brief essay by Judy Brady, "Why I Want a Wife," in which she humorously lists all the many reasons she would find having a wife useful to her in her life (this essay can be found at the end of this introduction). While reading this essay actively, you might circle a point that you want to come back to review later, or you might argue with her assumptions about gender roles. In whatever way you mark this text, your markings will be your own and will indicate how you have connected to the essay.

Even when reading and responding to a text, you make decisions about it at an unconscious level. In every part of life, we unknowingly block out much of the information that comes at us simply because we cannot possibly take it all in. Children who have been blind from birth are overwhelmed if they regain their sight, because they cannot select from the mass of information that comes at them from all sides. They have not developed an unconscious ability to select what to notice and in what order. Reading is like this, and part of learning to read college work involves learning how to manage the reading demands of college courses. At first, college reading can feel to a student the way the world must feel to a newly-sighted person. What should you notice first? How can you take it all in and make sense of it? That is where active reading such as Adler's can come in handy. You can control how and what you notice in any essay or book by responding actively in writing *to* that text. By doing this, you begin to control your ability to select what you will think and feel about the vast quantity of material you are asked to read.

Prereading

As a beginning reader, you learned over time to block incoming signals in many quite subtle ways. As you scan the page of a newspaper looking for a sports score or a weather report, all the rest of the information on the page disappears from your notice. Actually, this kind of reading used to be called "speed reading," but in 1949, reading specialist Louise Rosenblatt named it "*efferent reading*," from the Latin word *efferare*, to carry away. She meant that when reading for information, we scan the text quickly to catch the information needed for a specific purpose. Study skills courses often suggest that students *preview* a text before reading it. The purpose of this preview is to scan for the gist of the information, its basic outline, the main points, and anything the writer has highlighted as important information that a reader will want to carry away from the reading. This kind of previewing can help you to read and remember the important concepts in a text. These concepts can in turn help you to fit subordinate points into the overall order of the reading. Finding what you want to "carry away" is the key to rapid and efficient reading. Just the opposite will occur when you are distracted and unable to select effectively.

Vocabulary and Concepts

We need to feel in control of the meaning of a book or essay that we are reading. Too many unfamiliar concepts or words can distract us from our response to a text. A pattern of unfamiliar words will confuse or discourage us. Each text has its optimal mix of known and unknown words and concepts for any particular reader. We tend to be most attracted to a book or essay that contains just the right mix of old and new information for our own personal store of knowledge. For example, if you have an amateur interest in science but are not an expert in paleontology, a science writer such as Stephen Jay Gould might provide an interesting and stimulating reading experience, especially if you have a fairly extensive science vocabulary. If you don't, however, a reading such as this can at first appear quite complex and challenging. Any reader should understand that the tools (appropriate vocabulary, concepts, and interest) he or she brings to a reading will strongly affect his or her efficiency and enjoyment of that reading.

Authority

Another aspect of reading selectivity concerns the authority that the reader gives to the text. If you know, for instance, that Stephen Jay Gould is not only an expert in paleontology, biology, and the history of science, but also a talented science writer, and you are reading his essay "Evolution as Fact and Theory," you can more easily overlook a lack of clarity in certain passages, or even distracting misprints (if they are there), because of your underlying trust in the author and his authority on his subject. What minor problems you do encounter can be overlooked, not only because of the enjoyment you experience reading his essay, but because you give the author the benefit of the doubt because of his considerable knowledge.

Purpose and Freedom of Choice

To understand how the reading process works best, we should think about what happens when we read. First, we have to consider *why we are reading*. What is the purpose of the task? Our purpose determines almost everything else that happens when we read. As we mentioned earlier, Louise Rosenblatt divides reading into two major types: reading for pleasure and reading for information. Pleasure reading usually occurs when we choose a Web site, book, newspaper, or magazine and read whatever strikes our fancy. We feel comfortable and easy, or if we do not, we move on to something else we do like to read. Reading for information can also be comfortable and easy. For example, most of us enjoy finding out about sports stars or gleaning health information from the newspaper.

On the other hand, if we have been assigned by a teacher to read a book or essay, the process can differ considerably from what happens at the kitchen table over coffee and a newspaper, or at our desk as we surf the Web. When *we choose* the reading material, even that with detailed technical information that is demanding to read, we still tend to enjoy the experience. When we stop enjoying it, we simply stop reading. If a reading is assigned, however, and we have no choice but to get through it, reading becomes a different kind of task, especially if we do not find the topic already intrinsically interesting. When someone else tells us what to read, we may have to *find* ways to enjoy reading!

Much of academic reading is assigned reading. With this type of reading, it may become necessary to look for personal motivators for reading, since we sometimes do not concentrate well when someone else directs our concentration. It is not much use just saying that you need an "A" in a course, because external motivations like grades can wear thin quickly. In effect, you want to persuade yourself that you have your own reasons for reading a class assignment.

Read closely the brief essay, "Why I Want a Wife." First, and not to be underestimated, it is an "easy read." On the surface, it is simple to understand and "fits into" what most of us already know and think. In this essay, Brady tells the reader that husbands have it easy, or at least they did before wives began to act like husbands. She also tells us that the person who takes care of a household has a lot to do and earns little appreciation. That, too, is common knowledge in this time and era. The only aspect of the essay that might cause comment or dissonance is its sarcastic and critical tone, which leaves us feeling a bit accused, even if we aren't anyone's wife or husband. So though we might find something to disagree with in this very "readable" and comfortable essay, still so much of it is familiar to us that we do feel in control as readers. Thus, responding to Brady's essay is easy because the text gives us the chance to feel confident and successful when we have completed it.

Suggestions for Learning How to Read Actively

One of the difficulties with college reading may be that many students try to read everything as if they were reading Brady's familiar and comfortable essay. In fact, readings vary considerably depending on whether we are familiar and comfortable with the text or whether we find the text challenging or beyond our usual scope. Often, college readings can be complex, and by their very nature are likely to contain materials that are unfamiliar. The task of reading then becomes more difficult. Selecting what to read and how to read when we are faced with unfamiliar and complex texts challenges even the most experienced readers. For someone just getting used to college, the task can be daunting. Here are some suggestions for ways to attack the problem.

Read as if you were interested in the subject. As noted earlier, when we read what we like, reading is much more interesting and vital. A natural interest in the subject certainly makes the task easier, but when you do not have a natural interest in the subject, some other way must be found. Take again the example of a science essay by Stephen Jay Gould. You are not interested in science, but the essay has been assigned. The question then becomes how to find a way to "get into" the essay. Surveying the first sentences in the text and getting an idea of the content will help. What is the issue of the essay? Consider what you already know and what you need to know to get involved in the subject matter of the essay. Consider what you could learn from the essay. Think of what there might be to argue with in the essay. Do you agree with it? What might be wrong in the essay? However you decide to approach it, be creative and brave in finding ways to focus your attention and interest on the reading.

Read as if you know what is going on. This suggestion may seem contradictory, since the problem usually is just the opposite: the reader of college texts may be quite perplexed by unfamiliar vocabulary and concepts. Prereading the reading can help here. Skim the headings, noting what makes sense, and speculating on what the whole text will be about. Read over the first sentence in each paragraph (usually the thesis sentence of that paragraph), trying to get the gist of the information or the mood of the writer. Select what is known from what is unknown and move forward by reading the material on the assumption that the text does make sense. When the reading becomes confusing, return to the overview you gleaned from your prereading of the material and decide how the new information fits into the already familiar. Find ways to identify the information in the text with things you already know. If necessary, ask for help so that you have enough familiar information to begin to "own" the work you are reading.

Read as if you had an expert next to you to ask questions about the text.
If the reading does not capture your attention, the problem may be simply total incompatibility of interests. If so, an expert could help to explain why the topic is important. Imagine what to ask that expert. The same would be true if the concepts and vocabulary are too

complex. What questions would an expert be able to answer? Where could that expert be found? Would anyone else in class know more? What could the library or the Web offer? The point is to approach the reading *as if* an expert could help with vocabulary and concepts that might distract and diffuse your attention.

Read as if you were as knowledgeable, important, and powerful as the writer.   Readers often become discouraged when the text seems frighteningly important. No one likes to admit it, but works in print tend to be believed more readily than the spoken word. We unconsciously think to ourselves, "This person managed to have her work printed in a major journal or magazine. It must be important, so I had better not question it. In fact, if I cannot 'get it' on first reading, I must have a problem, not the writer." Assume, rather, that you can "get" the text, that you may even be able to think critically about it, and that you have the power as a reader to add a new perspective to the text. Although the writer has written with the intention of being read, it is also true that the writer may even be wrong or misguided. If after a close reading the material still is not clear, you might want to suggest to the writer that she or he could write more clearly next time!

Read as if you were going to help the writer revise the text.   Reading specialists tend to talk a great deal about *active reading*, a concept that means that the reader has as much authority over the text as the writer. Read with the assumption that you can ask important questions of the writer and that you can even suggest revisions to the writer, both of which could have made the writer's points more effective or his or her argument stronger. Again, the reader has to be creative and brave. Ask questions like, "How could this essay have been organized more effectively?" "What other points could have made it more interesting?" "What information might be missing that would fill in gaps?" "What other examples could have been given to enrich the reading?" For example, the reader might imagine asking Gould to explain a scientific concept behind an argument or to give more details in an example. An active reader assumes he or she has the right to ask these types of questions when reading.

Read as if you were going to write a response to the text. This suggestion extends the concepts already presented. Read a piece of writing as if the writer had asked for written feedback and suggestions for improving the text, or for counter-arguments. When writing about the text, write as if the writer has asked for reader responses and reactions. Explain how the text could have been more interesting, clearer, or better argued. What kind of response could you then expect from reading the text? Reading in this way helps to keep you active and alert and also helps you in selecting how and what to concentrate on in the text.

Suggestions for Responding to Literature

We use various techniques to write about literature depending on our reasons for writing and the audience we have in mind when we write. The following discussions of writing about literature will give you a sense of the kind of questions readers ask about a text when they use a particular analytical technique. If you think about a piece of literature using these explanations, you will get a feel for how a technique works, but keep in mind that these points are not meant to be detailed instruction in writing about literature.

Basic Techniques

Techniques familiar to you probably include using **journal** writing to help yourself understand or appreciate a piece of literature; **explication**, the detailed interpretive or supportive comments you may have read or perhaps written in a literature course; and **reviews** such as you may have read in a newspaper or magazine.

Journals. Your instructor may ask you to write a journal response to a reading, which simply expresses how you feel about the text and attempts to sort out your reactions to it. Often literary critics and English or theater professors will begin this way because they first need to know how they respond to a text before they can translate their initial thoughts into publishable work. Reactions and thoughts written while we are experiencing a particular text can give us new insight. You may find yourself discovering new ideas about the text as you begin to write. Keeping a reading journal may enrich your experience and let you know in later years how your responses have changed with time. It actually helps to write as we read, especially if we are trying to see a story in a new way. What is going to happen? How do we feel about the characters? Do the actions of the characters suit our values? Do they startle or amaze us? Is the author writing in a style that is new or different? What is our reaction to it?

Explicating. The word *explication*, which means "to make clear," is most often used in reference to written texts. Once you have explicated a text, you understand it quite thoroughly. An explication of a poem, for example, involves a line-by-line discussion of meaning, symbols, metaphors, unusual word choices, rhythm, and meter— anything that contributes to the experience of the poem. If you are reading a story, you may talk about setting, conflict, characters, tone, theme, and symbols. Sometimes writers tell readers about the general content of a text in order to make discussion possible. Teachers sometimes provide supportive explications that outline or summarize plays or novels. The kind of summary or simple statement of theme found in an explication may be a first assignment from your instructor, or it might be used in a group project. Each person in the group might read a different story and write an explication to share with the group so that the others can judge for themselves whether they too want to read the story.

Reviewing. This kind of writing about literature is common in magazines and newspapers that review books and other types of art, where it serves to persuade the reader about the quality of the work. Thus the *New York Times* might review a new book by a famous author, or *Rolling Stone* might review a new music CD (the lyrics count as "popular" literature). Your instructor might assign you to write a review of a story, asking that you assess its value to readers in general or that you discuss the importance of the story to you and other readers like you.

Advanced Critical Techniques

More advanced writing about literature, called literary analysis or criticism, involves the focused use of a particular theory on how to read literature. Of the many reading theories available, we will mention eight that are relatively well-known among students of literature. **Formalist** (also called New Critical) theory exploits irony and other multiple meanings found in the words and ideas in a literary work. You might use a **reader-response** theory to explain your personal reactions to the literary text. Or you could try some kind of psychological theory—**Freudian** or **Jungian**—to analyze the characters and images in a literary text. Some theories emphasize literature's tendency to criticize the dominant customs and ideas in society: in particular, **feminist** and **deconstructionist** interpreters of literature hope to foster social and intellectual change. If you are interested in politics or history, you might refer to **Marxist** thought or use **New Historicist** theory to demonstrate the systems of ideas (also called "ideologies") inherent in the text.

Formalism and Reader-Response. These approaches produce what has been called "close reading" or "critical reading" of a literary text. In formalist readings of a text, you concentrate on unpacking the language of the text to help the reader enjoy the complexity of literature, to learn how to understand the many meanings in a literary text, and to renew the excitement of the first experience of reading a literary text. When you do a formalist reading, you don't bring in the author's life or intentions, nor do you talk about the historical context, because both biography and history lead outside the text. This kind of reading has some practical uses as well. Written essay tests, for example, often involve this type of approach.

Your instructor may ask you to explain your personal reaction to a literary text. In sharing your reader-response, you allow another reader to participate vicariously in your experience of the text and to learn something about your individual emotional or aesthetic values. By reading a collection of readers' responses to a text, you can increase your own repertoire of potential responses, thereby becoming a more skillful and flexible student of literature. Naturally, other people's reader-responses will differ from yours because their life experiences differ. However, you probably will find that you share assumptions with some people, and as you come to know one another more intimately, you may become a community of readers who understand texts in similar ways. Perhaps you'll even form a reading group outside of class.

Freudian and Jungian Psychological Interpretation. Freud and Jung were among the founders of psychoanalysis, a medical technique for dealing with mental illnesses by bringing to conscious awareness the thoughts and feelings that people can't deal with, which they force into the unconscious part of their minds. In psychoanalysis, the doctor and patient discuss the unconscious material that is expressed in the patient's dreams, memories, fantasies, and reflections on life. It is only natural that psychoanalytic theories about human nature and behavior are useful in explaining the motivations and meanings in literary texts. If a character in fiction unconsciously behaves in self-defeating ways, seeming to experience internal conflicts based on repressed sexual feelings about her father, Sigmund Freud's theories about the Electra complex may help give the story meaning. Likewise Carl Jung's psychological theories may apply to stories in which the plot seems similar to the plots we find in mythology—such as the conflicts between gods and mortal in Greco-Roman literature. Psychoanalytic theories help us to see the logic and cause that underlie even the oddest patterns of human behavior, and they help us to see the universal human experiences that create the possibility for transformation, new growth, and development in the human character. As we grow older and reread our favorite pieces of literature, our psychological interpretations may change. We may find that Freud suits us better at first, and that Jung, who has been called the psychologist of the second half of life, suits us later.

Feminist and Deconstructionist Interpretation. In recent years writers and teachers have followed the lead of French intellectuals such as Hélène Cixous and Michel Foucault in stressing the ways in which texts, especially literary texts, reflect their time and contemporary political and social values. In a sense, the texts that we read also hold society together by conveying assumptions so basic that we don't even recognize we have them. You can see that every culture has hidden assumptions when you look at a culture different from your own. In reading Shakespeare, for example, you might notice that he makes assumptions about race and gender that would be quite shocking to most readers if they were presented today. What do our own cultural assumptions about gender bring to our reading of a work? Why were almost all the "great books" of the early 1900s written by men? What do we know about life in the South in the 1930s when we read a story by Maya Angelou? These can be exciting questions for writers to contemplate. The feminist criticism that results from these readings helps to point out the ways in which a society prefers and promotes men over women, and the understanding gained may serve as motivation for political action intended to help improve the status of women in society.

If you compare one literary text to another or look at the same text in different forms, you may start to see that some quite famous texts are neither so perfect nor so whole as they first appear. You may notice that the text was constructed with a point of view that is clearly different from yours or that it serves a political purpose, helping to keep the basic truths of the society safe from question. You may see where the text contradicts itself, where the author has overlooked or deliberately suppressed certain competing points of view. You may see that the text depends on oppositions (called "binaries") between male and female, sane and insane, legal and illegal, and that you must believe in the importance of binaries if the text is to make sense to you. If you stop believing in the truth or importance of binaries, you may find that the meaning of the text breaks down. If you continue thinking about how language works, you eventually will begin wondering about how it works to control you. Does your awareness of yourself originate in the language your mind creates? If so, is there really any reality outside language? Deconstructing a text in this way may help you see how language and culture work to control the way you think.

Marxist and New Historicist Interpretation. Like feminist and deconstructionist interpretation, Marxism and New Historicism serve the purposes of cultural and social analysis. Marxist theory points out the ways that the concrete facts of everyday life affect the production of text. For example, a predominantly middle-class ("bourgeois") society will produce artistic works that promote the individualistic achievement and striving that characterize a capitalist economy. A predominantly working-class ("proletarian") society will produce works that value the collective over the individual. Reading from a Marxist view may encourage you to research more about the living conditions found in the setting of the literary work or during the time it was composed. A little research in Marxist theory may help you to understand how the class system in Renaissance England—which included an aristocracy, a middle class, and a large population of poor working people—affected what Shakespeare presented on stage.

If you like to read historical fiction, you will probably enjoy the "New Historicist" style of interpretation. In fact, the basic idea of new historicism is that there isn't much difference between history and literature. It won't do to think of history as objective fact, and fiction as artistic interpretation, because both contain fact and interpretation so intricately interwoven that you're never sure which you're reading at any given moment. For example, if you read what passed for "history" of the United States in the first half of the twentieth century, you'll notice that historians treated the white European settlers a lot more gently than they deserved, given the liberties that Europeans took with the environment and the people who were already living here. You may formulate historically-based research questions about a literary work. What do we know about the historical period in which Hawthorne wrote "Rappaccini's Daughter"? Was Hawthorne a Puritan? What were his responses to his ancestors and to his reading of their history? Having asked those questions, you may begin to see how those ideas that a culture values create the stories it tells itself, and that those stories then serve as the shared knowledge that holds the culture together.

Often, students doing academic reading assume that the reading can not be amusing or pleasing. Within this text, *The Mercury Reader*, there is a wide variety of reading. Of the essays and literature included, some are very factual and about issues we face as a society; others are fictional but nonetheless speak to many of the same concerns.

Use the suggestions above to get the most out of each selection. These readings can serve a variety of purposes, but the first should be to enjoy reading them. You also may find that reading these and other writings helps you develop your own writing voice or style by consciously (or unconsciously) imitating those writers you like. Even for those writers you do not "resonate" with, there can be a certain pleasure in successfully mastering a reading that you have not particularly liked or agreed with. If a reading gives you the energy to agree or disagree with it, or the idea for a way to write an interesting essay of your own, it has served you well. So there are lots of ways to enjoy a selection. Perhaps the greatest gift to be gained through reading is how we grow and change through it. The reading process is organic and continues as we learn to be more critical readers and to take personal "possession" of the essays and books we read.

The Writing Process

Writing ought to be as natural a process as talking or reading, but for a variety of reasons most writers find classroom composition challenging. The root of this problem lies in the ways that writers have learned to read and write. Readers must focus their attention and bring certain interests and capacities to their reading experiences, whereas writers have to diffuse their attention to consider all the possible items that could go into the text being composed. In addition, writers usually have to consider the potential reader's many responses to the text being written. Thus, a reader concentrates on understanding a text, but a writer concentrates on making the text understandable to others. A piece of writing that is meant to communicate clearly contains many qualities and characteristics in one seemingly simple text. Brady's "Why I Want a Wife" appeals to a variety of readers in a variety of times and places because the writer has managed to express not only her own frustrations but also those of others with experiences similar to hers. Such an essay appears to be easy to write because it is easy to read and understand, but the ingredients that go into the composition of such a text are many.

Rhetorical Considerations

Traditional writing instruction has focused on the qualities of a completed text: organization (thesis, support, elaboration), style (diction, figures of speech, tone, voice), and surface conventions important to final copyediting and proofreading (punctuation, format, word choice, etc.). These qualities are called *rhetorical* considerations, in that they focus on the final output or form of writing—the *product*—rather than the *process* of writing.

Classical divisions of writing have been built around the rhetorical triangle of ethos, logos, and pathos. These divisions are based on the emphasis of the writing and assume that a writer has a purpose in mind when producing a text: to express (ethos), to explain (logos), or to move or persuade (pathos). In expressive writing, the writer emphasizes personal beliefs and feelings and emphasizes his or her own perspective. In expository or explanatory writing, the writer emphasizes the "message" in order to clarify an idea or process. In persuasive writing, the writer emphasizes the reader, trying to convince that reader to think in a new way or to persuade that reader to some sort of action.

The rhetorical contexts of ethos, logos, and pathos can be further subdivided into a number of rhetorical strategies. As a student, you may find that your teacher asks you to explain the overall rhetorical context for each paper that you write, or to write an essay using a particular writing strategy. Every essay that you read or write is developed according to one or more rhetorical strategies. Most, if not all, essays make use of *several* rhetorical strategies, with individual paragraphs being developed according to a specific strategy, depending upon the topic of the paragraph. The primary rhetorical strategy of an essay, if there is one, depends again on the purpose of the essay. The writer uses different strategies to organize and develop the thesis, while the reader responds by thinking about the topic in different ways. These strategies include the following:

- *Narration* tells a story, answering such questions as who? what? when? where? why? and how?

- *Description* creates an image of the subject, relying on the senses of sight, touch, hearing, taste, and smell.

- *Example* provides specific illustrations of an idea, presenting abstract ideas in concrete ways.

- *Comparison and Contrast* shows how things are similar to, and different from, each other, pointing out common features and distinctions.

- *Cause and Effect* explains what makes something happen, emphasizing reasons and consequences.

- *Process Analysis* explains how something happens, focusing on steps or sequence.

- *Classification and Division* arranges things according to categories or divides something into its parts, emphasizing shared characteristics.

- *Definition* explains or limits meaning, pointing out distinguishing features.

- *Persuasion* justifies or validates a position on an issue, relying on reason and emotion to convince readers.

All of these rhetorical descriptions assume that the purpose of writing is to communicate with an audience in some way. The choice of a topic often revolves around these rhetorical considerations, simply because we often write in response to external stimulation. Brady no doubt wrote "Why I Want a Wife" as an expressive piece in response to her own personal life pressures and to those of women around her at the time. Even though the piece stresses her own feelings about the life of a "wife," it also becomes a kind of expressive manifesto for many women who have read the piece. At the time it was written, it was also persuasive because the audience for the essay tended to be women who were themselves realizing that they were trying to "do it all" and were always running out of time and energy. The essay was both funny and sad at the same time for that audience.

Writers do not usually sit down and say, "I think I'll write an expressive essay today," or, "I think I'm feeling persuasive, so I'll write a persuasive essay." Rather, most writers write in response to experiences they have, to books and articles they read, to media reports they see and hear, or to conversations they have with their classmates, co-workers, friends, and families.

Topic focus often comes from the rhetorical desire to join a *discourse community*, that is, a group of people reading, talking, or writing about a given subject. Many listservs and moos are examples of such discussion groups. More and more writers are finding topics, beginning essays, and revising essays in response to computer-based discussions. Whatever the source of the topic, the rhetorical context comes into consideration both in the choice of topic and in the shaping of the topic into a paper.

It is a good idea to write notes to yourself about who your audience is and about where your essay might appear in print when finished. It is important, however, not to let the rhetorical context—for example, considerations of audience—drive the focus and content of the paper too early in the writing process. If only rhetorical considerations drive the writing, new and interesting ideas could be lost or ignored. At the same time, however, knowing your purpose and audience can save wasted time and energy.

A beginning writer may be a person who has little experience with writing long papers, but a beginning writer is also like *any* writer faced with a blank sheet of paper or computer screen. Each new writing task demands a kind of naïve beginning from each writer. Let us look at the ongoing, difficult process many writers go through in developing any new piece of writing.

Prewriting

Prewriting, or *discovery writing*, stresses the writer's internal processes—how and where the writer discovers what to write about. It can be a category of writing by itself, but it is also an important part of every writing task. A writer may have a problem to solve or a process to discover. In this case, the writer may talk extensively with others about their ideas for what they might want to write about, and may read widely about the potential subject of the paper before drafting a text. All this kind of writing and talking will be done for the sole purpose of *discovering* the solution to the problem or simply finding what the essay is really going to be about. This type of writing is not meant for a reader, at least not in its early stages.

In classical rhetoric, the sources of ideas were called *topoi*, which means something like "places to go for ideas." In most writing situations, we have the "places" or topics spelled out for us. Even writers of fiction tend to give themselves assignments by collecting newspaper clippings of real events that can lead to stories or by bringing up memories of people, places, and experiences that will provide the roots of a new story. Professional fiction and nonfiction writers also keep collections of their previously written stories and essays so that they can use old ideas in new ways. Other ways of discovering a topic include:

Brainstorming and "Webbing"

Either alone or in a classroom group, or possibly in a computer-classroom talk group, you could discuss a potential topic—or brainstorm—coming up with as many random ideas as possible about the subject. You could also build a web of association with a word or an idea from which to build an essay. For example, you could use, from "Why I Want a Wife," the word *wife* or other words that might be used ironically, for example, *teacher*. A webbing activity built around the concept of teacher might look like the following: ideas would develop from the word *teacher* in conjunction with the ironic concept of the essay. Some concepts might include: "Teachers are always there when you come to class. They have to read your writing no matter what. They have to be nice to you even when they have headaches. Teachers work for very little money compared to others with the same amount of education. Teachers cannot stop paying attention to you even if you are not at your best that day."

When the webbing activity is under way, you can work with the ideas generated to expand the topic or to find new "angles" on the topic. The aim of brainstorming and webbing is always to open up options and possibilities, not to limit or narrow ideas. Order and narrowing will come a bit later for most writers, though some writers tend to move quickly to structure and planning. The quickness with which any writer seizes on a topic and limits the topic depends on both the writing situation and the writerly inclinations of the particular person. For the most part, it is a good idea to keep the options wide open at the early stages of brainstorming a paper.

Searching Your Storehouse of Ideas and Information

Everyone has a collection of thoughts and ideas, including memories, about most topics. If the task were to write an ironic essay similar to "Why I Want a Wife," it might be a good idea to work on mining your memories about questions relating to feminism and gender roles, again either alone or in a group. The benefits of working in a writing group might be that the pool of experience is broader, and so might operate to generate more ideas than if you worked alone. For example, one member of the group might have had two working parents, while another had a stay-at-home mother. The two could compare memories and develop papers along the lines of their different experiences. Similarly, members of the group may have read articles about the effects of changing lifestyles on families. They also could compare notes. Such outside ideas and resources can encourage the writer to rethink his or her original idea. Rethinking what may at first seem obvious is an important part of discovering topics for writing. It is important to draw on as many areas of reading, viewing, and listening as possible. The more information that a writer considers before writing, the better the final essay will be.

Research and Survey Activities

Ideas often come from a decision to look further than the obvious materials available within the writer's memory or writing group. It may be necessary to look beyond what is already known and open up the topic by investigating possible sources of new ideas. Researching a topic for ideas is different from researching for specific support, although it is important to keep track of any information discovered (it may be needed in the actual paper). Bookstores, the library, and the Web are excellent sources of new ideas. To find more ideas about the issues in "Why I Want a Wife," you might go to a good bookstore and browse the section on gender issues or on home and family. The library search engines would provide perhaps more information than could be sorted at one time, but a browse through sections on sociology and social issues might turn up new ideas. The Web, of course, will give more ideas than most of us know what to do with, but it never hurts to browse on a few search words like *wife* and *family*. A completely new angle may turn up. Finally, surveys often change a writer's perspective radically. An informal survey that asks men and women who does the housework, who finds the child care, who has the car serviced, who takes the dog to the groomer, and who figures the taxes, could offer some interesting information that might help to expand ideas for the essay. Again, this kind of information should be kept with preplanning for the actual paper because it can all be handy in the actual writing as well as in topic expansion and discovery.

Settling on a Topic and Getting Started

Deciding to choose a topic rests on several considerations. First, you very well may be writing because you have been given a particular type of writing assignment. As mentioned above, most of us write in response to a particular request. The teacher has assigned a persuasive paper on a current social issue; the boss has asked for a report on the cost/benefit analysis of investing in a new product; the newspaper editor has sent the reporter out to cover a general interest story involving the local community.

Second, you may have a deadline. Your teacher, editor, or boss will simply say, "Have the topic [or book proposal or report outline] in by next Tuesday." That kind of deadline focuses the mind quite effectively. Even when the time frame is more flexible, the time will come when the writing project will *have* to find a focus.

With a topic chosen and a blank screen or page before you, it might be a good idea to take stock of your own writing processes. Each writer attacks a new writing project in his or her own way, and each project, depending on its complexity, demands different approaches from a writer. Some writers are "discovery" writers who dive in and start to write in order to discover what they think. Other writers take time to jot down rough outlines and to plan ways of finding support materials. Our experience tells us that these groups divide into two-thirds those who dive in and one-third those who make a plan. Both groups can learn from one another, though we are all likely to stick to our own preferred style even when we see advantages in someone else's way of composing.

Whichever approach you take, it is still important not to close down options too quickly. If you are the type who dives in and starts to write, be careful to remember that everything in the first attempt may have to be thrown away when the final draft goes to press! All of us hate to give up a word we have written, but discovery writers have to learn that part of discovery may mean going down the wrong trail and having to retrace the track. On the other hand, wonderful new ideas and new ways of saying things can be found on that discovery path.

Outliners may be in even more danger of closing down too soon. A first draft is only a first draft, and an outline should always be subject to major restructuring. The outline becomes a comforting template for the rest of the essay. Consider a potential paper on working couples and tax laws. The writer may decide to investigate three areas: tax law; personal experiences of married couples who both work; and attitudes of the intended audience (perhaps a congressperson to whom they plan to write about the issue) toward the tax structure. The danger of closing down on these three issues is great, yet the three are not really parallel, nor does one grow logically from another. All are areas for investigation, but the three areas may appear in different relationships in the final paper, or one or more of the areas might not appear at all. Thus, the person who writes a tentative outline or notes that look like an outline could short-circuit his or her own writing process. The writer who outlines needs to keep options open and to realize that any outline or plan may change as the paper develops or as new ideas appear.

A Word on Research

Contrary to common lore, writers do *not* research a paper and then sit down to write. Real writing is far messier and far more complex. A discovery draft (or part of one) or a tentative outline may clearly indicate that more outside information is necessary before the writing can continue. A search of the Web for tax laws or interviews with several married couples who both work and several who have only one working individual may stop the actual writing for a bit. A call to a congressperson may be in order. The drafting of an essay can involve several research stops and starts. Every paper can turn into a researched paper if the writer is sensitive to the questions and issues that develop as the draft takes shape.

A Word about Composing Styles

Writers differ in more ways than whether they outline or not. Some writers tend to plan early and start early whereas other writers have to wait until the last minute. Some writers write for hours without moving; others take frequent breaks for soft drinks or chocolate bars. Some writers start over and erase many times before finishing a first draft, while others pour out words without stopping until the first draft is fully down on paper or up on the screen. The best advice composition researchers can give you about your writing method is that you need to learn what works best for you and then follow the best writing pattern for your own comfort and success. Sometimes trying a different pattern can be helpful, just as lacing your fingers or crossing your legs differently challenges the body, but the truth is that you will revert to your preferred pattern most of the time, both in writing and in physical habits.

Revision—What to Do with a Draft

Somewhere in this messy drafting process, it is important to stop and get feedback from others. *You* get to decide when you have a draft, *or* your deadline may decide for you. In either case, bringing a draft to other readers is essential. These readers may not be the intended audience for the paper, but they can look at the draft in its intended rhetorical context and make suggestions. You will receive better suggestions if you ask the readers *specific* questions about the draft you have written. Do not ask questions like, "Does it make sense?"

or, "How do you like it?" Ask questions that have crossed your mind as you composed the draft. An example might be, "Tell me what else I could add to persuade the congressperson that I *do* understand the tax laws." Another possible question could be, "Can you think of other people I should interview to make my case more effectively?" It is also a good idea to ask readers to suggest at least one other source, such as an article or Web site, that would improve your draft. Ask questions that will help your reader help you make the draft better on the next revision. Remember that *revision* means "re-vision," or to "see again." That means to look at the paper from a new angle or from a new perspective. Ask your readers questions that will help them help you to find new perspectives.

Strategies

At this point, your knowledge of strategies can come in handy, too. As we have already discussed, you are aware that writers use different kinds of strategies to focus a paper. You may want to ask readers to suggest comparisons that would enrich a paper whose primary strategy is that of comparison and contrast. Or you could ask readers to suggest places in the paper where you need to add definitions and examples to clarify or illustrate the narrative more effectively. Remember to ask readers (and yourself) to use the strategies not only as writing forms but as tools for revision as well.

When your readers have made suggestions, take some time to decide whether or not you find the suggestions useful and helpful. If you *do* find them useful, incorporate the suggestions or new research findings into your next draft. As a student, you may find that your teacher will ask for a summary of how you used revision suggestions, including your teacher's suggestions. Also, editors for professional publications often want a detailed account of how writers used reviewers' responses, noting what responses were used and why others were ignored, just as bosses also want a sense of the sources for your writing and the reasons you approached the specific writing task the way you did. For these and many other reasons, becoming aware of your writing process in this way is an important skill to cultivate.

These activities of drafting and responding and revising can go on indefinitely. (Some biographers claim that the great Irish author James Joyce died in bed still rewriting his novel *Finnegans Wake* one more time, despite its publication years before!) In truth, rarely is the revision process ever "done." In some ways, because of deadlines and similar requirements, there can almost be a sense of "abandoning" a piece of writing, rather than fully "completing" it. Some writing projects reach this state of being "abandoned" to publication (or turned in to the teacher) sooner than others. All sorts of artificial deadlines may intervene, but working at making the arguments, support, and concepts as complete and effective as possible is the goal of every writing project.

Style and Voice

Different writing projects demand quite different voices. "Why I Want a Wife" is casual and a bit sarcastic in tone. Since Brady is expressing her own frustration, that tone is just right for her essay. Writing to a congressperson would demand a quite different tone. You would still want your own voice in the essay, but more formality and a more measured tone would suit the occasion more appropriately. Here again, attentive readers can help. In the final drafting stages, it is a good idea to ask readers to gauge whether the tone and voice of the essay fit the purpose and whether these stylistic qualities are maintained. Ask readers to mark places where the tone varies or the voice waivers from the appropriate choice for the intended audience and purpose. This is the point at which you will want to work on vocabulary. The more formal the paper, the more formal the vocabulary. These variations are called *registers*. When a writer changes from an informal tone and vocabulary to a more formal approach, the writer is said to *change registers*. Unless a writer wants to be funny, it is best not to mix registers.

Copyediting and Proofreading

When everything else is right in a paper (or as right as time and energy will allow), it is time to give those final attentive checks that will persuade the audience that you are an authoritative writer. A thoughtless typographical error or a punctuation mistake can destroy credibility in a reader more quickly than anything else. The simpler and more obvious the error, the more likely the reader is to notice it and to make negative judgments. Everyone should know that *too* means "very," and that *to* is a preposition or a part of an infinitive.

Since everyone *should* know these things, it is especially important not to confuse the words. If you do, you have a nearly 100% chance of being thought careless and negligent. Leaving a *too* where you need a *to* is like going on a date with spinach in your teeth. Everyone but you will notice, and the person you want to impress the most (the reader) will more than likely think less of your writing than the content and other aspects of its style and composition warrant.

This final copyediting is the point at which you need your trusty group of readers the most. We all have trouble seeing these glitches in our own writing, especially since we are more likely to be concentrating on the content and meaning than on the mechanics of the piece. *Always* ask other readers to read over a final draft before turning it in to a teacher or turning it over for publication. Even professional writers ask colleagues to look at their work before submission.

A Few Last Words on Writing

Here are a few rules that may lead to better writing:

1. Don't short-circuit your own writing process. Keep the possibilities for new ideas and approaches open and flexible.

2. Continue to ask readers for feedback, and talk to readers about how to expand and improve your text at every stage.

3. Never assume that a paper is finished. You can *always* make it better.

Just as we spoke about reading for pleasure, there is also much to be said for writing for the sheer pleasure of doing it. This is a type of writing known as aesthetic writing—for example poetry, journals, and diaries. Aesthetic writing may or may not be intended to communicate with a reader. Examples of essays that fit into this category include writing by Maya Angelou and Joan Didion. Often, these writers begin by musing in their journals or diaries and then turn their texts into literary essays that readers enjoy reading as much as the authors enjoyed writing them. Sometimes an essay that begins with another purpose ends up being admired for its craft. "Why I Want a Wife" may actually have moved into that category. It began as an expressive piece, but it has become a kind of classic that is read not just for its power, but also for its powerful language and forceful imagery. Although all writers aspire to aesthetic writing at least some of the time, most of us will probably not have the time or discipline to become full-time writers of elegantly crafted texts. Still, becoming aware of, and learning to pay attention to, *all* the elements of writing help to make each writing project pleasing to both writer *and* reader and effective for the intended audience.

WHY I WANT A WIFE

Judy Brady

Judy Brady (1937–), born in San Francisco, studied painting and received a B.F.A. in 1962 in art from the University of Iowa. Then she married and raised a family in a traditional housewife role. She later commented that her male professors had talked her out of pursuing a career in education. In the late 1960s, she became active in the women's movement and began writing articles on feminism and other social issues. In 1990, she was the editor of Women and Cancer, *an anthology by women. The essay "Why I Want a Wife" appeared in the first issue of* Ms. *magazine in 1972.*

1   I belong to that classification of people known as wives. I am a Wife. And, not altogether incidentally, I am a mother.

Not too long ago a male friend of mine appeared on the scene fresh from a recent divorce. He had one child, who is, of course, with his ex-wife. He is looking for another wife. As I thought about him while I was ironing one evening, it suddenly occurred to me that I, too, would like to have a wife. Why do I want a wife?

I would like to go back to school so that I can become economically independent, support myself, and, if need be, support those dependent upon me. I want a wife who will work and send me to school. And while I am going to school I want a wife to take care of my children. I want a wife to keep track of the children's doctor and dentist appointments. And to keep track of mine, too. I want a wife to make sure my children eat properly and are kept clean. I want a wife who will wash the children's clothes and keep them mended. I want a wife who is a good nurturant attendant to my children, who arranges for their schooling, makes sure that they have an adequate social life with their peers, takes them to the park, the zoo, etc. I want a wife who takes care of the children when they are sick, a wife who arranges to be around when the children need special care, because, of course, I cannot miss classes at school. My wife must arrange to lose time at work and not lose the job. It may mean a small cut in my wife's income from time to time, but I guess I can tolerate that. Needless to say, my wife will arrange and pay for the care of the children while my wife is working.

I want a wife who will take care of *my* physical needs. I want a wife who will keep my house clean. A wife who will pick up after me. I want a wife who will keep my clothes clean, ironed, mended, replaced when need be, and who will see to it that my personal things are kept in their proper place so that I can find what I need the minute I need it. I want a wife who cooks the meals, a wife who is a *good* cook. I want a wife who will plan the menus, do the necessary grocery shopping, prepare the meals, serve them pleasantly, and then do the cleaning up while I do my studying. I want a wife who will care for me when I am sick and sympathize with my pain and loss of time from school. I want a wife to go along when our family takes a vacation so that someone can continue to care for me and my children when I need a rest and change of scene.

5   I want a wife who will not bother me with rambling complaints   5
about a wife's duties. But I want a wife who will listen to me when I feel the need to explain a rather difficult point I have come across in my course of studies. And I want a wife who will type my papers for me when I have written them.

I want a wife who will take care of the details of my social life. When my wife and I are invited out by friends, I want a wife who will take care of the babysitting arrangements. When I meet people at school that I like and want to entertain, I want a wife who will have the house clean, will prepare a special meal, serve it to me and my friends, and not interrupt when I talk about the things that interest me and my friends. I want a wife who will have arranged that the children are fed and ready for bed before my guests arrive so that the children do not bother us. I want a wife who takes care of the needs of my guests so that they feel comfortable, who makes sure that they have an ashtray, that they are passed the hors d'oeuvres, that they are offered a second helping of the food, that their wine glasses are replenished when necessary, that their coffee is served to them as they like it. And I want a wife who knows that sometimes I need a night out by myself.

I want a wife who is sensitive to my sexual needs, a wife who makes love passionately and eagerly when I feel like it, a wife who makes sure that I am satisfied. And, of course, I want a wife who will not demand sexual attention when I am not in the mood for it. I want a wife who assumes the complete responsibility for birth control, because I do not want more children. I want a wife who will remain sexually faithful to me so that I do not have to clutter up my intellectual life with jealousies. And I want a wife who understands that *my* sexual needs may entail more than strict adherence to monogamy. I must, after all, be able to relate to people as fully as possible.

If, by chance, I find another person more suitable as a wife than the wife I already have, I want the liberty to replace my present wife with another one. Naturally, I will expect a fresh, new life; my wife will take the children and be solely responsible for them so that I am left free.

When I am through with school and have a job, I want my wife to quit working and remain at home so that my wife can more fully and completely take care of a wife's duties.

10   My God, who *wouldn't* want a wife?   10

～ NARRATION ～

Throughout most of our lives, we read, write, listen to, and tell stories. Our religious and cultural values are often passed on through stories, as is our history. And of course, stories have always entertained us.

Narration is the act of relating a story; the story itself is called a *narrative*. While narrative is a complex form with a variety of purposes, most meaningful narratives, particularly essays, have a point. Fairy tales, religious stories, and historical narratives are all told in order to drive home a point—about behavior, belief, or national identity. To convey that point, the writer of narrative must pay attention to the *conventions* of narration.

Often, the point of a narrative essay is stated or implied in the first paragraph, but sometimes the writer waits until the end. The clarity of that point is dependent on the writer's ability to *show* the reader what happens rather than simply *tell* about the action. A writer can achieve this goal by paying careful attention to organization, detail, and word choice. Organization in a narrative is almost always chronological; the story is told in a specific time sequence. Such organization allows readers to follow the action without becoming confused. Organization is supported by clear, precise details; readers must be able to envision the action in order to understand the story. These details are created by descriptive word choice, or diction. The following narrative, from Maya Angelou's "Graduation," illustrates these features:

> *Amazingly the great day finally dawned and I was out of bed before I knew it. I threw open the back door to see it more clearly, but Momma said, "Sister, come away from that door and put your robe on." I hoped the memory of that morning would never leave me. Sunlight was itself young, and the day had none of the insistence maturity would bring it in a few hours. In my robe and barefoot in the backyard, under cover of going to see about my new beans, I gave myself up to the*

gentle warmth and thanked God that no matter what evil I had done in my life He had allowed me to live to see this day. Somewhere in my fatalism I had expected to die, accidentally, and never have the chance to walk up the stairs in the auditorium and gracefully receive my hard-earned diploma. Out of God's merciful bosom I had won reprieve. Bailey came out in his robe and gave me a box wrapped in Christmas paper. He said he had saved his money for months to pay for it. It felt like a box of chocolates, but I knew Bailey wouldn't save money to buy candy when we had all we could want under our noses. He was as proud of the gift as I. It was a soft-leather-bound copy of a collection of poems by Edgar Allan Poe, or, as Bailey and I called him, "Eap." I turned to "Annabel Lee" and we walked up and down the garden rows, the cool dirt between our toes, reciting the beautifully sad lines.

Notice how Angelou organizes her story in simple chronological order: she goes to the door in the early morning, relishes the sweetness of the day, is joined by her brother, receives his gift, and then recites poetry with him as they walk through the garden. The author also brings readers into the narrative through the use of specific details: the warmth of the day is "gentle," Bailey's present is wrapped in Christmas paper and feels like a box of chocolates, the book is bound in soft leather, and she and her brother feel "the cool dirt between [their] toes." Both organization and detail, supported by precise diction, make the scene real to readers.

While narration may be the primary rhetorical strategy employed in an essay, it may also be used in an essay employing a different strategy. For example, a persuasive essay might use a brief story to support its argument, or a cause-and-effect essay might use a narrative to illustrate a sequence of events. In these cases, narrative is used as an *example*. In fact, one could argue that the narrative "Graduation" is an extended example of the evils of segregation and the resilience of African Americans in the face of discrimination. As the excerpt illustrates, regardless of how it is used, an effective narrative will command the reader's attention.

⌁ DESCRIPTION ⌁

If you have ever tried to recreate for someone who has not seen it a sunset over the ocean, an unusual animal in a zoo, or a building with unique architectural features, then you know how important description is. When a writer describes something, she or he creates an image with words. In order to do that, the writer must also be a careful observer of the world around him or her. Sometimes writers offer readers *objective* descriptions, recreating for the reader, in precise detail, the image as it might appear to anyone observing it. But sometimes writers create *subjective* descriptions, reproducing the image as it appears to the writer, including the writer's emotional response to the image. A sunset, for example, might be described purely in terms of the colors of the sky, the size of the sun relative to the horizon, and the time required for the sun to sink below the horizon. Subjectively, on the other hand, the sunset might be described as infusing the sky with hopeful illumination, or instilling in the observer a sense of peace, or creating in the observer an awe of nature.

In "Graduation," Angelou describes class valedictorian Henry Reed in objective terms, as "a small, very black boy with hooded eyes, a long, broad nose and an oddly shaped head." She describes the days preceding graduation, however, in subjective terms: "The faded beige of former times had been replaced with strong and sure colors. . . . Clouds that lazed across the sky were objects of great concern to me. Their shiftier shapes might have held a message that in my new happiness and with a little bit of time I'd soon decipher."

Whatever the description, there must be a *purpose* for presenting it, an impression that the writer wants to leave with the reader. That purpose might be simply to create an image in the reader's mind, as Angelou does in her description of the days before her graduation. But description may also be used in conjunction with other rhetorical strategies, for example, to describe an effect. Angelou does this in "Graduation" when she describes her feelings as she listens to the white speaker denigrating her people: "The man's dead words fell like bricks around the auditorium and too many settled in my belly. . . . Every girl in my row had found something new to do with her handkerchief. Some folded the tiny squares into love knots, some into triangles, but most were wadding them, then pressing them flat on their yellow laps." The vivid detail of this description shows the reader how Angelou and her classmates felt rather than simply telling the reader about it. The good writer of description will try to arouse the reader's senses—of sight, smell, touch, taste, hearing, and movement. Unlike narrative, a description rarely involves a time sequence (unless the thing described involves time) and arrangement is spatial rather than chronological. But like narrative, a description must include clear details if it is to be successful. A good description, as the Angelou examples illustrate, will leave the reader with the sense that he or she has experienced the image along with the writer.

⌁ EXAMPLE ⌁

If you have ever been asked to explain a theory or concept so that the average person can understand it, then you are aware of the importance of example. Examples are particularly useful in making abstractions concrete. A political scientist might offer the examples of Great Britain and Israel to explain the parliamentary system of government; a psychologist might offer the examples of particular patients to explain certain neuroses; a literary critic might offer the examples of Edith Wharton and Henry James to explain the concept of realism and naturalism. For examples like these to be effective, they must be relevant to the concept being explained. The examples must also be typical and not an exception; the concrete example must truly be representative of the concept.

In "Graduation," Maya Angelou presents the concept of segregation and racial discrimination through the example of Edward Donleavy's speech to the graduates, but within that example, she also provides specific examples of what segregation meant to her and her friends. When Donleavy sings the praises of African American athletes like Olympic star Jesse Owens and world heavyweight champion Joe Louis (known as the "Brown Bomber"), the young Angelou thinks,

> *Owens and the Brown Bomber were great heroes in our world, but what school official in the white-goddom of Little Rock had the right to decide that those two men must be our only heroes? Who decided that for Henry Reed to become a scientist he had to work like George Washington Carver, as a bootblack, to buy a lousy microscope? Bailey was obviously always going to be too small to be an athlete, so which concrete angel glued to what country seat had decided that if my brother wanted to become a lawyer he had to first pay penance for his skin by picking cotton and hoeing corn and studying correspondence books at night for twenty years?*

Angelou's examples of African Americans facing overwhelming obstacles in their quest for success are obvious to the reader. Not all examples are so obvious, however, and thus the writer who uses examples must be careful to explain or analyze how they relate to some concept. It is only when the example is as clearly relevant as Angelou's that the writer can leave it to the reader to figure out the connection.

As with other strategies of development, example requires that the writer use specific details in order to *show* rather than simply *tell*. Thus, Angelou uses names such as Jesse Owens, the Brown Bomber, and George Washington Carver; she also uses details such as the concrete angel glued to the country seat, as well as specific images of hoeing corn and picking cotton. All of these details help make the example clearer and more concrete in readers' minds. Example leaves the reader with a specific impression of the concept being explained; to that end, organization is crucial.

Sometimes a writer will use different examples to illustrate specific features of a concept. One patient, for example, might illustrate the idea that obsessive-compulsive disorder often interferes with an individual's capacity to perform at work, while another patient illustrates the impact of the disorder on family life. Or a writer may move from the least significant example to the most significant, and sometimes even from most to least significant. In Angelou's piece, the less important (to her) example of Henry Reed is presented first, with the more important example of her brother Bailey presented second—and in greater detail.

While example can be used as the primary rhetorical strategy of an essay, often it is used in support of other strategies. Writers of *argument* often use examples to provide *evidence* in support of a position, while writers of *definition* use examples to *clarify* the term being described. Often, a narrative is an extended example: "Graduation" might be considered, in its entirety, an example of the evils of segregation and the resilience of African Americans. Whatever the strategy, it is essential to remember that whether it is used as the primary or secondary strategy, example must always contribute to the specific point that the writer is trying to make.

COMPARISON AND CONTRAST

O ne of the easiest ways for us to understand a thing is to consider it alongside something else, emphasizing either similarities, differences, or both. We are always making comparisons: of products, in order to determine which is the best buy; of restaurants, in order to determine which is most appropriate for a given occasion; of candidates for office, in order to determine which will best serve our interests. What these three examples illustrate is that we use comparison and contrast not for its own sake but to support a point. Thus, if you use this strategy in your writing, you should always keep the *point* of your comparison in mind.

Usually, the two subjects under comparison will have something in common; that common feature will constitute the basis for comparison. When you were deciding on a college, for example, you may have considered a large public university, a small private college, or a community college. These kinds of schools are quite different, but they all share at least one common basis for comparison: they are all institutions of higher education. When making comparisons, it is important to maintain the *same basis* for each subject being compared. For example, if you scrutinize the liberal arts *curriculum* of the first two schools, but then focus on the *location* of the third school, you have undermined your comparison by changing the basis. By focusing on the same qualities of each subject, you maintain that basis.

In "Graduation," Maya Angelou uses comparison and contrast briefly when she refers to Mr. Donleavy's speech praising the accomplishments of both white and African American children in the school district. In response to his words, she thinks, "The white kids were going to have a chance to become Galileos and Madame Curies and Edisons and Gaugins, and our boys (the girls weren't even in on it) would try to be Jesse Owenses and Joe Louises." In this case, the basis for comparison is the field in which children might hope to succeed.

Later in the essay, Angelou contrasts her appreciation of "Lift Ev'ry Voice and Sing," known as "the Negro National Anthem," to her response to Patrick Henry's "Give me liberty or give me death" speech:

> *Each child I know had learned ["Lift Ev'ry Voice"] with his ABC's and along with "Jesus Loves Me This I Know." But I personally had never heard it before. Never heard the words, despite the thousand of times I had sung them. Never thought they had anything to do with me. On the other hand, the words of Patrick Henry had made such an impression on me that I had been able to stretch myself tall and trembling and say, "I know not what course others may take, but as for me, give me liberty or give me death."*

Angelou's basis for comparison in this example is the child's misunderstanding of the relevance of famous words.

The Angelou examples represent *comparison* and *contrast* used in support of other rhetorical strategies (e.g., *narrative* and *persuasion*). At times, however, an entire essay can be written using the comparison-and-contrast strategy. In such essays, appropriate organization is essential. Most writers recognize two primary methods of organization for comparison and contrast: point-by-point or subject-by-subject. Consider the educational institutions mentioned earlier, for example: if you were to write an essay on the topic, you might organize your comparison by looking at curriculum, cost, and location of the institutions. For each of these categories, you would consider each school in turn. This is a point-by-point organization. But you might also choose to consider the individual school, focusing on curriculum, cost, and location of each before moving on to a discussion of the next school. This organization is subject-by-subject. In outline form, the two organizations would look like this:

Point-by-Point	Subject-by-Subject
Curriculum	Large Public University
large public university	curriculum
small private college	cost
community college	location
Cost	Small Private College
large public university	curriculum
small private college	cost
community college	location
Location	Community College
large public university	curriculum
small private college	cost
community college	location

Occasionally, a writer will combine the two organizing strategies. Regardless of the strategy you choose, establishing a *pattern* for the comparison will make the essay clearer and easier for the reader to understand.

Whether a comparison is used in support of another rhetorical strategy or presented as the primary strategy in an essay, the same guidelines apply: the comparison must have a *point*, it must operate on a common *basis*, and (in the case of an essay) it must be *organized* appropriately.

PROCESS ANALYSIS

Whenever we follow instructions in putting something together (a bicycle, for example) or try to explain why something happens (leaves changing color in autumn, for example), we engage in *process analysis*. Process analysis breaks a process down into logical steps; for example, in putting the bicycle together, it is necessary to construct the entire handlebar unit before attaching it to the frame of the bike. Such an analysis has a purpose, as does any good process analysis. A *directive process analysis* (constructing the bicycle) tells readers *how to do something*, while an *informative process analysis* (leaves turning color) *explains a phenomenon*. If either type of process analysis is to be effective, the steps must be delineated in clear detail. (Anyone who has tried to put a bicycle together using inadequate instructions can attest to the need for clear detail!)

In "Graduation," Maya Angelou recounts the usual process followed during an assembly at the Lafayette County Training School:

> *The school band struck up a march and all classes filed in as had been rehearsed. We stood in front of our seats, as assigned, and on a signal from the choir director, we sat. No sooner had this been accomplished than the band started to play the national anthem. We rose again and sang the song, after which we recited the pledge of allegiance.*

The significance of clearly delineated steps becomes clear in this piece immediately following the recitation of the pledge of allegiance, when the next step in the process is changed:

> *We remained standing for a brief minute before the choir director and the principal signaled to us, rather desperately I thought, to take our seats. The command was so unusual that our carefully rehearsed and smooth-running machine was thrown off. For a full minute we fumbled for our chairs and*

bumped into each other awkwardly. Habits change or solidify under pressure, so in our state of nervous tension we had been ready to follow our usual assembly pattern: the American national anthem, then the pledge of allegiance, then the song every Black person I knew called the Negro National Anthem. All done in the same key, with the same passion and most often standing on the same foot.

The significance of a well-defined process is illustrated in this passage when Angelou and her classmates become convinced that this disruption signals "worse things to come," which of course is precisely what happens when the white politician Edward Donleavy addresses the assembly.

The process outlined by Angelou is a chronological one, but processes can be simultaneous or cyclical as well. An example of a simultaneous process might be the signs of autumn: leaves turn color, daylight becomes shorter, and temperatures drop. Autumn itself, of course, is part of the cyclical process of changing seasons. Understanding a process allows us to see an object or an event in a new way, sometimes helping us understand how something happens and sometimes helping us understand why it happens.

When using process analysis as a strategy, it is important to appreciate the audience. Angelou, for example, knows that her readership extends beyond African Americans who grew up in the rural South, so she explains the song that follows the pledge of allegiance. In recreating the sequence accurately, she allows her audience to understand the unease felt by the graduates when the process is disrupted. If Angelou knew that her audience was unfamiliar with American patriotic rituals, she would also have to define the term *pledge of allegiance*. The concept of a national anthem is a fairly universal one, but many countries do not feature a pledge of allegiance to the flag. Similarly, a biologist explaining the signs of autumn would have to define terms such as "photosynthesis" for a general audience.

As evidenced in Maya Angelou's "Graduation," process analysis need not constitute the primary rhetorical strategy for an essay. Essays outlining scientific or mechanical processes often use this as a primary strategy, but essays featuring narration, description, definition, and other rhetorical strategies may also employ process analysis. Regardless of whether the strategy is primary or secondary, following the guidelines above will ensure that the process analysis is effective.

CLASSIFICATION AND DIVISION

When we walk into a supermarket, we see individual items classified into categories: produce, dairy, bakery, and the like. And when we pursue a college major, we find the field of study divided into individual courses. Given the amount of information we must process every day, it would be difficult indeed to negotiate our way through life without classification and division. As a rhetorical strategy, classification and division allows writers to make sense of what might otherwise seem to be random ideas.

While the two strategies share similar principles, classification involves sorting items into categories, moving from the individual to the group, while division breaks a whole into parts, moving from group to individual. Thus, classification emphasizes similarities among items in a group, while division emphasizes differences. Such analyses allow us to understand how parts relate to wholes and how things work. In the supermarket, for example, products that share certain qualities are placed together: cheese, milk, cream, and butter can all be classified as dairy products. As a college major, the broad subject of American history is divided into courses that focus on different time periods: colonial, federal, Civil War, twentieth-century. Both classification and division help people to put information into a coherent order by identifying relationships either between parts and the whole or among parts.

For classification and division to be successful, the same *principle* must be used throughout the analysis. Think about how confusing it would be if the supermarket manager classified some products by *purpose*, some by *price*, and some by *brand*! There would be one aisle for dairy products, another for products over three dollars, and another for Kraft products. This failure to employ a uniform principle would result in some dairy products being in the dairy aisle, some in the over-three-dollar aisle, and some in the Kraft aisle. Shoppers would have an extremely difficult time finding their way around the store. Similarly, an essay dividing heads of state might use the categories of monarch, prime minister, and president. To also introduce male and female as categories would confuse the reader; no coherent order would emerge, because some of the categories are based on title and some on gender.

Maya Angelou uses classification and division to a limited extent in "Graduation." When she divides the general category academic honors, she uses a principle commonly used in elementary schools: "No absences, no tardiness, and my academic work was among the best of the year." And when she divides academic work into categories, she uses a performance principle more appropriate to a twelve year old: "I could say the preamble to the Constitution even faster than Bailey. . . . I had memorized the presidents of the United States from Washington to Roosevelt in chronological as well as alphabetical order."

In addition to ensuring that the same principle is used in classifying and dividing, it is also important to keep the *level* of the subclasses *parallel* and the treatment *equal*. Monarch, prime minister, and president, for example, are all parallel titles—each is a general category for a head of state. To introduce Ronald Reagan as a parallel category would not make sense; he represents a further subcategory, individual heads of state. Finally, the identification of categories should account for *every* significant item in the group: to neglect to include presidents as a class of heads of state would make for an incomplete treatment of the subject.

When Angelou classifies the opportunities open to children in the South in the 1940s, she creates two parallel classes: white children and African American children. She then creates several subclasses for each of the primary classes, treating each subclass equally: "The white kids were going to have a chance to become Galileos and Madame Curies and Edisons and Gaugins, and our boys (the girls weren't even in on it) would try to be Jesse Owenses and Joe Louises." The subclasses for white children include a variety of exalted occupations, including inventors, scientists, and painters; the subclasses for African American children are only two, both of them athletic: runners and boxers. That Angelou uses names of famous people keeps her classes equal; had she written, "inventors and women scientists and Gaugins," she would not have been treating the classes equally. And her limiting the classes open to African American children to only two accounts for what at that time constituted almost the only options open to those children.

As with other rhetorical strategies, classification and division must have a purpose. Dividing heads of state into subclasses allows a student of political science to examine different governmental systems; dividing a college major into separate courses allows a student to understand relationships among courses; classifying supermarket products into categories allows shoppers to find easily what they are looking for. Angelou's use of classification and division allows her readers to understand the mind of a twelve year old and to appreciate the limited options open to African American children as compared to white children in the 1940s. What matters is not whether the purpose is simple or profound; what matters is that there is a purpose.

CAUSE AND EFFECT

Whenever you try to answer the question "why?" you are engaging in cause-and-effect analysis. Sometimes the analysis is simple: if a car won't start on a winter morning, chances are the battery is too weak to get a cold engine moving. But often the analysis is complex: when war broke out in the Balkans after the fall of the Soviet Union, the causes ranged from economics, to religion, to nationalism, to ideology. Cause and effect can be used in support of another rhetorical strategy, for example, *persuasion*. Or it can be used as the primary rhetorical strategy in an essay. Whether the strategy is used as a primary or supporting strategy, or whether it focuses primarily on causes or effects, the features of the strategy remain the same.

One of those features is the identification of causes as either *immediate* or *remote*. In the case of the Balkans, for example, one of the immediate causes of the fighting was ethnic divisions among inhabitants of the area. These divisions became apparent shortly after the end of Soviet domination of the region, and thus were easily recognizable as a cause of the conflict. But the situation cannot be understood fully without considering remote causes, some of which go back to the redrawing of national boundaries following World War I. Since this cause is found in the history of a conflict that occurred over sixty years earlier, it is not so obvious as the more immediate causes. Nonetheless, remote causes are often even more significant than immediate causes in explaining an effect.

Maya Angelou analyzes both immediate and remote causes in "Graduation." The immediate cause, for example, of the graduates' discomfort at the beginning of the graduation ceremony is a change in the order of the program:

> *We remained standing for a brief minute [after singing the national anthem] before the choir director and the principal signaled to us, rather desperately I thought, to take our seats.*

The command was so unusual that our carefully rehearsed and smooth-running machine was thrown off.

The effect of this change in the program is profound: "Finding my seat at last, I was overcome with a presentiment of worse things to come. Something unrehearsed, unplanned, was going to happen, and we were going to be made to look bad." Later, valedictorian Henry Reed's leading the graduates in singing the Negro National Anthem constitutes the immediate cause for renewed pride: "We were on top again. As always, again. We survived. . . . I was no longer simply a member of the proud graduating class of 1940; I was a proud member of the wonderful, beautiful Negro race."

Throughout "Graduation," however, Angelou also implies remote causes for the emotions she feels throughout the ceremony. When she contemplates how "awful" it is "to be a Negro and have no control over my life," she is referring to the seventy-five years of segregation that followed the end of the Civil War. When she listens to Donleavy recount the great improvements to be made to the white schools, she is referring to the deep-seated inequality foisted on African Americans in the South. And later, when she sings the praises of "Black known and unknown poets" whose tales and songs have sustained her race, she is referring to the ongoing struggle of African Americans to achieve freedom and dignity. The imposition of segregation after the Civil War, the inequality built into the Southern social fabric, and the simmering rebellion within the African American community—all of these constitute remote causes for the young Angelou's reactions on her graduation night.

Another feature of cause-and-effect analysis is the distinction between *primary* and *contributory* causes. While the primary cause of the lengthy Balkan war can be found in the tensions within the region itself, a contributory cause might be the rest of the world's failure to intervene early in the conflict. Similarly, the primary cause of Angelou's dismay during the graduation ceremony is the denigrating speech delivered by Edward Donleavy. The remote cause is the reaction of the leaders of the African American community: the principal's normally powerful voice nearly fades into silence when he introduces Donleavy, and when the speaker's driver takes the principal's seat on the dais, confusion ensues and no one objects. The identification of immediate and remote, primary and contributory, causes enriches the analysis of complex issues.

By now it should be clear that cause-and-effect analysis normally includes multiple causes; it often includes multiple effects as well. Consider once again the Balkan war example: it has been determined that the conflict was the result of many causes. One of those causes, however, was itself responsible for more than just the Balkan war. The armistice that ended World War I not only set the stage for later conflict in the Balkans, but also resulted in conditions in Germany that led to the rise of Nazism under Adolf Hitler. In fact, an effect of a given cause often becomes the cause of yet another effect: The terms imposed on Germany after World War I, for example, resulted in humiliation and economic turmoil in that country. In turn, the national humiliation and deplorable economic conditions resulted in public unrest, which in turn resulted in the rise of the National Socialist, or Nazi Party. The rise of the Nazis led to World War II.

In "Graduation," Donleavy's speech causes the young Angelou to ponder the injustices heaped on her people, which, in turn, causes her not to hear her name when she is called to the stage to receive her diploma. The change in the program caused by Donleavy's appearance causes the graduates to lose their composure, which results in valedictorian Henry Reed's decision to change the program yet again and sing the Negro National Anthem, which causes the graduates to regain not only their composure but their pride. These multiple causes and multiple effects make cause-and-effect analysis more complicated than other rhetorical strategies such as description or comparison and contrast.

The key to handling this complex strategy effectively lies in recognizing legitimate causes and effects. For a cause to be credible, it must be both *necessary* and *sufficient* to produce an effect. To illustrate this requirement, consider the simple example of the car that fails to start. In determining the cause of the problem, a mechanic checks under the hood. If all other parts of the engine are working, then a weak or dead battery is both a necessary and sufficient cause of the car's failure to start. When the mechanic checks the engine, she is looking for connections or relationships to determine the cause of the problem. A car's failure to start is a mechanical or an electrical problem; therefore, the causes probably lie in the mechanical or electrical operations of the car. In a more complex problem such as determining the causes of the Balkan war, historians will also look for connections and relationships, in this case: economic conditions, nationalism, religious conflicts, and the history of the region. The mechanic and the historian are experts in their respective fields, so they are likely to avoid a common fallacy found in cause-and-effect analysis. Called *post-hoc reasoning*, this fallacy assumes that simply because a phenomenon or an event precedes another, the first is the cause of the second. If, for example, the owner of the car had lent it to a friend the day before, there is no reason why he should blame his friend for the problem; the two events may be merely *coincidental.*

In "Graduation," the arrival of an unanticipated speaker would not in itself constitute a necessary and sufficient cause for the turmoil that follows. It is Edward Donleavy's position as a white politician, as well as his treatment of both the dignitaries on the dais and the audience in the hall, that make his appearance a necessary and sufficient cause. Earlier in the essay, Angelou describes her youthful conviction that God would punish her evil deeds by somehow not allowing her to participate in graduation. Had she attributed the turmoil caused by Donleavy's speech to her own evil deeds, she would have been employing a post-hoc fallacy.

Another common problem found in cause-and-effect analysis involves *oversimplification.* This problem usually results from a failure to appreciate the complexity of causes and effects. For example, an uninformed writer might attribute the rise of Nazism solely to the economic conditions in Germany during the 1930s, ignoring the simmering anti-Semitism in the country, the disputes over territory along the borders with Austria and France, the inefficiency of the government, and a number of other causes. When analyzing the causes of a particular event or phenomenon, it is necessary to consider a variety of causes—immediate *and* remote, primary *and* contributing.

An essay employing cause-and-effect analysis can be organized by first describing the effect and then analyzing the causes that led to it, or by analyzing the causes first and then concluding with the effect. The writer should make this choice based on what he or she wants to emphasize in the analysis. For example, a writer who wants to emphasize the *history* of the Balkan war might elaborate on the various causes before discussing the war itself, while a writer who wants to emphasize possible *solutions* to the conflict might begin by focusing on the conflict, and then analyzing the causes that led to it. As in essays employing other strategies, the approach taken by the writer should reflect both the topic and the purpose of the essay.

DEFINITION

Definition of terms and concepts is essential to the clear understanding of any subject. If the reader is to share common ground with the writer, then the writer has the responsibility to clarify his or her meaning to the reader. In some cases, definitions are *formal*: short, dictionary-like explanations of a term. If you were asked to define *psychoanalytic criticism*, for example, you might offer a brief definition: it is a school of criticism that relies on Freud's theories of personality development in analyzing literary works. Frequently, however, definitions are *extended*, requiring a paragraph, an essay, or even an entire book to clarify the meaning of a term or concept. If you were expected to apply psychoanalytic criticism to a novel, for example, you would need to explain the intricacies of the school, and this would require an extended definition. In this case, your entire essay might constitute an extended definition, with the novel serving as an example of this particular school of literary criticism.

Maya Angelou provides a brief definition of "A & M (agricultural and mechanical schools)" in "Graduation": they were schools "which trained Negro youths to be carpenters, farmers, handymen, masons, maids, cooks and baby nurses." When she is wallowing in the self-loathing brought on by Donleavy's speech, she engages in an extended definition of humanity, especially for African Americans:

> It was awful to be a Negro and have no control over my life.
> It was brutal to be young and already trained to sit quietly
> and listen to charges brought against my color with no chance
> of defense. We should all be dead. I thought I should like to
> see us all dead, one on top of the other. A pyramid of flesh
> with the whitefolks on the bottom, as the broad base, then the
> Indians with their silly tomahawks and teepees and wigwams
> and treaties, the Negroes with their mops and recipes and
> cotton sacks and spirituals sticking out of their mouths. The
> Dutch children should all stumble in their wooden shoes and

break their necks. The French should choke to death on the Louisiana Purchase (1803) while silkworms ate all the Chinese with their stupid pigtails. As a species, we were an abomination. All of us.

Both formal and extended definitions comprise three parts: *term*, *class*, and *differentiation*. The *term* is that which is being defined, psychoanalytic criticism, for example. The *class* identifies the general category in which the term is found—in this case, a school of literary criticism. *Differentiation* distinguishes the term from other terms in the same class, such as feminist criticism, formalist criticism, and Marxist criticism. If the definition is to be effective, all three parts must be clear, complete, and detailed. Depending on the audience, the language used in the definition can be either technical or general. An audience unfamiliar with Freud's theories, for example, would need to have the terms *id*, *ego*, and *superego* explained in lay terms, while an audience familiar with his work would be able to understand a technical explanation that assumed knowledge of these key terms. Although Angelou's extended definition of humanity is metaphorical rather than literal, it is still possible to identify term (races), class (humanity), and differentiation (whites, Indians, Negroes, Dutch, French, and Chinese).

Writers employing this rhetorical strategy must be careful to avoid what is known as *circular definition*, in which the term is simply restated in different words. For example, "Organic food is food that is grown organically" is a circular definition. The definition does *nothing* to help the reader understand the concept!

Using definition as a strategy can be interesting because it almost always involves other rhetorical strategies. Example is frequently used in defining terms: a song by the Mighty Mighty Bosstones, for example, might be used to help define *ska music*. Comparison and contrast might be used in the same definition, contrasting ska to heavy metal music. A definition of contemporary music in general might involve division and classification, dividing it into ska, rap, reggae, and other categories. In addition, a definition might use metaphor or analogy, comparing the term imaginatively to something else, or negation, stating what the term is not.

Angelou employs some of these strategies in "Graduation." She uses examples of African American working tools (mops, recipes, and cotton sacks) to help define her race. She contrasts the aspirations of white children and African American children to help define opportunity. And finally, she defines the human species by dividing it into different races.

Definition may be used for its own purpose, or it may support another purpose—*persuasion*, for example. Regardless of purpose, however, a good definition must be detailed, complete, and presented in such a way that the audience can understand it.

⌒ PERSUASION ⌒

Whenever you take a position on a subject and seek to convince others to join you, you are engaging in **persuasion**. Almost always linked with **argument**, persuasion is a strategy that employs not only the logic and reason of argument but appeals to emotion as well. Because most of the arguments you encounter involve both logical and emotional appeals, this discussion will use the term *persuasion* exclusively.

The purpose of persuasion can vary: Sometimes a writer seeks only to establish the validity of a particular position; sometimes a writer wishes to convince readers to change their minds on an issue; sometimes a writer is determined to commit readers to a specific course of action. For example, if you are involved in a movement to prevent the building of a toxic waste dump in your community, you may seek to persuade your audience in several ways. In addressing those who consider only the economic impact of the dump on the community, you simply may want to establish that the environmental position is valid and must be considered in any debate. You also may want to convince those who see no harm in the dump to recognize the impact on the air and water quality in the surrounding areas. And you may seek to convince those who agree that the dump is a hazard to take such actions as picketing the company building the dump, engaging in a letter-writing campaign to the local newspaper, or petitioning the company's stockholders to oppose the move.

What these examples also illustrate is that writers of persuasion must pay careful attention to their **audience**. If you are seeking, for example, to convince the environmentalists to take action against the dump, your appeal will be different from the one you would make to a group whose money is invested in the company building the dump. Some audiences will be entirely sympathetic to your position, some antithetic to it, and many will fall somewhere between those two extremes. Your task as a writer of persuasion is to appeal to the **beliefs** and **values** of your audience. If you can find common beliefs and values, your task will be that much easier. For example, most members of a community will be sensitive to the economic impact of a toxic waste dump; a facility providing both jobs and tax dollars is an attractive prospect. You will be more persuasive, then, if you can address economic concerns. Perhaps you might balance the economic advantages of a dump with the increased costs of health care, loss of work due to illness, and decline of property values in order to appeal to those whose position stems from their sense of economic values. (It is worth noting here that such an appeal would also incorporate the strategies of comparison and contrast and cause and effect. It is common for other rhetorical strategies to be used in support of persuasion.)

In a persuasive piece a writer usually supports rational appeals with appeals to emotion and to her integrity or credibility as well. These appeals derive from the Greek concept of **logic**, which highlights three factors essential to an effective argument: *logos* (soundness of argument), *pathos* (emotional power of language), and *ethos* (credibility or integrity of writer). Emotional appeals, if legitimately related to your position, will strengthen a purely rational argument. Maya Angelou uses emotional appeals effectively in "Graduation" when she describes how she felt after Edward Donleavy's speech:

> Graduation, the hush-hush magic time of frills and gifts and congratulations and diplomas, was finished for me before my name was called. The accomplishment was nothing. The meticulous maps, drawn in three colors of ink, learning and spelling decasyllabic words, memorizing the whole of *The Rape of Lucrece*—it was for nothing. Donleavy had exposed us.

The demoralization of a young girl whose hopes only recently had included heading "for the freedom of open fields" supports the implicit argument against segregation that permeates Angelou's piece. By allowing her audience to focus not on statistics and principles but rather on a real girl's disillusionment with her life and her race, she brings the issue into clearer focus for her readers by providing a personal touch.

"Graduation" also illustrates the significance of language to *pathos*. When considering the meaning of words, it is important to distinguish between *denotation*, the dictionary definition of the word, and *connotation*, the implied meaning or emotional overtones of the word. The word *group*, for example, is rather neutral in both denotation and connotation; it refers to a number of people with some common purpose. Change the word to *gang*, however, and while the dictionary meaning may remain essentially the same, the sinister implications of the word, the sense of danger or violence, cannot be ignored. Thus a newspaper account referring to a *group* of environmental activists creates a different image than one referring to a *gang* of activists. Angelou uses connotation when she asks why her brother has to "pay penance for his skin" in order to become a lawyer. Her reference to penance calls up religious images of sinning against God, thereby heightening the impact of this condemnation of segregation.

Angelou's *ethos* is established both within and without the essay. Within "Graduation" she establishes her credibility by clearly presenting herself as one who has suffered the inequities of segregation; she has first-hand experience of her subject. A brief look at Angelou's biography also establishes her *ethos*. Growing up in the segregated South and San Francisco, she overcame numerous obstacles to become the first black female conductor on the San Francisco cable cars, to excel as an accomplished writer and actor, and to be chosen to compose and present the ceremonial poem at President Bill Clinton's first inauguration. Her credentials lend credibility to her position. If you wish to establish your credibility and integrity in the fight against the toxic waste dump, you would have to make your understanding of the issues clear, highlight any education or professional experience relating to the issues, and present yourself as a reasonable, trustworthy person.

There is no better way to present yourself as reasonable and trustworthy than to **address opposing views** within your persuasive piece. Acknowledging the economic benefits of a toxic waste dump, for example, establishes you as a person who understands the validity of different points of view, thus enhancing your credibility. At the same time, **refuting** that argument with evidence of the economic costs of the dump strengthens your position.

In preparing a persuasive piece it is important to consider various approaches to argument and persuasion. Two of the more common approaches used today are the **Rogerian** and the **Toulmin** models. Using the Rogerian model, you would first acknowledge your opposition and assert its validity. This process would lead to finding a common ground from which all sides can view the issue. Finally, you would present evidence to establish your position as the most reasonable.

Another effective approach to argument and persuasion is found in the work of philosopher Stephen Toulmin, whose model stresses the importance of a strong link between the thesis of a persuasive piece and the evidence supporting that thesis. The primary parts of the Toulmin model are **claim** (thesis), **grounds** (evidence or emotional appeal), and **warrant** (assumption linking claim to grounds).

In using reason rather than emotional appeals in persuasion, it is necessary to understand the distinction between the two primary types of reasoning. **Inductive reasoning** involves moving from specific evidence to a general conclusion, while **deductive reasoning** moves from a general statement to specific conclusions. Using inductive reasoning to persuade your audience to oppose the toxic waste dump, for example, would be based on a collection of specific pieces of evidence:

Evidence:

Toxic waste dumps cause health problems.

Toxic waste dumps pose environmental dangers.

Toxic waste dumps result in lower property values.

Toxic waste dumps result in higher health-care costs.

Conclusion:

A toxic waste dump in this community should be opposed.

A deductive approach, on the other hand, would probably involve presenting a **syllogism**. A syllogism comprises three parts: the **major premise** (a general statement about a category or class), the **minor premise** (a specific statement about one member of that category or class), and the **conclusion** (derived about the specific member). If presented in the form of a syllogism, Maya Angelou's argument against segregation might look like this:

Major premise:	Segregation is always unjust.
Minor premise:	The school system of Stamps, Arkansas was segregated in the 1940s.
Conclusion:	The school system of Stamps, Arkansas in the 1940s was unjust.

Looking at Angelou's piece in this way illustrates the interrelationship between rational arguments and emotional appeals. While the syllogism is valid, the real persuasive power of "Graduation" lies in the emotional response it engenders in readers. Similarly, the emotional appeal would lose its effectiveness if the rational argument were not valid.

It should be evident by now that persuasion is perhaps the most complex of the rhetorical strategies outlined here. The successful persuasive essay is directed at a specific audience, employs appropriate rational and emotional appeals, and follows the rules of logic.

⤳ THE TYGER ⤳

William Blake

William Blake (1757–1827) was born in London, the second of five children. From childhood, Blake claimed he saw visions: angels in a tree, and the prophet Ezekiel in a field. As a child, Blake educated himself by reading and by studying engravings from paintings of Renaissance masters. Later, Blake was apprenticed to an engraver and, in 1782, married a poor, illiterate woman. He set up a printshop in 1784, with his wife and brother Robert helping him. When Robert fell ill and died in 1787, Blake said that he had seen Robert's soul rising through the ceiling and that Robert had revealed to him a new method of engraving books. Blake wrote poetry and drew imaginative illustrations. He used the technique given him in his vision to engrave poems and illustrations together on copper plates from which books were printed. Considered one of the greatest poets ever to write in English, Blake produced a number of works in which religious feeling, sensuality, imagination, and technical brilliance were combined with words and pictures. Two of his most famous works are Songs of Innocence, *produced in 1789, and* Songs of Experience, *printed in a double collection with* Songs of Innocence *in 1794. Blake wanted the collection to show "the two contrary states of the human soul." Blake depicted the innocent child's soul, which simply grows, in contrast with the experienced adult's soul, which is repressed by law and morality. In the following poem, written in 1794, innocence is represented by the lamb while experience is represented by the strong, cruel tyger.*

1 Tyger, Tyger, burning bright
In the forests of the night,
What immortal hand or eye
Could frame thy fearful symmetry?

5 In what distant deeps or skies
Burnt the fire of thine eyes?
On what wings dare he aspire?
What the hand dare seize the fire?

And what shoulder and what art
10 Could twist the sinews of thy heart?
And, when thy heart began to beat,
What dread hand and what dread feet?

What the hammer? What the chain?
In what furnace was thy brain?
15 What the anvil? What dread grasp
Dare its deadly terror clasp?

When the stars threw down their spears,
And watered heaven with their tears,
Did he smile his work to see?
20 Did he who made the Lamb make thee?

Tyger, Tyger, burning bright
In the forests of the night,
What immortal hand or eye
Dare frame thy fearful symmetry?

Questions on Meaning

1. Describe the scene that you see when you imagine the action described in this poem.
2. The phrase "fearful symmetry" is often quoted. What does it mean in the context of this poem?

Questions on Rhetorical Strategy and Style

1. A rhetorical question does not require an answer: in fact, it usually disguises a statement. Paraphrase Blake's rhetorical questions into the statements he is actually making.
2. Is Blake comparing the maker of the tiger to a metalworker of some kind? What evidence do you find for this interpretation? Why might that comparison be an appropriate way to depict the nature of a tiger? If you think some other comparison is intended, cite evidence to support your view, and explain the appropriateness of the comparison.

Writing Assignments

1. Tell the story of an experience during which you came face to face with a frightening element of the natural environment.
2. Spend an afternoon at the zoo or in a forest or garden. Make careful notes about your observations and write them up in an essay that focuses on the most vivid elements of the environment.

⤚ WE REAL COOL ⤙

Gwendolyn Brooks

Gwendolyn Brooks (1917-) was born in Topeka, Kansas, but has lived her life in Chicago and has become one of the most beloved of Illinois poets. She attended Wilson Junior College in Chicago and was graduated in 1938. Her first poem, "Eventide," appeared in the magazine American Childhood *when she was yet in her early teens. She published many poems in the* Chicago Defender, *a local paper. Her first book of poems,* A Street in Bronzeville *was published in 1945.* Annie Allen *(1949) won Brooks a Pulitzer Prize. Other collections of her poetry include* Bronzeville Boy and Girls *(1956),* The Bean Eaters *(1960),* Selected Poems *(1963),* In the Mecca *(1968),* Riot *(1969),* Blacks *(1987), and* Children Coming Home *(1991). She also has written an autobiographical novel,* Maud Martha *(1953) and a book of memoirs,* Report from Part One *(1972). "We Real Cool" expresses the quality of life in the city for young African-American men in the early 1960s.*

The Pool Players.
Seven at the Golden Shovel.

We real cool. We
Left school. We

Lurk late. We
Strike straight. We

Sing sin. We
Thin gin. We

Jazz June. We
Die soon.

"We Real Cool," from *Blacks* by Gwendolyn Brooks. Copyright © 1991 by Gwendolyn Brooks. Published by Third World Press, Chicago, 1991. Reprinted by permission of the author.

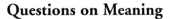

Questions on Meaning

1. The subtitle of "We Real Cool" is "The Pool Players. Seven at the Golden Shovel." What associations does the poem make with pool playing and the life of young men?
2. Does Brooks' poem have a political edge? What persuasive intention might she have for the speakers in the poem and for her readers?
3. The speakers in "We Real Cool" may become an example to other young people. Does Brooks seem to be giving a reason for picking these particular young men for her example of the dangerous life? Why?

Questions on Rhetorical Strategy and Style

1. What kind of language is Brooks approximating in the poem? What kinds of reactions might readers have to that language?
2. Who is speaking in the poem, and what is the reader supposed to think and feel about the speakers?
3. The life of the youngsters in the poem will clearly lead to a bad end, or so says the poem. What chain of causation does the poem imply? Do young people believe that their actions will lead to bad effects?

Writing Assignments

1. Find current rap lyrics that use the same types of rhythm and style as Brooks' poem. Write about your reaction to the effects of these rhythms.
2. Does the social commentary in the poem have as strong an effect in the beginning of the twenty-first century as it did in the middle of the twentieth century? What does your answer to this question say about human progress?
3. "We Real Cool" appears to be about not growing up, but what does it say about the need to grow up? Write an essay or poem that give examples of behaviors that imply acceptance of adult responsibilities.

BECAUSE I COULD NOT STOP FOR DEATH—

Emily Dickinson

Emily Dickinson (1830-1886) was born in Amherst, Massachusetts, where she lived an almost hidden life. She attended Mount Holyoke Female Seminary (1847-1848); in 1854 she met the Reverend Charles Wadsworth, who some say became her imaginary lover. Whatever the facts, he soon left for California and reclusiveness became Dickinson's permanent way of life. She wrote many poems, some of which she showed to her sister-in-law Susan, but most of her work remained hidden until after her death. The poems first began to be published in 1890, but the definitive edition, The Poems of Emily Dickinson, *edited by Thomas H. Johnson, did not appear until 1955.*

1 Because I could not stop for Death—
He kindly stopped for me—
The Carriage held but just Ourselves—
And Immortality.

5 We slowly drove—He knew no haste
And I had put away
My labor and my leisure too,
For His Civility—

We passed the School, where Children strove
At Recess—in the Ring—
We passed the Fields of Gazing Grain—
We passed the Setting Sun—

Or rather—He passed Us—
The Dews drew quivering and chill—
For only Gossamer, my Gown—
My Tippet—only Tulle—

We paused before a House that seemed
A Swelling of the Ground—
The Roof was scarcely visible—
The Cornice—in the Ground—

Since then—'tis Centuries—and yet
Feels shorter than the Day
I first surmised the Horses' Heads
Were toward Eternity—

Questions on Meaning

1. Dickinson may have had an unhappy love affair, after which she seems to have withdrawn from all social life. How does the death imagery in the poem reflect feelings of lost love?
2. The speaker says that she has put away her "labor and leisure" and that she has done so for death's "civility." What kind of values about death does the word "civility" imply? Is death always a bad thing?
3. How does Dickinson leave the reader with more questions about death than answers? Do these kinds of questions still trouble people? Find a current news event or news report that brings up these same questions and write about the meaning of the story.

Questions on Rhetorical Strategy and Style

1. Death is compared to a kindly coachman who stops his horse and carriage for the poem's speaker. What effect does the comparison have on the reader? Is death at all like a coachman? How?
2. What does the use of the words gossamer (like a spider web) and tulle (fine net) to describe the speaker's clothing suggest about the state of the speaker? Is she a ghost or a corpse? How do we know?
3. What is the "house"? Why is it a "swelling"? Does comparing the grave to a house make the poem more or less disturbing? How does the comparison make the reader respond to both graves and houses?

Writing Assignments

1. Critics have noted that all Dickinson's poems can be sung to hymn tunes. Find a popular song that deals with the kinds of issues that Dickinson takes up in this poem and compare both the meaning and the rhythms of the two works.
2. Dickinson lived to be only fifty-six years old and lived most of her life by herself. Did she appear to have an unhappy life? Find other stories about people, especially women, who have lived private lives alone, either as scholars or as religious people. How do such lives contrast with society's expectations about happiness? Write about your beliefs or values on this subject.
3. Dickinson did not publish her poems but appears to have written them for her personal pleasure. What do you write for pleasure? If you do not write for pleasure, try keeping a journal or log book for a week. Read back over your entries at the end of the week, and write about what you discovered from them.

INDIAN BOARDING SCHOOL:
THE RUNAWAYS

Louise Erdrich

Karen Louise Erdrich (1954-) was born in Little Falls, Minnesota and grew up in Wahpeton, North Dakota, where her parents worked at the Bureau of Indian Affairs School. She attended Dartmouth and Johns Hopkins universities. She claims a French Ojibwe heritage from her mother and is a member of the Turtle Mountain Band of Chippewa. A prize-winning fiction writer, Erdrich is probably best known for her novels, which include the acclaimed Love Medicine *(1984) and* Beet Queen *(1986). She and her husband, writer Michael Dorris, separated in 1995; Dorris committed suicide in 1997. Erdrich now lives in Minneapolis, Minnesota with their children. In this poem, she writes from the point of view of the Native American child struggling in the environment of the government school.*

1   Home's the place we head for in our sleep.
    Boxcars stumbling north in dreams
    don't wait for us. We catch them on the run.
    The rails, old lacerations that we love,
5   shoot parallel across the face and break
    just under Turtle Mountains. Riding scars
    you can't get lost. Home is the place they cross.

    The lame guard strikes a match and makes the dark
    less tolerant. We watch through cracks in boards
10 as the land starts rolling, rolling till it hurts
    to be here, cold in regulation clothes.

We know the sheriff's waiting at midrun
to take us back. His car is dumb and warm.
The highway doesn't rock, it only hums
15   like a wing of long insults. The worn-down welts   15
of ancient punishments lead back and forth.
All runaways wear dresses, long green ones,
the color you would think shame was. We scrub
the sidewalks down because it's shameful work.
20   Our brushes cut the stone in watered arcs   20
and in the soak frail outlines shiver clear
a moment, things us kids pressed on the dark
face before it hardened, pale, remembering
delicate old injuries, the spines of names and leaves.

Questions on Meaning

1. Erdrich uses the conflict between Native Americans and the white culture to set the background of the poem's similes and metaphors. Consider the lines, "The highway doesn't rock, it only hums / like a wing of long insults. The worn-down welts / of ancient punishments lead back and forth." Explain the literal and figurative meanings implied in these lines.
2. The punishment given runaways is to clean sidewalks, yet another in the series of references to hard surfaces that are the signs of white civilization. What is Erdrich's point?

Questions on Rhetorical Strategy and Style

1. In the first verse paragraph of the poem, the train's rails are "lacerations" or "scars." Explain the implied comparison between railroads and highways.
2. Erdrich uses language in complex ways. For example, she refers to the car as "dumb and warm." The words' sounds are similar, but their meanings seem odd together. She probably means you to understand *dumb* in the sense of "silent," but the other meanings of *dumb* provide interesting alternate possibilities for meaning. Define the words and explain how you would interpret the line.

Writing Assignments

1. Investigate the history of the boarding schools for Native American children administered by the United States government. Write an essay that explains the historical background of this poem.
2. The runaways in this poem have boarded a freight train to try to return to their homes on a reservation, fleeing from one form of imprisonment to another. Does their situation resemble any that you have experienced? Write a narrative essay that describes a time when you were in flight.

 BIRCHES

Robert Frost

Robert Frost (1874-1963), the American poet everyone knows, was born in San Francisco, studied at Dartmouth and Harvard, worked in a mill, taught school, and farmed in New Hampshire before his first volume of poems was published. Having achieved prominence in the United States by 1915, he taught at many colleges and universities as well as at the famous Bread Loaf Writer's Conference. He won the Pulitzer four times, had a mountain in Vermont named after him, and read at John F. Kennedy's inauguration. He aspired to write a few poems it would be hard to get rid of, an ambition he achieved in "Stopping by Woods on a Snowy Evening," "The Death of the Hired Man," and "Birches," among others. "Birches" is typical of Frost's work in its rural themes and philosophical reflection.

1   When I see birches bend to left and right   1
    Across the lines of straighter darker trees,
    I like to think some boy's been swinging them.
    But swinging doesn't bend them down to stay
5   As ice storms do. Often you must have seen them   5
    Loaded with ice a sunny winter morning
    After a rain. They click upon themselves
    As the breeze rises, and turn many-colored
    As the stir cracks and crazes their enamel.
10 Soon the sun's warmth makes them shed crystal shells   10
    Shattering and avalanching on the snow crust—
    Such heaps of broken glass to sweep away
    You'd think the inner dome of heaven had fallen.
    They are dragged to the withered bracken by the load,

15 And they seem not to break; though once they are bowed
So low for long, they never right themselves:
You may see their trunks arching in the woods
Years afterwards, trailing their leaves on the ground
Like girls on hands and knees that throw their hair
20 Before them over their heads to dry in the sun.
But I was going to say when Truth broke in
With all her matter of fact about the ice storm,
I should prefer to have some boy bend them
As he went out and in to fetch the cows—
25 Some boy too far from town to learn baseball,
Whose only play was what he found himself,
Summer or winter, and could play alone.
One by one he subdued his father's trees
By riding them down over and over again
30 Until he took the stiffness out of them,
And not one but hung limp, not one was left
For him to conquer. He learned all there was
To learn about not launching out too soon
And so not carrying the tree away
35 Clear to the ground. He always kept his poise
To the top branches, climbing carefully
With the same pains you use to fill a cup
Up to the brim, and even above the brim.
Then he flung outward, feet first, with a swish,
40 Kicking his way down through the air to the ground.
So was I once myself a swinger of birches.
And so I dream of going back to be.
It's when I'm weary of considerations,
And life is too much like a pathless wood
45 Where your face burns and tickles with the cobwebs
Broken across it, and one eye is weeping
From a twig's having lashed across it open.
I'd like to get away from earth awhile
And then come back to it and begin over.
50 May no fate willfully misunderstand me
And half grant what I wish and snatch me away
Not to return. Earth's the right place for love:
I don't know where it's likely to go better.

I'd like to go by climbing a birch tree,
55 And climb black branches up a snow-white trunk 55
Toward heaven, till the tree could bear no more,
But dipped its top and set me down again.
That would be good both going and coming back.
One could do worse than be a swinger of birches.

Questions on Meaning

1. List the references to things from or in the sky. What point is being made with these references?
2. Why does Frost capitalize the word "Truth"? And what is the Truth to which he refers?

Questions on Rhetorical Strategy and Style

1. Bending birches evidently involves climbing a young tree and then shifting one's weight until the tree bends slowly down, a little like an escalator, and deposits the rider on the ground. But the bent birches appear to Frost's imagination to be like girls drying their hair. Is the comparison appropriate? Why do you think he chose that comparison and not something like the escalator comparison we suggested?
2. The poem is divided into two parts—the first having to do with the effects of ice storms and the second with the effects of boys on the birches. What is the point of the implied comparison between ice storms and boys? (Hint: if you don't know where to start, make a list of details about boys and ice storms.)

Writing Assignments

1. Read the poem aloud to a partner, and then listen while the partner reads it to you. As you read, ignore the ends of the lines; read the poem as if it were prose, noticing that Frost creates pleasant rhythms with his sentence structure. Then turn to some of your own writing and revise a paragraph or two, striving to create a rhythm that is pleasant to hear aloud.
2. In an essay, tell the story of a favorite preadolescent game you played. Start by drawing a map of the place you played in, and then describe the game and the people you played with. Strive to recapture the experience using words that *evoke* emotional states rather than words that *name* emotional states. (For example, don't write, "Racing made me excited." Instead, describe the actions of someone who is experiencing the emotion you want to evoke. "I gripped the handlebars of my bike harder and pumped furiously as Alan closed the distance between us.")

THOSE WINTER SUNDAYS

Robert Hayden

Robert Hayden (1913-1980) was born and raised in Detroit, Michigan and studied at Detroit City College (now Wayne State University) and the University of Michigan (M.A., 1944). He taught at Fisk University and the University of Michigan, where he remained until his death. Hayden was awarded many literary prizes and was honored as Consultant in Poetry to the Library of Congress. He published ten books of poems in his lifetime and often wrote on African-American themes. Notable works include Mourning Time: Poems *(1971) and* The Night-Blooming Cereus *(1972). "Those Winter Sundays" is among his most famous poems. It originally appeared in the 1975 collection* Angle of Ascent *and is a powerful statement on the complexities of love in the family.*

1   Sundays too my father got up early   1
    and put his clothes on in the blueblack cold,
    then with cracked hands that ached
    from labor in the weekday weather made
5   banked fires blaze. No one ever thanked him.   5

    I'd wake and hear the cold splintering, breaking.
    When the rooms were warm, he'd call,
    and slowly I would rise and dress,
    fearing the chronic angers of that house,

10 Speaking indifferently to him,
who had driven out the cold
and polished my good shoes as well.
What did I know, what did I know
of love's austere and lonely offices?

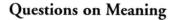
Questions on Meaning

1. How would you characterize the atmosphere in the house during those cold mornings Hayden recalls? What is the significance of describing things in this way?
2. What does the season of Winter bring to Hayden's image of familial relations, that Spring, Summer, or Fall might not?

Questions on Rhetorical Strategy and Style

1. Hayden's poem relies on detailed images drawn from his memory. Point out some examples of descriptive language in the poem. What senses does the author rely upon?
2. Hayden makes a point of describing the condition of his father's hands. What does this description contribute to the overall meaning?
3. What picture of his father does the poet paint? How does he create this image?

Writing Assignments

1. Recall a childhood memory you have of one of your parents. What meaning does that memory have for you?
2. Write about a time when you made a discovery about your father or mother. What did you realize, and how did you come to that understanding?

MID-TERM BREAK

Seamus Heaney

Seamus Heaney (1939-) was born in Londonderry in Northern Ireland, studied in Belfast at St. Joseph's College, and moved to Dublin in 1976. He has won many honors as a poet, most significantly the Nobel Prize for Literature in 1995 "for works of lyrical beauty and ethical depth, which exalt everyday miracles and the living past." He has taught at Oxford, Berkeley, and Harvard. Noteworthy collections include Haw Lantern *(1987),* Seeing Things *(1991),* Selected Poems: 1966-1987 *(1990), and his most recent collection,* The Spirit Level *(1996). Heaney has also written plays and essays. "Mid-term Break" was first published in 1980.*

1 I sat all morning in the college sick bay   1
Counting bells knelling classes to a close.
At two o'clock our neighbors drove me home.

In the porch I met my father crying—
5 He had always taken funerals in his stride —   5
And Big Jim Evans saying it was a hard blow.

The baby cooed and laughed and rocked the pram
When I came in, and I was embarrassed
By old men standing up to shake my hand

10 And tell me they were "sorry for my trouble,"   10
Whispers informed strangers I was the eldest,
Away at school, as my mother held my hand

In hers and coughed out angry tearless sighs.
At ten o'clock the ambulance arrived
15 With the corpse, stanched and bandaged by the nurses. 15

Next morning 1 went up into the room. Snowdrops
And candles soothed the bedside; I saw him
For the first time in six weeks. Paler now,

Wearing a poppy bruise on his left temple,
20 He lay in the four foot box as in his cot. 20
No gaudy scars, the bumper knocked him clear.

A four foot box, a foot for every year.

Questions on Meaning

1. What event does Heaney recount in this poem? What is the significance of the title?
2. Why does the poet mention that his father "had always taken funerals in his stride"?

Questions on Rhetorical Strategy and Style

1. We can discover much about a poem's meaning by examining its tone. How would you describe Heaney's tone here? What is his attitude toward the event?
2. You might notice that the poet never mentions the child's name. Why?
3. Each stanza in the poem, except for the last, is three lines in length. How does this form serve its overall meaning?

Writing Assignments

1. Write an essay about a sad event in your life. Try to capture your state of mind at the time by describing in detail things you remember seeing and hearing. As you recount these details, consider what dominant impression you want to create.
2. Write an essay in which you recount your memories of returning home for the first time. Was it on the occasion of a significant family event? How did you feel at the time? In what way were things different?

⌒ WHEN I WAS ⌒
ONE-AND-TWENTY

A. E. Housman

Alfred Edward Housman was born in England in 1859 and died in 1936. He attended Oxford University but failed his final examinations, probably because of an unhappy love affair, and took a job working at the Patent Office. Determined to return to the academic world, he contributed articles to learned journals and by 1911 had won a position as a professor of Latin at Cambridge University. Although he remained a Latin scholar all his life, he is best remembered for his sentimental poetry, and especially for the poems of A Shropshire Lad, *the volume from which this poem is taken. In "When I Was One-and-Twenty," Housman tells a sad truth about being in love that is as hard to remember when one is older as it is to learn when one is younger.*

1 When I was one-and-twenty   1
  I heard a wise man say,
"Give crowns and pounds and guineas
  But not your heart away;

5 Give pearls away and rubies   5
  But keep your fancy free."
But I was one-and-twenty,
  No use to talk to me.

When I was one-and-twenty
10   I heard him say again,
"The heart out of the bosom
        Was never given in vain;

'Tis paid with sighs a plenty
        And sold for endless rue."
15   And I am two-and-twenty,
        And oh, 'tis true, 'tis true.

Questions on Meaning

1. Summarize the poem in prose. Do your very best to change it entirely into your own words. Find out your school's or teacher's policy on plagiarism, exchange your summaries with a classmate, and discuss whether you have avoided plagiarizing. Consult with your teacher as well.

2. Using only the summary you prepared for question 4, attempt to reconstruct the original poem. Noting which parts were easiest for you to remember, speculate about what makes writing clear and effective.

Questions on Rhetorical Strategy and Style

1. Housman's poem is on the theme of lost love, yet the narrator leaves out the whole story of losing his love, revealing only that it has happened. Comment on this strategy. Would it have been more effective to insert the details of the unhappy love affair? Why?

2. Listen to some popular music and try to match the words of "When I Was One-and-Twenty" to the music and rhythm. Once you have made a close match, see if you can remember the words without looking back at the text. Does setting them to music help? How does the music change the way you perceive organization and emphasis in the poem?

Writing Assignments

1. In the sixth line, what does the word *fancy* mean? Find other words in a college dictionary that are related to fancy (e.g., start with fanciful and fantasy) and write a short essay that describes the meaning and development of the word.

2. Does twenty-one seem young or old to be having one's first unhappy love affair? Use a study to attempt to learn what age is the norm. Use a questionnaire that asks people for both simple facts (e.g., "What age were you when you first fell in love?") and open-ended narratives (e.g., "How and why did you lose your first love?") and prepare a report from your results. You'll probably get better results with your questionnaire if you allow your respondents to remain anonymous. In any case, you must tell anyone who fills out your questionnaire exactly how you plan to use the information, and you must get each person's written permission to use the responses in your research.

THE NEGRO SPEAKS OF RIVERS

Langston Hughes

Langston Hughes (1902–1967) was born in Joplin, Missouri, in 1902 and grew up in Kansas and Ohio. A poet from childhood, he attended Columbia University to study engineering but dropped out. In 1923, Hughes shipped out on a freighter to Africa, and later to Italy and France, Russia and Spain. He eventually returned to college at Lincoln University, from which he was graduated in 1929. In his long career as a writer, Hughes published sixteen books of poetry. The poem reprinted here is the first one he published.

I've known rivers:
I've known rivers ancient as the world and older than the
    flow of human blood in human veins.

My soul has grown deep like the rivers.

I bathed in the Euphrates when dawns were young.
I built my hut near the Congo and it lulled me to sleep.
I looked upon the Nile and raised the pyramids above it.
I heard the singing of the Mississippi when Abe Lincoln
    went down to New Orleans, and I've seen its muddy
    bosom turn all golden in the sunset.

I've known rivers:
Ancient, dusky rivers.

My soul has grown deep like the rivers.

Questions on Meaning

1. Working with a classmate, recall as many stories, poems, songs, and other art works as you can that give a place of importance to rivers. What does this list tell you about Hughes's decision to use the river as the central image of this poem?
2. Find the word *soul* in a dictionary and describe its various meanings.

Questions on Rhetorical Strategy and Style

1. What logical progression is created in the lines that describe the four rivers?
2. What point is Hughes making about the special relationship between "Negro" peoples and rivers? Is he comparing them? Does he suggest a causal relationship between the spirit of Negro peoples and the river? Explain.

Writing Assignments

1. Draw a map of the river with which you are most familiar. On your map, mark where you fished, or swam, or sailed, or threw rocks, or in some other way experienced the river. Then write an essay that details one experience or a few related experiences having to do with the river.
2. Map an imaginary river that represents your life. Note where there were shallows and deep spots, note the source and hint at the destination, include the traffic that the river carried, the streams that flowed into it, and the places it flowed through.

 DADDY

Sylvia Plath

Sylvia Plath (1932-1963) grew up in Boston, the daughter of a Boston University entomologist who died when she was eight years old. Plath was a good student, as children of university faculty often are, but she sometimes found herself unable to go on with her writing or her academic work. She attended Smith College, where she was graduated summa cum laude. She then earned a Fulbright Scholarship to Oxford where she met the English poet, Ted Hughes, whom she quickly married. Her poetry and her one novel, The Bell Jar *(1963), indicate the stresses in her life and her marriage. Separated and living with her two small children in a flat in London, she succumbed to those stresses and committed suicide in 1963. Her books of poetry include* A Winter Ship *(1960) and* The Colossus and Other Poems *(1960). "Daddy" (1962) embodies some of the more negative features of feminist attitudes but also expresses a kind of anger that many women suppress.*

1 You do not do, you do not do
Any more, black shoe
In which I have lived like a foot
For thirty years, poor and white,
5 Barely daring to breathe or Achoo.

Daddy, I have had to kill you.
You died before I had time——
Marble-heavy, a bag full of God,
Ghastly statue with one grey toe
10 Big as a Frisco seal

And a head in the freakish Atlantic
Where it pours bean green over blue
In the waters off beautiful Nauset.
I used to pray to recover you.
15 Ach, du.

In the German tongue, in the Polish town
Scraped flat by the roller
Of wars, wars, wars.
But the name of the town is common.
20 My Polack friend

Says there are a dozen or two.
So I never could tell where you
Put your foot, your root,
I never could talk to you.
25 The tongue stuck in my jaw.

It stuck in a barb wire snare.
Ich, ich, ich, ich,
I could hardly speak.
I thought every German was you.
30 And the language obscene

An engine, an engine
Chuffing me off like a Jew.
A Jew to Dachau, Auschwitz, Belsen.
I began to talk like a Jew.
35 I think I may well be a Jew.

The snows of the Tyrol, the clear beer of Vienna
Are not very pure or true.
With my gypsy ancestress and my weird luck
And my Taroc pack and my Taroc pack
40 I may be a bit of a Jew.

I have always been scared of *you*,
With your Luftwaffe, your gobbledygoo.
And your neat moustache

And your Aryan eye, bright blue.
45 Panzer-man, panzer-man, O You——— 45

Not God but a swastika
So black no sky could squeak through.
Every woman adores a Fascist,
The boot in the face, the brute
50 Brute heart of a brute like you. 50

You stand at the blackboard, daddy,
In the picture I have of you,
A cleft in your chin instead of your foot
But no less a devil for that, no not
55 Any less the black man who 55

Bit my pretty red heart in two.
I was ten when they buried you.
At twenty I tried to die
And get back, back, back to you.
60 I thought even the bones would do 60

But they pulled me out of the sack,
And they stuck me together with glue.
And then I knew what to do.
I made a model of you,
65 A man in black with a Meinkampf look 65

And a love of the rack and the screw.
And I said I do, I do.
So daddy, I'm finally through.
The black telephone's off at the root,
70 The voices just can't worm through. 70

If I've killed one man, I've killed two———
The vampire who said he was you
And drank my blood for a year,
Seven years, if you want to know.
75 Daddy, you can lie back now. 75

There's a stake in your fat black heart
And the villagers never liked you.
They are dancing and stamping on you.
They always *knew* it was you.
Daddy, daddy, you bastard, I'm through.

80

80

Questions on Meaning

1. Psychologists suggest that all adults carry images of their parents and early caregivers in their personalities. What kind of man does Plath carry in her psyche? What kind of man does she appear to marry?

2. Most people pass through stages when they have blamed their parents for their problems. Is it fair to blame a parent for dying during a person's childhood? Discuss the idea of anger as Plath expresses it in the poem.

3. At the end of the poem, Plath says, "Daddy, daddy, . . ., I'm through." What is she through with? Has she escaped her obsession with her father, or is she saying that she has been overcome by his image and influence? Use evidence from the poem to argue either way.

Questions on Rhetorical Strategy and Style

1. Plath seems to be showing in this poem that her father has caused her life's distress. What evidence in the poem seems to confirm this causal link?

2. Why does Plath compare her life to the lives of Jews who were captured and carried off to concentration camps during World War II? Discuss this comparison. Does she persuade the reader that her suffering is so severe?

Writing Assignments

1. What is the difference between the words "daddy," "dad," and "father"? Why do we have these separate words? Do a survey of people you know asking them what words they use for their fathers or father figures, then write about the power of such words and their meanings. Discuss what the choice of a particular word can mean. How do these kinds of words change our family values and feelings?

2. Write about the "parent" you carry in your head. It doesn't have to be your biological parent or your caregiver, but think about the part of your personality that makes rules for you. What internalized rules run your life? Where did they come from?

3. "Daddy" works with stereotypes of blue-eyed Germans and images of World War II. What stereotypes of war does your generation carry and how do those images affect the way you see the world? Who is the "enemy" now, and how do we treat certain people unfairly because of those images?

MY PAPA'S WALTZ

Theodore Roethke

Theodore Roethke (1908–1963) was born in Saginaw, Michigan. He attended the University of Michigan and Harvard University and taught at Pennsylvania State University, Bennington College, and the University of Washington. His fourth volume of poetry, The Waking *(1953) won the Pulitzer Prize for Poetry and led to his popularity as an American poet.* Words for the Wind *(1958) became his best known work, which included a selection of poems from his previous work. His* Collected Poems *was published posthumously in 1968. "My Papa's Waltz" is the adult son's recollection of, and coming to grips with, the sometimes frenzied behavior of his father.*

The whiskey on your breath
Could make a small boy dizzy;
But I hung on like death:
Such waltzing was not easy.

We romped until the pans
Slid from the kitchen shelf;
My mother's countenance
Could not unfrown itself.

The hand that held my wrist
Was battered on one knuckle;
At every step I missed
My right ear scraped a buckle.

You beat time on my head
With a palm caked hard by dirt,
Then waltzed me off to bed
Still clinging to your shirt.

From *The Collected Poems of Theodore Roethke.* Published by Doubleday, a division of Bantam Doubleday Dell Publishing Group, Inc. Copyright © 1942 by Hearst Magazines, Inc.

Questions on Meaning

1. Why is this waltzing not easy for the small boy? Why does he hang on "like death"?
2. What sort of relationship do you think the young boy has with his father? What phrases or images in the poem give you this impression?

Questions on Rhetorical Strategy and Style

1. Describe the tone of the poem. What attitude is revealed in a phrase like "Could not unfrown itself"?
2. What is the effect of the rhythm and rhymes? Describe how this effect interacts with the apparently serious reality of his drunk father.

Writing Assignments

1. We all had moments in our childhood when we experienced fear, or pain, or embarrassment because of some action or behavior by a parent or guardian. Search your memory for one such specific moment. Recall it in as much detail as you can. Without using abstract terms such as "unhappy" or "painful," make a list of some of the facts you would use to describe what happened.
2. Write a narrative passage in which you describe a scene in a film or television program. Your goal is only to describe the scene in an objective way—do not make any judgments, do not summarize, do not generalize. Use only concrete words that physically describe what you see and hear. After you have written this description, read it and analyze what feeling arises from your description. Does it reveal your attitude toward what happens, as you are "objectively" describing it?

SONNET 18: SHALL I COMPARE THEE TO A SUMMER'S DAY?

William Shakespeare

According to tradition, William Shakespeare was born on April 23, 1564 in Stratford-upon-Avon, England. He was the third of eight children born to John and Mary Shakespeare. At age 18, he married 26-year-old Anne Hathaway, six months before the birth of their son. Two years later, there were twins to support as well. It is well known that by the time he was 25, he was a working actor and playwright in London. When he died on his birthday in 1616, he had completed a body of work that ensured his place as the greatest poet and playwright ever to write in English. In addition to writing the nearly forty plays for the stage in London that are best known to the public, Shakespeare wrote a number of poems, including a series (or "cycle") of sonnets that includes the sonnet reprinted here. In it, Shakespeare opens with a rhetorical question, "Shall I compare thee to a summer's day," that represents a conventional kind of flattering overstatement used in love poems of the time.

1   Shall I compare thee to a summer's day?   1
Thou art more lovely and more temperate:
Rough winds do shake the darling buds of May,
And summer's lease hath all too short a date;
5   Sometime too hot the eye of heaven shines,   5
And often is his gold complexion dimmed,
And every fair from fair sometime declines,
By chance or nature's changing course untrimmed:
But thy eternal summer shall not fade,

10

Nor lose possession of that fair thou ow'st,
Nor shall Death brag thou wand'rest in his shade,
When in eternal lines to time thou grow'st.
    So long as men can breathe or eyes can see,
    So long lives this, and this gives life to thee.

Questions on Meaning

1. The word *untrimmed* meant "stripped of its beauty" in the Early Modern English of Shakespeare's time. Are the words *temperate, lease*, and *date* used in their modern senses? Look them up in a college dictionary or the *Oxford English Dictionary* and identify the definition you think is being used.

2. Paraphrase the poem, writing it as if it were a love letter. Then summarize the argument that the poet is making to his beloved. Is it logical? Persuasive? What do you think he hoped to accomplish?

3. Poets phrase their lines very economically to create rhyme and meter without sounding awkward. This sometimes results in ambiguity, as in the line "And every fair from fair sometime declines . . . ." What are the meanings of the word *fair* in that line?

Questions on Rhetorical Strategy and Style

1. Notice that the poet's argument comes in two parts—the first eight lines (called an "octave") express a sentiment and the last six lines (the "sestet") present an observation based on the sentiment. Describe the change in tone from the octave to the sestet.

2. This poem is a sonnet. That is, it consists of fourteen lines in a meter called iambic pentameter (ten syllables per line with weak and strong stress alternating from one syllable to the next). Which lines sound "poetic" to you, and which might be written as prose? Explain.

Writing Assignments

1. This sonnet is the eighteenth in a series (or "cycle") that Shakespeare wrote. Its theme is the impermanence of youth and beauty. Find the rest of the series in the library (or on the Internet at the Gutenberg electronic text site at http://www.gutenberg.net/). Read some of the sonnets and report on other themes that you find there.

2. In a book on literary terms, find the term *Petrarchan Sonnet*. Compare and contrast Shakespeare's sonnet with the Petrarchan form.

DO NOT GO GENTLE INTO THAT GOOD NIGHT

Dylan Thomas

Dylan Thomas was born on October 27, 1914, in Swansea, Glamorgan, Wales. The son of an English teacher, he became an excellent student of English and a failure at almost everything else. He dropped out of school when he was sixteen, and he went to work as a reporter. When he was twenty, his first book, Eighteen Poems, *was published. Suddenly he was famous. Subsequent research has suggested that most of his best work was begun before he turned twenty-one. Depressive, incapable of handling money, and inclined to alcoholism, Thomas struggled for the next fifteen years to make a living in England while his eloquent books of poetry continued to appear:* Twenty-Five Poems, *1936;* The World I Breath, *1939;* The Map of Love, *1939;* New Poems, *1942;* New Poems, *1943; and* Deaths and Entrances, *1946. In 1950, at the age of thirty-five, Thomas visited America where he delivered a series of passionate poetry readings that made him famous on this side of the Atlantic. The books published during this period—*In Country Sleep, and Other Poems, *1952; and* Collected Poems, *1952—further contributed to his legendary status as a romantic hero. Unfortunately, he also became famous for roaring bouts of drunkenness, one of which killed him at the age of thirty-nine. He died in New York City on November 9, 1953, of an alcohol overdose, leaving behind him a wife, two sons, a daughter, and an exquisite body of poetic work. The elegant villanelle, "Do not go gentle into that good night," a meditation on death*

*and dying, is among the most memorable poems that he
wrote. As you read the poem, try to puzzle out the complex rules by which he composed the lines—a villanelle is
a great test of a poet's skill—and note that, despite the
complex form, his lines sound easy and natural. You may
wonder, as others have done, how a man who could not
discipline himself at all could discipline language so
beautifully.*

1 Do not go gentle into that good night,
Old age should burn and rave at the close of day;
Rage, rage against the dying of the light.

Though wise men at their end know dark is right,
5 Because their words had forked no lightning they
Do not go gentle into that good night.

Good men, the last wave by, crying how bright
Their frail deeds might have danced in a green bay,
Rage, rage against the dying of the light.

10 Wild men who caught and sang the sun in flight,
And learn, too late, they grieved it on its way,
Do not go gentle into that good night.

Grave men, near death, who see with blinding sight
Blind eyes could blaze like meteors and be gay,
15 Rage, rage against the dying of the light.

And you, my father, there on the sad height,
Curse, bless, me now with your fierce tears, I pray.
Do not go gentle into that good night.
Rage, rage against the dying of the light.

Questions on Meaning

1. Read the poem aloud and then paraphrase it in writing.
2. A villanelle is an extremely challenging and complex poetic form. Here are the rules: it must contain nineteen lines divided into six stanzas. The first five must be three-line stanzas (called tercets), and the sixth must be a four-line stanza (called a quatrain). The first and third lines of the first tercet must be repeated alternately as a refrain in tercets two through five and repeated as the last two lines of the quatrain. What is gained and lost when a writer commits to a complex organizational scheme like this one? Cite specific instances from the poem to illustrate your answer.

Questions on Rhetorical Strategy and Style

1. The poem works with an extended analogy in which night and day become death and life. Explain the meaning and appropriateness of the analogy.
2. Two of the lines—"Do not go gentle into that good night" and "Rage, rage against the dying of the light"—are repeated. They seem to restate the same idea. Why do you think the poet chose to restate the same idea? What advantages does he gain in making his message clear? What advantages does he gain in satisfying the requirements of writing a villanelle?

Writing Assignments

1. Write an essay about someone you have known who did not go gentle into that good night.
2. The poem's plea—do not go gentle into that good night—may be more a young person's than an older person's view of death. Ask some older people, perhaps grandparents or people in a nursing home, their views about death and report what you learn.

⌒ THE SECOND COMING ⌒

William Butler Yeats

William Butler Yeats (1865-1939), though born in Dublin, spent his early years in London. His father was the painter John Butler Yeats; his mother's family was from County Sligo in Ireland. Yeats began as a painter but quickly turned to poetry and drama. His fascination with pagan Irish mythology and the occult led him to produce works that reflected Irish legends and other mysterious stories and beings. He founded the Irish National Theatre in 1899. After the Irish rebellion of 1916, he became an avid nationalist and served as a senator from 1922 through 1928. In 1923 he received the Nobel Prize for literature. His first book of poems was The Wanderings of Oisin and Other Poems *(1889) and his first play* The Countess Cathleen *(1892). Later works include* The Green Helmet and Other Poems *(1910),* Michael Robartes and the Dancer *(1921), the autobiographical* A Vision *(1925), and* The Tower *(1928). "The Second Coming" contains many of Yeats' most important symbols and images compacted into a powerful twenty-two lines.*

1   Turning and turning in the widening gyre   1
   The falcon cannot hear the falconer;
   Things fall apart; the center cannot hold;
   Mere anarchy is loosed upon the world,
5   The blood-dimmed tide is loosed, and everywhere   5
   The ceremony of innocence is drowned;
   The best lack all conviction, while the worst
   Are full of passionate intensity.

Surely some revelation is at hand;
10 Surely the Second Coming is at hand.   10
The Second Coming! Hardly are those words out
When a vast image out of *Spiritus Mundi*
Troubles my sight: somewhere in sands of the desert
A shape with lion body and the head of a man,
15 A gaze blank and pitiless as the sun,   15
Is moving its slow thighs, while all about it
Reel shadows of the indignant desert birds.
The darkness drops again; but now I know
That twenty centuries of stony sleep
20 Were vexed to nightmare by a rocking cradle,   20
And what rough beast, its hour come round at last,
Slouches toward Bethlehem to be born?

Questions on Meaning

1. What does "the second coming" traditionally refer to in Christian imagery?

2. A common theme in "modernist" literature of the early twentieth century was the indifference and lack of passion in most powerful and intellectual people. What do lines 7-8 of "The Second Coming" say to a reader at the beginning of the twenty-first century? Does the description still fit?

3. When "The Second Coming" appeared in 1921, the Irish revolution had been accomplished and Yeats was about to become a civic leader. What kinds of fears would a person of great responsibility have in an era just following World War I, the sinking of the Titanic, and the beginnings of technological revolutions?

Questions on Rhetorical Strategy and Style

1. How does Yeats contrast and compare his desert beast to the expected deity?

2. Yeats begins the poem with one of his favorite images but turns the image on its head. The great hunting bird usually swoops through the sky in beautiful spirals, drops for its prey, and returns to its master. Yeats describes the bird in this poem as unable to "hear the falconer." Who might the falconer be, and what could the bird represent?

Writing Assignments

1. At the time of the poem's publication, boundaries were changing in Europe and political alliances were being redrawn in new configurations. Among other things, the Russian Communist revolution had just occurred: The Czar and his family had been shot by rebels. Such changes could certainly have promised anarchy and chaos. Did Yeats accurately predict the rest of the twentieth century? Give examples from your understanding of history.

2. Much mythology has developed around the ending of the second millennium. Find a written account of reactions to the year 1000 and describe the fears and fantasies of that time. What kinds of fears do "postmodern" people have about the year 2000? Write about the reasons for those fears.

3. Yeats brings bird and lion images together in this poem. Draw pictures of the creatures depicted in this poem, and then write about the drawings you have created. What do they represent?

"THE SONG OF WANDERING AENGUS"

William B. Yeats,

William Butler Yeats (1865–1939), though born in Dublin, spent his early years in London. His father was the painter John Bulter Yeats; his mother's family was from County Silgo in Ireland. Yeats began as a painter but quickly turned to poetry and drama. His facisnation with pagan Irish mythology and the occult led him to produce works that reflected Irish legends and other mysterious stories and beings. He founded the Irish National Theatre in 1899. After the Irish rebellion of 1916, he became an avid nationalist and served as a senator from 1922 through 1928. In 1923 he received the Nobel Prize for literature. His first book of poems was The Wanderings of Oisin and Other Poems *(1889) and his first play* The Countess Cathleen *(1892). Later works include* The Green Helmet and Other Poems *(1910),* Michael Robartes and the Dancer *(1921), the autobiographical* A Vision *(1925), and the* Tower *(1928). In "The Song of Wandering Aengus" Yeats asks what a person learns from spititual encounters: does one come away with new knowledge or is one simply overcome by awe?*

1   I went out to the hazel wood,   1
       Because a fire was in my head,
       And cut and peeled a hazel wand,
       And hooked a berry to a thread;
5   And when white moths were on the wing,   5

And moth-like stars were flickering out,
I dropped the berry in a stream
And caught a little silver trout.

When I had laid it on the floor
I went to blow the fire aflame,
But something rustled on the floor,
And some one called me by my name:
It had become a glimmering girl
With apple blossom in her hair
Who called me by my name and ran
And faded through the brightening air.

Though I am old with wandering
Through hollow lands and hilly lands,
I will find out where she has gone,
And kiss her lips and take her hands;
And walk among long dappled grass,
And pluck till time and times are done
The silver apples of the moon,
The golden apples of the sun.

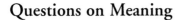

Questions on Meaning

1. What "fire" was in the narrator's head? Why does he go fishing?
2. The first part of the poem takes place in the early morning. Is it a dream? Why does the trout turn into a girl as it becomes light?
3. What has happened to the young man's dreams as he has aged?

Questions on Rhetorical Strategy and Style

1. Each line of the poem has eight syllables divided into four poetic feet (two syllables with the beat on the second), and every second and fourth line rhymes. What effect does this rhythm and rhyme have on the reader?
2. What imagery comes to mind with the last two lines: "the silver apples of the moon,/the golden apples of the sun"? How does this imagery change the rest of the poem?
3. The narrator is telling about early dreams. What is the tone of the poem?

Writing Assignments

1. Look up fire and trout or fish in a book of symbols. What does each represent? Write an essay about the symbolism of these words, especially noting where they appear in everyday symbols that we see frequently (for example, the fish symbol some people put on their cars).
2. Ray Bradbury has written a science fiction book called *The Golden Apples* of the Sun. Read the book and write about why he used the Yeats line for his title.
3. Try to remember one or more of your dreams. Write them down and then try to imagine what they symbolize in your life.

⌐ THE STORM ⌐

Kate Chopin

Kate Chopin (b. Katherine O'Flaherty, 1851–1904) began her life in St. Louis, Missouri. Her father died when she was four years old, so she was reared by three widows: her mother, her grandmother, and her great-grandmother. She graduated from Sacred Heart convent in 1870 and then married Oscar Chopin, following him to New Orleans and later to his plantation in northern Louisiana. The mother of six children, she was widowed in 1882 and moved back to St. Louis where she began to write stories and publish in stylish literary magazines. Her novels, At Fault *(1890) and* The Awakening *(1899), shocked conservative Victorian society but are praised by modern critics. Her collections of short stories,* Bayou Folk *(1894) and* A Night in Acadie *(1897), draw on her years of experience on a Louisiana plantation among Creole people. She died of a brain hemmorage at only fifty-three. In "The Storm" Chopin exlpores the unpredictable results of an adulterous encounter between two former sweethearts during a sudden, violent storm.*

I

The leaves were so still that even Bibi thought it was going to rain. Bobinôt, who was accustomed to converse on terms of perfect equality with his little son, called the child's attention to certain somber clouds that were rolling with sinister intention from the west, accompanied by a sullen, threatening roar. They were at

Friedheimer's store and decided to remain there till the storm had passed. They sat within the door on two empty kegs. Bibi was four years old and looked very wise.

"Mama'll be 'fraid, yes," he suggested with blinking eyes.

"She'll shut the house. Maybe she got Sylvie helpin' her this evenin'," Bobinôt responded reassuringly.

"No; she ent got Sylvie. Sylvie was helpin' her yistiday," piped Bibi.

5   Bobinôt arose and going across to the counter purchased a can of   5
shrimps, of which Calixta was very fond. Then he returned to his perch on the keg and sat stolidly holding the can of shrimps while the storm burst. It shook the wooden store and seemed to be ripping great furrows in the distant field. Bibi laid his little hand on his father's knee and was not afraid.

II

Calixta, at home, felt no uneasiness for their safety. She sat at a side window sewing furiously on a sewing machine. She was greatly occupied and did not notice the approaching storm. But she felt very warm and often stopped to mop her face on which the perspiration gathered in beads. She unfastened her white sacque at the throat. It began to grow dark, and suddenly realizing the situation she got up hurriedly and went about closing windows and doors.

Out on the small front gallery she had hung Bobinôt's Sunday clothes to air and she hastened out to gather them before the rain fell. As she stepped outside, Alcée Laballière rode in at the gate. She had not seen him very often since her marriage, and never alone. She stood there with Bobinôt's coat in her hands, and the big rain drops began to fall. Alcée rode his horse under the shelter of a side projection where the chickens had huddled and there were plows and a harrow piled up in the corner.

"May I come and wait on your gallery till the storm is over, Calixta?" he asked.

"Come 'long in, M'sieur Alcée."

10   His voice and her own startled her as if from a trance, and she   10
seized Bobinôt's vest. Alcée, mounting to the porch, grabbed the trousers and snatched Bibi's braided jacket that was about to be carried away by a sudden gust of wind. He expressed an intention to re-

main outside, but it was soon apparent that he might as well have been out in the open: the water beat in upon the boards in driving sheets, and he went inside, closing the door after him. It was even necessary to put something beneath the door to keep the water out.

"My! what a rain! It's good two years sence it rain' like that," exclaimed Calixta as she rolled up a piece of bagging and Alcée helped her to thrust it beneath the crack.

She was a little fuller of figure than five years before when she married; but she had lost nothing of her vivacity. Her blue eyes still retained their melting quality; and her yellow hair, dishevelled by the wind and rain, kinked more stubbornly than ever about her ears and temples.

The rain beat upon the low, shingled roof with a force and clatter that threatened to break an entrance and deluge them there. They were in the dining room—the sitting room—the general utility room. Adjoining was her bed room, with Bibi's couch along side her own. The door stood open, and the room with its white, monumental bed, its closed shutters, looked dim and mysterious.

Alcée flung himself into a rocker and Calixta nervously began to gather up from the floor the lengths of a cotton sheet which she had been sewing.

15 "If this keeps up, *Dieu sait* if the levees goin' to stan' it!" she exclaimed.

"What have you got to do with the levees?"

"I got enough to do! An' there's Bobinôt with Bibi out in that storm—if he only didn' left Friedheimer's!"

"Let us hope, Calixta, that Bobinôt's got sense enough to come in out of a cyclone."

She went and stood at the window with a greatly disturbed look on her face. She wiped the frame that was clouded with moisture. It was stiflingly hot. Alcée got up and joined her at the window, looking over her shoulder. The rain was coming down in sheets obscuring the view of far-off cabins and enveloping the distant wood in a gray mist. The playing of the lightning was incessant. A bolt struck a tall chinaberry tree at the edge of the field. It filled all visible space with a blinding glare and the crash seemed to invade the very boards they stood upon.

20 Calixta put her hands to her eyes, and with a cry, staggered backward. Alcée's arm encircled her, and for an instant he drew her close and spasmodically to him.

"Bonté!" she cried, releasing herself from his encircling arm and retreating from the window, "the house'll go next! If I only knew w'ere Bibi was!" She would not compose herself; she would not be seated. Alcée clasped her shoulders and looked into her face. The contact of her warm, palpitating body when he had unthinkingly drawn her into his arms, had aroused all the old-time infatuation and desire for her flesh.

"Calixta," he said, "don't be frightened. Nothing can happen. The house is too low to be struck, with so many tall trees standing about. There! aren't you going to be quiet? say, aren't you?" He pushed her hair back from her face that was warm and steaming. Her lips were as red and moist as pomegranate seed. Her white neck and a glimpse of her full, firm bosom disturbed him powerfully. As she glanced up at him the fear in her liquid blue eyes had given place to a drowsy gleam that unconsciously betrayed a sensuous desire. He looked down into her eyes and there was nothing for him to do but to gather her lips in a kiss. It reminded him of Assumption.

"Do you remember—in Assumption, Calixta?" he asked in a low voice broken by passion. Oh! she remembered; for in Assumption he had kissed her and kissed and kissed her; until his senses would well nigh fail, and to save her he would resort to a desperate flight. If she was not an immaculate dove in those days, she was still inviolate; a passionate creature whose very defenselessness had made her defense, against which his honor forbade him to prevail. Now—well, now— her lips seemed in a manner free to be tasted, as well as her round, white throat and her whiter breasts.

They did not heed the crashing torrents, and the roar of the elements made her laugh as she lay in his arms. She was a revelation in that dim, mysterious chamber; as white as the couch she lay upon. Her firm, elastic flesh that was knowing for the first time its birthright, was like a creamy lily that the sun invites to contribute its breath and perfume to the undying life of the world.

The generous abundance of her passion, without guile or trickery, was like a white flame which penetrated and found response in depths of his own sensuous nature that had never yet been reached.

When he touched her breasts they gave themselves up in quivering ecstasy, inviting his lips. Her mouth was a fountain of delight. And when he possessed her, they seemed to swoon together at the very borderland of life's mystery.

He stayed cushioned upon her, breathless, dazed, enervated, with his heart beating like a hammer upon her. With one hand she clasped his head, her lips lightly touching his forehead. The other hand stroked with a soothing rhythm his muscular shoulders.

The growl of the thunder was distant and passing away. The rain beat softly upon the shingles, inviting them to drowsiness and sleep. But they dared not yield.

The rain was over; and the sun was turning the glistening green world into a palace of gems. Calixta, on the gallery, watched Alcée ride away. He turned and smiled at her with a beaming face; and she lifted her pretty chin in the air and laughed aloud.

III

30 Bobinôt and Bibi, trudging home, stopped without at the cistern to make themselves presentable.

"My! Bibi, w'at will yo' mama say! You ought to be ashame'. You oughtn' put on those good pants. Look at 'em! An' that mud on yo' collar! How you got that mud on yo' collar, Bibi? I never saw such a boy!" Bibi was the picture of pathetic resignation. Bobinôt was the embodiment of serious solicitude as he strove to remove from his own person and his son's the signs of their tramp over heavy roads and through wet fields. He scraped the mud off Bibi's bare legs and feet with a stick and carefully removed all traces from his heavy brogans. Then, prepared for the worst—the meeting with an over-scrupulous housewife, they entered cautiously at the back door.

Calixta was preparing supper. She had set the table and was dripping coffee at the hearth. She sprang up as they came in.

"Oh, Bobinôt! You back! My! but I was uneasy. W'ere you been during the rain? An' Bibi? he ain't wet? he ain't hurt?" She had clasped Bibi and was kissing him effusively. Bobinôt's explanations and apologies which he had been composing all along the way, died on his lips as Calixta felt him to see if he were dry, and seemed to express nothing but satisfaction at their safe return.

"I brought you some shrimps, Calixta," offered Bobinôt, hauling the can from his ample side pocket and laying it on the table.

35 "Shrimps! Oh, Bobinôt! you too good fo' anything!" and she gave him a smacking kiss on the cheek that resounded. *"J'vous reponds,'* we'll have a feas' to-night! umph-umph!"

Bobinôt and Bibi began to relax and enjoy themselves, and when the three seated themselves at table they laughed much and so loud that anyone might have heard them as far away as Laballière's.

IV

Alcée Laballière wrote to his wife, Clarisse, that night. It was a loving letter, full of tender solictude. He told her not to hurry back, but if she and the babies liked it at Biloxi, to stay a month longer. He was getting on nicely; and though he missed them, he was willing to bear the separation a while longer—realizing that their health and pleasure were the first things to be considered.

V

As for Clarisse, she was charmed upon receiving her husband's letter. She and the babies were doing well. The society was agreeable; many of her old friends and acquaintances were at the bay. And the first free breath since her marriage seemed to restore the pleasant liberty of her maiden days. Devoted as she was to her husband, their intimate conjugal life was something which she was more than willing to forego for a while.

So the storm passed and everyone was happy.

Questions on Meaning

1. How does the violence of the storm anticipate the passion of Calixta and Alcée? How do nature and human behavior interact in the story?
2. How is Calixta portrayed as something other than the conventional wife and mother of the era? How is Bobinôt portrayed as something other than the conventional husband and father?
3. How do you interpret the ending of the story? What is Chopin saying about conventional attitudes toward adultery?

Questions on Rhetorical Strategy and Style

1. A good narrative relies heavily on vivid description. Choose one passage in which Chopin describes either the storm or the encounter between the lovers, and explain its significance to the narrative.
2. Chopin plays with cause and effect in this story. Choose two instances in which a cause results in an unexpected effect, and explain their significance to the story.

Writing Assignments

1. Write an essay comparing the effect of the storm on Calixta and Alcée and on Bobinôt and Bibi. Using references to the story, explain how the storm's impact illustrates the differences between Calixta and her husband.
2. Do you find Chopin's treatment of adultery in this story troublesome or not? Write an essay exploring the moral and ethical implications of the story from your own point of view.
3. Chopin concludes the story with letters written between Alcée and his wife. Compose letters between Alcée and Calixta in which the two explain what they believe happened during the storm and whether or not they intend to continue their relationship.

THE STORY OF AN HOUR

Kate Chopin

Kate Chopin (b. Katherine O'Flaherty, 1851–1904) began her life in St. Louis, Missouri. Her father died when she was four years old, so she was reared by three widows: her mother, her grandmother, and her great-grandmother. She was graduated from Sacred Heart convent in 1870 and then married Oscar Chopin, following him to New Orleans and later to his plantation in northern Louisiana. The mother of six children, she was widowed in 1882 and moved back to St. Louis where she began to write stories and publish in stylish literary magazines. Her novels, At Fault *(1890) and* The Awakening *(1899), shocked conservative Victorian society but are praised by modern critics. Her collections of short stories,* Bayou Folk *(1894) and* A Night in Acadie *(1897) draw on her years of experience on a Louisiana plantation among Creole people. She died of a brain hemorrhage at only fifty-three. "The Story of an Hour" caused Chopin to be shunned by both her literary club and magazine publishers at the close of the nineteenth century, but it has persevered to become especially appealing to women in the late twentieth century.*

1   Knowing that Mrs. Mallard was afflicted with a heart trouble, great care was taken to break to her as gently as possible the news of her husband's death.

It was her sister Josephine who told her, in broken sentences, veiled hints that revealed in half concealing. Her husband's friend Richards was there, too, near her. It was he who had been in the newspaper office when intelligence of the railroad disaster was received, with Brently Mallard's name leading the list of "killed." He had only taken the time to assure himself of its truth by a second telegram, and had hastened to forestall any less careful, less tender friend in bearing the sad message.

She did not hear the story as many women have heard the same, with a paralyzed inability to accept its significance. She wept at once, with sudden, wild abandonment, in her sister's arms. When the storm of grief had spent itself she went away to her room alone. She would have no one follow her.

There stood, facing the open window, a comfortable, roomy arm-chair. Into this she sank, pressed down by a physical exhaustion that haunted her body and seemed to reach into her soul.

5   She could see in the open square before her house the tops of trees   5
that were all aquiver with the new spring life. The delicious breath of rain was in the air. In the street below a peddler was crying his wares. The notes of a distant song which someone was singing reached her faintly, and countless sparrows were twittering in the eaves.

There were patches of blue sky showing here and there through the clouds that had met and piled above the other in the west facing her window.

She sat with her head thrown back upon the cushion of the chair, quite motionless, except when a sob came up into her throat and shook her, as a child who has cried itself to sleep continues to sob in its dreams.

She was young, with a fair, calm face, whose lines bespoke re-pression and even a certain strength. But now there was a dull stare in her eyes, whose gaze was fixed away off yonder on one of those patches of blue sky. It was not a glance of reflection, but rather indicated a sus-pension of intelligent thought.

There was something coming to her and she was waiting for it, fearfully. What was it? She did not know; it was too subtle and elusive to name. But she felt it, creeping out of the sky, reaching toward her through the sounds, the scents, the color that filled the air.

10   Now her bosom rose and fell tumultuously. She was beginning to   10
recognize this thing that was approaching to possess her, and she was striving to beat it back with her will—as powerless as her two white slender hands would have been.

When she abandoned herself a little whispered word escaped her slightly parted lips. She said it over and over under her breath: "Free, free, free!" The vacant stare and the look of terror that had followed it went from her eyes. They stayed keen and bright. Her pulses beat fast, and the coursing blood warmed and relaxed every inch of her body.

She did not stop to ask if it were or were not a monstrous joy that held her. A clear and exalted perception enabled her to dismiss the suggestion as trivial.

She knew that she would weep again when she saw the kind, tender hands folded in death; the face that had never looked save with love upon her, fixed and gray and dead. But she saw beyond that bitter moment a long procession of years to come that would belong to her absolutely. And she opened and spread her arms out to them in welcome.

There would be no one to live for her during those coming years; she would live for herself. There would be no powerful will bending her in that blind persistence with which men and women believe they have a right to impose a private will upon a fellow-creature. A kind intention or a cruel intention made the act seem no less a crime as she looked upon it in that brief moment of illumination.

And yet she had loved him—sometimes. Often she had not. What did it matter! What could love, the unsolved mystery, count for in face of this possession of self-assertion which she suddenly recognized as the strongest impulse of her being!

"Free! Body and soul free!" she kept whispering.

Josephine was kneeling before the closed door with her lips to the keyhole, imploring for admission. "Louise, open the door! I beg; open the door—you will make yourself ill. What are you doing, Louise? For heaven's sake open the door."

"Go away. I am not making myself ill." No; she was drinking in a very elixir of life through that open window.

Her fancy was running riot along those days ahead of her. Spring days, and summer days, and all sorts of days that would be her own. She breathed a quick prayer that life might be long. It was only yesterday she had thought with a shudder that life might be long.

She arose at length and opened the door to her sister's importunities. There was a feverish triumph in her eyes, and she carried herself unwittingly like a goddess of Victory. She clasped her sister's waist, and together they descended the stairs. Richards stood waiting for them at the bottom.

Someone was opening the front door with a latchkey. It was Brently Mallard who entered, a little travel-stained, composedly carrying his grip-sack and umbrella. He had been far from the scene of accident, and did not even know there had been one. He stood amazed at Josephine's piercing cry; at Richards' quick motion to screen him from the view of his wife.

But Richards was too late.

When the doctors came they said she had died of heart disease—of joy that kills.

Questions on Meaning

1. The main character dies at the end of the story. What causes her death, and why?
2. The St. Louis literary society refused to accept Chopin into their ranks because her stories shocked their polite sensibilities. What issues of gender and gender conflicts in this story would have caused this reaction?
3. Chopin was the mother of six children in only twelve years of marriage. What picture of family might Chopin have had from such an experience, and what "family" emotions might she be injecting into her story?

Questions on Rhetorical Strategy and Style

1. "The Story of an Hour" limits its narrative time to exactly one hour. How does it stay within that limit and yet capture the reader's close attention?
2. The story illustrates the need for freedom that some people, both men and women feel. How does Chopin describe scenes that convey this desire for freedom?
3. The woman in the story appears to be in shock when she hears of her husband's death but is actually shocked by his being alive. How does this reaction illustrate literary irony (the reader's knowing more about the character than the character knows or appears to know)?

Writing Assignments

1. Write a paper about some common cultural expectation (for example, that all mothers will bond with their children or that all fathers will be happy to share their incomes with their families). How do we respond when a storyteller challenges those expectations?
2. Illustrate an event in your life when your emotions did not appropriately fit the situation (maybe you didn't like your holiday presents or you weren't glad to have a little sister). How did you react emotionally to the contrast between your feelings and your family's expectations?
3. Learning that things are not always as they seem may be the first step in coming of age. Illustrate a time in your life when you suddenly realized that someone you knew was different from the

person you had imagined her or him to be, or describe a time when you found out that a prominent figure was not the person everyone had imagined. Discuss and describe your experience of this discovery.

THE YELLOW WALLPAPER

Charlotte Perkins Gilman

Born in Hartford, Connecticut to a branch of the famous New England Beecher family, Charlotte Perkins Gilman (1860-1935) grew up in near poverty after her father abandoned the family. She married at twenty-three, had a child a year later, and immediately plunged into depression. The treatment prescribed by the highly respected nerve specialist S. Weir Mitchell—to avoid writing and intellectual activity of any kind—only served to deepen her depression. Divorcing her husband, she resumed writing and lecturing on women's rights and eventually married a cousin, George Gilman, in 1900. Unlike her first marriage, the marriage to Gilman was based on equality and lasted until his death in 1934. Gilman was a prolific writer, publishing a highly acclaimed exploration of women's status in Women and Economics *(1898) and a thoughtful, witty feminist-utopian novel,* Herland *(1915). She also published the magazine* The Forerunner, *for which she was the sole contributor, from 1910 to 1916; and wrote several novels and more than 200 short stories. In 1935, a year after her husband's death and upon being diagnosed with breast cancer, she committed suicide. "The Yellow Wallpaper," published in 1892 in* New England Magazine *after having been rejected by* The Atlantic Monthly, *draws from her experience with the common treatment of depression in women at the turn of the last century. The story is all the more disturbing for its ring of truth.*

1   It is very seldom that mere ordinary people like John and myself   1
secure ancestral halls for the summer.

A colonial mansion, a hereditary estate, I would say a haunted house and reach the height of romantic felicity—but that would be asking too much of fate!

Still I will proudly declare that there is something queer about it.

Else, why should it be let so cheaply? And why have stood so long untenanted?

5   John laughs at me, of course, but one expects that.   5

John is practical in the extreme. He has no patience with faith, an intense horror of superstition, and he scoffs openly at any talk of things not to be felt and seen and put down in figures.

John is a physician, and *perhaps*—(I would not say it to a living soul, of course, but this is dead paper and a great relief to my mind)—*perhaps* that is one reason I do not get well faster.

You see, he does not believe I am sick! And what can one do?

If a physician of high standing, and one's own husband, assures friends and relatives that there is really nothing the matter with one but temporary nervous depression—a slight hysterical tendency—what is one to do?

10   My brother is also a physician, and also of high standing, and he   10
says the same thing.

So I take phosphates or phosphites—whichever it is—and tonics, and air and exercise, and journeys, and am absolutely forbidden to "work" until I am well again.

Personally, I disagree with their ideas.

Personally, I believe that congenial work, with excitement and change, would do me good.

But what is one to do?

15   I did write for a while in spite of them; but it *does* exhaust me a   15
good deal—having to be so sly about it, or else meet with heavy opposition.

I sometimes fancy that in my condition, if I had less opposition and more society and stimulus—but John says the very worst thing I can do is to think about my condition, and I confess it always makes me feel bad.

So I will let it alone and talk about the house.

The most beautiful place! It is quite alone, standing well back from the road, quite three miles from the village. It makes me think of English places that you read about, for there are hedges and walls and gates that lock, and lots of separate little houses for the gardeners and people.

There is a *delicious* garden! I never saw such a garden—large and shady, full of box-bordered paths, and lined with long grape-covered arbors with seats under them.

There were greenhouses, but they are all broken now.

There was some legal trouble, I believe, something about the heirs and co-heirs; anyhow, the place has been empty for years.

That spoils my ghostliness, I am afraid, but I don't care—there is something strange about the house—I can feel it.

I even said so to John one moonlight evening, but he said what I felt was a draught, and shut the window.

I get unreasonably angry with John sometimes. I'm sure I never used to be so sensitive. I think it is due to this nervous condition.

But John says if I feel so I shall neglect proper self-control; so I take pains to control myself—before him, at least, and that makes me very tired.

I don't like our room a bit. I wanted one downstairs that opened onto the piazza and had roses all over the window, and such pretty old-fashioned chintz hangings! But John would not hear of it.

He said there was only one window and not room for two beds, and no near room for him if he took another.

He is very careful and loving, and hardly lets me stir without special direction.

I have a schedule prescription for each hour in the day; he takes all care from me, and so I feel basely ungrateful not to value it more.

He said he came here solely on my account, that I was to have perfect rest and all the air I could get. "Your exercise depends on your strength, my dear," said he, "and your food somewhat on your appetite; but air you can absorb all the time." So we took the nursery at the top of the house.

It is a big, airy room, the whole floor nearly, with windows that look all ways, and air and sunshine galore. It was nursery first, and then playroom and gymnasium, I should judge, for the windows are barred for little children, and there are rings and things in the walls.

The paint and paper look as if a boys' school had used it. It is stripped off—the paper—in great patches all around the head of my bed, about as far as I can reach, and in a great place on the other side of the room low down. I never saw a worse paper in my life. One of those sprawling, flamboyant patterns committing every artistic sin.

It is dull enough to confuse the eye in following, pronounced enough constantly to irritate and provoke study, and when you follow the lame uncertain curves for a little distance they suddenly commit suicide—plunge off at outrageous angles, destroy themselves in un-heard-of contradictions.

The color is repellent, almost revolting: a smouldering unclean yellow, strangely faded by the slow-turning sunlight. It is a dull yet lurid orange in some places, a sickly sulphur tint in others.

35 No wonder the children hated it! I should hate it myself if I had to live in this room long.

There comes John, and I must put this away—he hates to have me write a word.

We have been here two weeks, and I haven't felt like writing be-fore, since that first day.

I am sitting by the window now, up in this atrocious nursery, and there is nothing to hinder my writing as much as I please, save lack of strength.

John is away all day, and even some nights when his cases are se-rious.

40 I am glad my case is not serious!

But these nervous troubles are dreadfully depressing.

John does not know how much I really suffer. He knows there is no reason to suffer, and that satisfies him.

Of course it is only nervousness. It does weigh on me so not to do my duty in any way!

I meant to be such a help to John, such a real rest and comfort, and here I am a comparative burden already!

45 Nobody would believe what an effort it is to do what little I am able—to dress and entertain, and order things.

It is fortunate Mary is so good with the baby. Such a dear baby!

And yet I *cannot* be with him, it makes me so nervous.

I suppose John never was nervous in his life. He laughs at me so about this wallpaper!

At first he meant to repaper the room, but afterward he said that I was letting it get the better of me, and that nothing was worse for a nervous patient than to give way to such fancies.

50 He said that after the wallpaper was changed it would be the heavy bedstead, and then the barred windows, and then that gate at the head of the stairs, and so on.

"You know the place is doing you good," he said, "and really, dear, I don't care to renovate the house just for a three months' rental."

"Then do let us go downstairs," I said. "There are such pretty rooms there."

Then he took me in his arms and called me a blessed little goose, and said he would go down cellar, if I wished, and have it whitewashed into the bargain.

But he is right enough about the beds and windows and things.

55 It is as airy and comfortable a room as anyone need wish, and, of course, I would not be so silly as to make him uncomfortable just for a whim.

I'm really getting quite fond of the big room, all but that horrid paper.

Out of one window I can see the garden—those mysterious deep-shaded arbors, the riotous old-fashioned flowers, and bushes and gnarly trees.

Out of another I get a lovely view of the bay and a little private wharf belonging to the estate. There is a beautiful shaded lane that runs down there from the house. I always fancy I see people walking in these numerous paths and arbors, but John has cautioned me not to give way to fancy in the least. He says that with my imaginative power and habit of story-making, a nervous weakness like mine is sure to lead to all manner of excited fancies, and that I ought to use my will and good sense to check the tendency. So I try.

I think sometimes that if I were only well enough to write a little it would relieve the press of ideas and rest me.

60 But I find I get pretty tired when I try.

It is so discouraging not to have any advice and companionship about my work. When I get really well, John says we will ask Cousin Henry and Julia down for a long visit; but he says he would as soon put fireworks in my pillow-case as to let me have those stimulating people about now.

I wish I could get well faster.

But I must not think about that. This paper looks to me as if it *knew* what a vicious influence it had!

There is a recurrent spot where the pattern lolls like a broken neck and two bulbous eyes stare at you upside down.

65 I get positively angry with the impertinence of it and the everlastingness. Up and down and sideways they crawl, and those absurd unblinking eyes are everywhere. There is one place where two breadths didn't match, and the eyes go all up and down the line, one a little higher than the other.

I never saw so much expression in an inanimate thing before, and we all know how much expression they have! I used to lie awake as a child and get more entertainment and terror out of blank walls and plain furniture than most children could find in a toy-store.

I remember what a kindly wink the knobs of our big old bureau used to have, and there was one chair that always seemed like a strong friend.

I used to feel that if any of the other things looked too fierce I could always hop into that chair and be safe.

The furniture in this room is no worse than inharmonious, however, for we had to bring it all from downstairs. I suppose when this was used as a playroom they had to take the nursery things out, and no wonder! I never saw such ravages as the children have made here.

70 The wallpaper, as I said before, is torn off in spots, and it sticketh closer than a brother—they must have had perseverance as well as hatred.

Then the floor is scratched and gouged and splintered, the plaster itself is dug out here and there, and this great heavy bed, which is all we found in the room, looks as if it had been through the wars.

But I don't mind it a bit—only the paper.

There comes John's sister. Such a dear girl as she is, and so careful of me! I must not let her find me writing.

She is a perfect and enthusiasitic housekeeper, and hopes for no better profession. I verily believe she thinks it is the writing which made me sick!

75 But I can write when she is out, and see her a long way off from these windows.

There is one that commands the road, a lovely shaded winding road, and one that just looks off over the country. A lovely country, too, full of great elms and velvet meadows.

This wallpaper has a kind of subpattern in a different shade, a particularly irritating one, for you can only see it in certain lights, and not clearly then.

But in the places where it isn't faded and where the sun is just so— I can see a strange, provoking, formless sort of figure that seems to skulk about behind that silly and conspicuous front design.

There's sister on the stairs!

Well, the Fourth of July is over! The people are all gone, and I am tired out. John thought it might do me good to see a little company, so we just had Mother and Nellie and the children down for a week.

Of course I didn't do a thing. Jennie sees to everything now.

But it tired me all the same.

John says if I don't pick up faster he shall send me to Weir Mitchell in the fall.

But I don't want to go there at all. I had a friend who was in his hands once, and she says he is just like John and my brother, only more so!

Besides, it is such an undertaking to go so far.

I don't feel as if it was worthwhile to turn my hand over for anything, and I'm getting dreadfully fretful and querulous.

I cry at nothing, and cry most of the time.

Of course I don't when John is here, or anybody else, but when I am alone.

And I am alone a good deal just now. John is kept in town very often by serious cases, and Jennie is good and lets me alone when I want her to.

So I walk a little in the garden or down that lovely lane, sit on the porch under the roses, and lie down up here a good deal.

I'm getting really fond of the room in spite of the wallpaper. Perhaps *because* of the wallpaper.

It dwells in my mind so!

I lie here on this great immovable bed—it is nailed down, I believe—and follow that pattern about by the hour. It is as good as gymnastics, I assure you. I start, we'll say, at the bottom, down in the corner over there where it has not been touched, and I determine for the thousandth time that I *will* follow that pointless pattern to some sort of a conclusion.

I know a little of the principle of design, and I know this thing was not arranged on any laws of radiation, or alternation, or repetition, or symmetry, or anything else that I ever heard of.

95 It is repeated, of course, by the breadths, but not otherwise. 95

Looked at in one way, each breadth stands alone; the bloated curves and flourishes—a kind of "debased Romanesque" with dilirium tremens go waddling up and down in isolated columns of fatuity.

But, on the other hand, they connect diagonally, and the sprawling outlines run off in great slanting waves of optic horror, like a lot of wallowing sea-weeds in full chase.

The whole thing goes horizontally, too, at least it seems so, and I exhaust myself trying to distinguish the order of its going in that direction.

They have used a horizontal breadth for a frieze, and that adds wonderfully to the confusion.

100 There is one end of the room where it is almost intact, and there, 100 when the crosslights fade and the low sun shines directly upon it, I can almost fancy radiation after all—the interminable grotesque seems to form around a common center and rush off in headlong plunges of equal distraction.

It makes me tired to follow it. I will take a nap, I guess.

I don't know why I should write this.

I don't want to.

I don't feel able.

105 And I know John would think it absurd. But I *must* say what I 105 feel and think in some way—it is such a relief!

But the effort is getting to be greater than the relief.

Half the time now I am awfully lazy, and lie down ever so much. John says I mustn't lose my strength, and has me take cod liver oil and lots of tonics and things, to say nothing of ale and wines and rare meat.

Dear John! He loves me very dearly, and hates to have me sick. I tried to have a real earnest reasonable talk with him the other day, and tell him how I wish he would let me go and make a visit to Cousin Henry and Julia.

But he said I wasn't able to go, not able to stand it after I got there; and I did not make out a very good case for myself, for I was crying before I had finished.

110 It is getting to be a great effort for me to think straight. Just this nervous weakness, I suppose.

And dear John gathered me up in his arms, and just carried me upstairs and laid me on the bed, and sat by me and read to me till it tired my head.

He said I was his darling and his comfort and all he had, and that I must take care of myself for his sake, and keep well.

He says no one but myself can help me out of it, that I must use my will and self-control and not let any silly fancies run away with me.

There's one comfort—the baby is well and happy, and does not have to occupy this nursery with the horrid wallpaper.

115 If we had not used it, that blessed child would have! What a fortunate escape! Why, I wouldn't have a child of mine, an impressionable little thing, live in such a room for worlds.

I never thought of it before, but it is lucky that John kept me here after all; I can stand it so much easier than a baby, you see.

Of course I never mention it to them anymore—I am too wise—but I keep watch for it all the same.

There are things in the wallpaper that nobody knows about but me, or ever will.

Behind that outside pattern the dim shapes get clearer every day.

120 It is always the same shape, only very numerous.

And it is like a woman stooping down and creeping about behind that pattern. I don't like it a bit. I wonder—I begin to think—I wish John would take me away from here!

It is so hard to talk with John about my case, because he is so wise, and because he loves me so.

But I tried it last night.

It was moonlight. The moon shines in all around just as the sun does.

125 I hate to see it sometimes, it creeps so slowly, and always comes in by one window or another.

John was asleep and I hated to waken him, so I kept still and watched the moonlight on that undulating wallpaper till I felt creepy.

The faint figure behind seemed to shake the pattern, just as if she wanted to get out.

I got up softly and went to feel and see if the paper *did* move, and when I came back John was awake .

"What is it, little girl?" he said. "Don't go walking about like that—you'll get cold."

130 I thought it was a good time to talk, so I told him that I really was 130 not gaining here, and that I wished he would take me away.

"Why, darling!" said he. "Our lease will be up in three weeks, and I can't see how to leave before."

"The repairs are not done at home, and I cannot possibly leave town just now. Of course, if you were in any danger, I could and would, but you really are better, dear, whether you can see it or not. I am a doctor, dear, and I know. You are gaining flesh and color, your appetite is better, I feel really much easier about you."

"I don't weigh a bit more," said I, "nor as much; and my appetite may be better in the evening when you are here but it is worse in the morning when you are away!"

"Bless her little heart!" said he with a big hug. "She shall be as sick as she pleases! But now let's improve the shining hours by going to sleep and talk about it in the morning!"

135 "And you won't go away?" I asked gloomily. 135

"Why, how can I, dear? It is only three weeks more and then we will take a nice little trip for a few days while Jennie is getting the house ready. Really, dear, you are better!"

"Better in body perhaps—" I began, and stopped short, for he sat up straight and looked at me with such a stern, reproachful look that I could not say another word.

"My darling," said he, "I beg you, for my sake and for our child's sake, as well as for your own, that you will never for one instant let that idea enter your mind! There is nothing so dangerous, so fascinating, to a temperament like yours. It is a false and foolish fancy. Can you trust me as a physician when I tell you so?" So of course I said no more on that score, and we went to sleep before long. He thought I was asleep first, but I wasn't, and lay there for hours trying to decide whether that front pattern and the back pattern really did move together or separately.

140 On a pattern like this, by daylight, there is a lack of sequence, a 140 defiance of law, that is a constant irritant to a normal mind.

The color is hideous enough, and unreliable enough, and infuriating enough, but the pattern is torturing.

You think you have mastered it, but just as you get well under way in following, it turns a back-somersault and there you are. It slaps you in the face, knocks you down, and tramples upon you. It is like a bad dream.

The outside pattern is a florid arabesque, reminding one of a fungus. If you can imagine a toadstool in joints, an interminable string of toadstools, budding and sprouting in endless convolutions—why, that is something like it.

That is, sometimes!

145   There is one marked peculiarity about this paper, a thing nobody seems to notice but myself, and that is that it changes as the light changes.   145

When the sun shoots in through the east window—I always watch for that first long, straight ray—it changes so quickly that I never can quite believe it.

That is why I watch it always.

By moonlight—the moon shines in all night when there is a moon—I wouldn't know it was the same paper.

At night in any kind of light, in twilight, candlelight, lamplight, and worst of all by moonlight, it becomes bars! The outside pattern, I mean, and the woman behind it is as plain as can be.

150   I didn't realize for a long time what the thing was that showed behind, that dim subpattern, but now I am quite sure it is a woman.   150

By daylight she is subdued, quiet. I fancy it is the pattern that keeps her so still. It is so puzzling. It keeps me quiet by the hour.

I lie down ever so much now. John says it is good for me, and to sleep all I can.

Indeed he started the habit by making me lie down for an hour after each meal.

It is a very bad habit, I am convinced, for you see, I don't sleep.

155   And that cultivates deceit, for I don't tell them I'm awake—oh, no!   155

The fact is I am getting a little afraid of John.

He seems very queer sometimes, and even Jennie has an inexplicable look.

It strikes me occasionally, just as a scientific hypothesis, that perhaps it is the paper!

I have watched John when he did not know I was looking, and come into the room suddenly on the most innocent excuses, and I've caught him several times *looking at the paper*! And Jennie too. I caught Jennie with her hand on it once.

160 She didn't know I was in the room, and when I asked her in a 160 quiet, a very quiet voice, with the most restrained manner possible, what she was doing with the paper, she turned around as if she had been caught stealing, and looked quite angry—asked me why I should frighten her so!

Then she said that the paper stained everything it touched, that she had found yellow smooches on all my clothes and John's and she wished we would be more careful!

Did not that sound innocent? But I know she was studying that pattern, and I am determined that nobody shall find it out but myself!

Life is very much more exciting now than it used to be. You see, I have something more to expect, to look forward to, to watch. I really do eat better, and am more quiet than I was.

John is so pleased to see me improve! He laughed a little the other day, and said I seemed to be flourishing in spite of my wallpaper.

165 I turned it off with a laugh. I had no intention of telling him it 165 was *because* of the wallpaper—he would make fun of me. He might even want to take me away.

I don't want to leave now until I have found it out. There is a week more, and I think that will be enough.

I'm feeling so much better!

I don't sleep much at night, for it is so interesting to watch developments; but I sleep a good deal during the daytime.

In the daytime it is tiresome and perplexing.

170 There are always new shoots on the fungus, and new shades of 170 yellow all over it. I cannot keep count of them, though I have tried conscientiously.

It is the strangest yellow, that wallpaper! It makes me think of all the yellow things I ever saw—not beautiful ones like buttercups, but old, foul, bad yellow things.

But there is something else about that paper—the smell! I noticed it the moment we came into the room, but with so much air and sun it was not bad. Now we have had a week of fog and rain, and whether the windows are open or not, the smell is here.

It creeps all over the house.

I find it hovering in the dining-room skulking in the parlor, hiding in the hall, lying in wait for me on the stairs.

175 It gets into my hair.

Even when I go to ride, if I turn my head suddenly and surprise it—there is that smell!

Such a peculiar odor, too! I have spent hours in trying to analyze it to find what it smelled like.

It is not bad—at first—and very gentle, but quite the subtlest, most enduring odor I ever met.

In this damp weather it is awful. I wake up in the night and find it hanging over me.

180 It used to disturb me at first. I thought seriously of burning the house—to reach the smell.

But now I am used to it. The only thing I can think of that it is like is the *color* of the paper! A yellow smell.

There a very funny mark on this wall, low down, near the mopboard. A streak that runs round the room. It goes behind every piece of furniture, except the bed, a long, straight, even *smooch*, as if it had been rubbed over and over.

I wonder how it was done and who did it, and what they did it for. Round and round and round—round and round and round—it makes me dizzy!

I really have discovered something at last.

185 Through watching so much at night, when it changes so, I have finally found out.

The front pattern *does* move—and no wonder! The woman behind shakes it!

Sometimes I think there are a great many women behind, and sometimes only one, and she crawls around fast, and her crawling shakes it all over.

Then in the very bright spots she keeps still, and in the very shady spots she just takes hold of the bars and shakes them hard.

And she is all the time trying to climb through. But nobody could climb through that pattern—it strangles so; I think that is why it has so many heads.

190 They get through and then the pattern strangles them off and turns them upside down, and makes their eyes white!

If those heads were covered or taken off it would not be half so bad.

I think that woman gets out in the daytime!

And I'll tell you why—privately—I've seen her!

I can see her out of every one of my windows!

195 It is the same woman, I know, for she is always creeping and most women do not creep by daylight.

I see her in that long shaded lane, creeping up and down. I see her in those dark grape arbors, creeping all round the garden.

I see her on that long road under the trees, creeping along, and when a carriage comes she hides under the blackberry vines.

I don't blame her a bit. It must be very humiliating to be caught creeping by daylight!

I always lock the door when I creep by daylight. I can't do it at night, for I know John would suspect something at once.

200 And John is so queer now that I don't want to irritate him. I wish he would take another room! Besides, I don't want anybody to get that woman out at night but myself.

I often wonder if I could see her out of all the windows at once.

But, turn as fast as I can, I can only see out of one at one time.

And though I always see her, she *may* be able to creep faster than I can turn! I have watched her sometimes away off in the open country, creeping as fast as a cloud shadow in a wind.

If only that top pattern could be gotten off from the under one! I mean to try it, little by little.

205 I have found out another funny thing, but I shan't tell it this time! It does not do to trust people too much.

There are only two more days to get this paper off, and I believe John is beginning to notice. I don't like the look in his eyes.

And I heard him ask Jennie a lot of professional questions about me. She had a very good report to give.

She said I slept a good deal in the daytime.

John knows I don't sleep very well at night, for all I'm so quiet!

210 He asked me all sorts of questions too, and pretended to be very loving and kind.

As if I couldn't see through him!

Still, I don't wonder he acts so, sleeping under this paper for three months.

It only interests me, but I feel sure John and Jennie are affected by it.

Hurrah! This is the last day, but it is enough. John is to stay in town over night, and won't be out until this evening.

215 Jennie wanted to sleep with me—the sly thing; but I told her I should undoubtedly rest better for a night all alone.

That was clever, for really I wasn't alone a bit! As soon as it was moonlight and that poor thing began to crawl and shake the pattern, I got up and ran to help her.

I pulled and she shook. I shook and she pulled, and before morning we had peeled off yards of that paper.

A strip about as high as my head and half around the room.

And then when the sun came and that awful pattern began to laugh at me, I declared I would finish it today!

220 We go away tomorrow, and they are moving all my furniture down again to leave things as they were before.

Jennie looked at the wall in amazement, but I told her merrily that I did it out of pure spite at the vicious thing.

She laughed and said she wouldn't mind doing it herself, but I must not get tired.

How she betrayed herself that time!

But I am here, and no person touches this paper but Me—not *alive*!

225 She tried to get me out of the room—it was too patent! But I said it was so quiet and empty and clean now that I believed I would lie down again and sleep all I could, and not to wake me even for dinner—I would call when I woke.

So now she is gone, and the servants are gone, and the things are gone, and there is nothing left but that great bedstead nailed down, with the canvas mattress we found on it.

We shall sleep downstairs tonight, and take the boat home tomorrow.

I quite enjoy the room, now it is bare again.

How those children did tear about here!

230 This bedstead is fairly gnawed!

But I must get to work.

I have locked the door and thrown the key down into the front path.

I don't want to go out, and I don't want to have anybody come in, till John comes.

I want to astonish him.

235 I've got a rope up here that even Jennie did not find. If that woman does get out, and tries to get away, I can tie her!

But I forgot I could not reach far without anything to stand on! This bed will *not* move!

I tried to lift and push it until I was lame, and then I got so angry I bit off a little piece at one corner—but it hurt my teeth.

Then I peeled off all the paper I could reach standing on the floor. It sticks horribly and the pattern just enjoys it! All those strangled heads and bulbous eyes and waddling fungus growths just shriek with derision!

240 I am getting angry enough to do something desperate. To jump out of the window would be admirable exercise, but the bars are too strong even to try.

Besides I wouldn't do it. Of course not. I know well enough that a step like that is improper and might be misconstrued.

I don't like to *look* out of the windows even—there are so many of those creeping women, and they creep so fast.

I wonder if they all come out of that wallpaper as I did!

But I am securely fastened now by my well-hidden rope—you don't get *me* out in the road there!

245 I suppose I shall have to get back behind the pattern when it comes night, and that is hard!

It is so pleasant to be out in this great room and creep around as I please!

I don't want to go outside. I won't, even if Jennie asks me to.

For outside you have to creep on the ground, and everything is green instead of yellow.

But here I can creep smoothly on the floor, and my shoulder just fits in that long smooch around the wall, so I cannot lose my way.

250 Why, there's John at the door!

It is no use, young man, you can't open it!

How he does call and pound!

Now he's crying to Jennie for an axe.

It would be a shame to break down that beautiful door!

"John, dear!" said I in the gentlest voice. "The key is down by the front steps, under a plantain leaf!"

That silenced him for a few moments.

Then he said, very quietly indeed, "Open the door, my darling!"

"I can't," said I. "The key is down by the front door under a plantain leaf!" And then I said it again, several times, very gently and slowly, and said it so often that he had to go and see, and he got it of course, and came in. He stopped short by the door.

"What is the matter?" he cried. "For God's sake, what are you doing!"

260   I kept on creeping just the same, but I looked at him over my 260 shoulder.

"I've got out at last," said I, "in spite of you and Jane. And I've pulled off most of the paper, so you can't put me back!"

Now why should that man have fainted? But he did, and right across my path by the wall, so that I had to creep over him every time!

Questions on Meaning

1. Of all the adult characters mentioned in this story, only the narrator remains nameless. Her husband refers to her as "my dear," "my darling," "little girl," and "she." Of what significance is the narrator's namelessness? How is the story affected by the fact that even the narrator herself does not offer her name?
2. At what point do you begin to suspect that the narrator is losing touch with objective reality? Trace her decline, citing passages that indicate a progressive separation from the world around her.
3. What leads the narrator to determine that there is a woman behind the wallpaper? Why does she eventually refer to the woman as herself?

Questions on Rhetorical Strategy and Style

1. A successful narrative can be enhanced by detailed description. Find several passages in which the narrator describes her surroundings and explain how those descriptions help readers understand what is happening to her.
2. Based on what the narrator states and implies, what do you think is the original cause of her condition? What causes contribute to her continuing decline? How does her assessment of the cause of her condition differ from her husband's?

Writing Assignments

1. Write an essay in which you compare the narrator's situation to the imprisonment of a convict. Consider the descriptions of the room, the behavior of John and Jennie, and the narrator's language in your analysis.
2. In order to understand the importance of perspective in this story, consider how the narrator's actions must appear to her sister-in-law and husband. Compose a letter from Jennie to John describing the narrator's behavior while he is away on one of his cases. Try to be as specific as the narrator is in her account.
3. Research the treatment of women's nervous disorders at the turn of the last century, particularly those therapies promoted by Dr. S. Weir Mitchell, who treated Charlotte Perkins Gilman and whose treatment is feared by the narrator. Write a report on the beliefs underlying such treatments for women.

⮞ TRIFLES ⮜

Susan Glaspell

Susan Glaspell (1876-1948) worked as a reporter for a Des Moines newspaper after graduating from Drake University with a degree in philosophy. Intent upon cultivating her fiction rather than pursuing a career in journalism, Glaspell returned to her hometown of Davenport, Iowa, in 1902. There she met and later married the liberal utopian George Cram Cook. The pair moved to Greenwich Village to write for the theater, eventually settling on Cape Cod, where they helped found the Provincetown Players with such notable playwrights as Eugene O'Neill. Glaspell's play Trifles, *written for the new company, has endured for almost a century. So successful was the play that Glaspell translated it into a short story, "A Jury of Her Peers." In addition to these two works, Glaspell also wrote forty-nine other short stories, thirteen other plays, and nine novels. Her play* Alison's House *won a Pulitzer Prize in 1930, and her work with the Provincetown Players is considered to have been instrumental in the development of serious theater in the United States. Both* Trifles *and "A Jury of Her Peers" reveal Glaspell's commitment to what was then considered the radical cause of women's rights. As the two women in the play and story unravel the real tale of John Wright's murder, they begin to question their loyalty to the very men who consider women's concerns "trifles."*

Characters

GEORGE HENDERSON, *County Attorney*
HENRY PETERS, *Sheriff*
LEWIS HALE, *A Neighboring Farmer*
MRS. PETERS
MRS. HALE

"Trifles," by Susan Glaspell. Reprinted by permission of the Estate of Susan Glaspell.

SCENE

1 *The kitchen in the now abandoned farmhouse of* JOHN WRIGHT, *a* 1
gloomy kitchen, and left without having been put in order—unwashed
pans under the sink, a loaf of bread outside the breadbox, a dish towel on
the table—other signs of incompleted work. At the rear the outer door
opens and the SHERIFF *comes in followed by the* COUNTY ATTORNEY *and*
HALE. *The* SHERIFF *and* HALE *are men in middle life, the* COUNTY
ATTORNEY *is a young man; all are much bundled up and go at once to*
the stove. They are followed by two women—the SHERIFF's *wife first; she*
is a slight wiry woman, a thin nervous face. MRS. HALE *is larger and*
would ordinarily be called more comfortable looking, but she is disturbed
now and looks fearfully about as she enters. The women have come in
slowly, and stand close together near the door.

COUNTY ATTORNEY. [*Rubbing his hands.*] This feels good. Come up
to the fire, ladies.

MRS. PETERS. [*After taking a step forward.*] I'm not—cold.

SHERIFF. [*Unbuttoning his overcoat and stepping away from the stove as*
if to mark the beginning of official business.] Now, Mr. Hale, before
we move things about, you explain to Mr. Henderson just what
you saw when you came here yesterday morning.

5 COUNTY ATTORNEY. By the way, has anything been moved? Are things 5
just as you left them yesterday?

SHERIFF. [*Looking about.*] It's just the same. When it dropped below
zero last night I thought I'd better send Frank out this morning
to make a fire for us—no use getting pneumonia with a big case
on, but I told him not to touch anything except the stove—and
you know Frank.

COUNTY ATTORNEY. Somebody should have been left here yesterday.

SHERIFF. Oh—yesterday. When I had to send Frank to Morris Center
for that man who went crazy—I want you to know I had my
hands full yesterday. I knew you could get back from Omaha by
today and as long as I went over everything here myself—

COUNTY ATTORNEY. Well, Mr. Hale, tell just what happened when
you came here yesterday morning.

10 HALE. Harry and I had started to town with a load of potatoes. We 10
came along the road from my place and as I got here I said, "I'm
going to see if I can't get John Wright to go in with me on a party
telephone." I spoke to Wright about it once before and he put me

off, saying folks talked too much anyway, and all he asked was peace and quiet—I guess you know about how much he talked himself; but I thought maybe if I went to the house and talked about it before his wife, though I said to Harry that I didn't know as what his wife wanted made much difference to John—

COUNTY ATTORNEY. Let's talk about that later, Mr. Hale. I do want to talk about that, but tell now just what happened when you got to the house.

HALE. I didn't hear or see anything; I knocked at the door, and still it was all quiet inside. I knew they must be up, it was past eight o'clock. So I knocked again, and I thought I heard somebody say, "Come in." I wasn't sure, I'm not sure yet, but I opened the door—this door [*Indicating the door by which the two women are still standing*] and there in that rocker—[*Pointing to it.*] sat Mrs. Wright. [*They all look at the rocker.*]

COUNTY ATTORNEY. What—was she doing?

HALE. She was rockin' back and forth. She had her apron in her hand and was kind of—pleating it.

15 COUNTY ATTORNEY. And how did she—look?   15

HALE. Well, she looked queer.

COUNTY ATTORNEY. How do you mean—queer?

HALE. Well, as if she didn't know what she was going to do next. And kind of done up.

COUNTY ATTORNEY. How did she seem to feel about your coming?

20 HALE. Why, I don't think she minded—one way or other. She didn't   20
pay much attention. I said, "How do, Mrs. Wright, it's cold, ain't it?" And she said " Is it?"—and went on kind of pleating at her apron. Well, I was surprised; she didn't ask me to come up to the stove, or to set down, but just sat there, not even looking at me, so I said, "I want to see John." And then she—laughed. I guess you would call it a laugh. I thought of Harry and the team outside, so I said a little sharp: "Can't I see John?" "No," she says, kind o' dull like. "Ain't he home?" says I. "Yes," says she, "he's home." "Then why can't I see him?" I asked her, out of patience. "'Cause he's dead," says she. *"Dead?"* says I. She just nodded her head, not getting a bit excited, but rockin' back and forth. "Why—where is he?" says I, not knowing what to say. She just pointed upstairs—like that [*Himself pointing to the room above.*] I

got up, with the idea of going up there. I walked from there to here—then I says, "Why, what did he die of?" "He died of a rope round his neck," says she, and just went on pleatin' at her apron. Well, I went out and called Harry. I thought I might—need help. We went upstairs and there he was lyin'—

COUNTY ATTORNEY. I think I'd rather have you go into that upstairs, where you can point it all out. Just go on now with the rest of the story.

HALE. Well, my first thought was to get that rope off. It looked . . . [*Stops, his face twitches*] . . . but Harry, he went up to him, and he said, "No, he's dead all right, and we'd better not touch anything." So we went back down stairs. She was still sitting that same way. "Has anybody been notified?" I asked. "No," says she, unconcerned. "Who did this, Mrs. Wright?" said Harry. He said it businesslike—and she stopped pleatin' of her apron. "I don't know," she says. "You don't *know?*" says Harry. "No," says she. "Weren't you sleepin' in bed with him?" says Harry. "Yes," says she, "but I was on the inside." "Somebody slipped a rope round his neck and strangled him and you didn't wake up?" says Harry. "I didn't wake up," she said after him. We must 'a looked as if we didn't see how that could be, for after a minute she said, "I sleep sound." Harry was going to ask her more questions but I said maybe we ought to let her tell her story first to the coroner, or the sheriff, so Harry went fast as he could to Rivers' place, where there's a telephone.

COUNTY ATTORNEY. And what did Mrs. Wright do when she knew that you had gone for the coroner?

HALE. She moved from that chair to this one over here [*Pointing to a small chair in the corner.*] and just sat there with her hands held together and looking down. I got a feeling that I ought to make some conversation, so I said I had come in to see if John wanted to put in a telephone, and at that she started to laugh, and then she stopped and looked at me—scared. [*The* COUNTY ATTORNEY, *who has had his notebook out, makes a note.*] I dunno, maybe it wasn't scared. I wouldn't like to say it was. Soon Harry got back, and then Dr. Lloyd came, and you, Mr. Peters, and so I guess that's all I know that you don't.

25 COUNTY ATTORNEY. [*Looking around.*] I guess we'll go upstairs first— 25
and then out to the barn and around there. [*To the* SHERIFF] You're

convinced that there was nothing important here—nothing that would point to any motive.

SHERIFF. Nothing here but kitchen things.

[*The* COUNTY ATTORNEY, *after again looking around the kitchen, opens the door of a cupboard closet. He gets up on a chair and looks on a shelf. Pulls his hand away, sticky.*]

COUNTY ATTORNEY. Here's a nice mess.

[*The women draw nearer.*]

MRS. PETERS. [*To the other woman.*] Oh, her fruit; it did freeze. [*To the* COUNTY ATTORNEY] She worried about that when it turned so cold. She said the fire'd go out and her jars would break.

SHERIFF. Well, can you beat the women! Held for murder and worryin' about her preserves.

COUNTY ATTORNEY. I guess before we're through she may have something more serious than preserves to worry about.

HALE. Well, women are used to worrying over trifles. [*The two women move a little closer together.*]

COUNTY ATTORNEY. [*With the gallantry of a young politician.*] And yet, for all their worries, what would we do without the ladies? [*The women do not unbend. He goes to the sink, takes a dipperful of water from the pail and pouring it into a basin, washes his hands. Starts to wipe them on the roller towel, turns it for a cleaner place.*] Dirty towels! [*Kicks his foot against the pans under the sink.*] Not much of a housekeeper, would you say, ladies?

MRS. HALE. [*Stiffly.*] There's a great deal of work to be done on a farm.

COUNTY ATTORNEY. To be sure. And yet [*With a little bow to her*] *I* know there are some Dickson county farmhouses which do not have such roller towels.

[*He gives it a pull to expose its full length again.*]

MRS. HALE. Those towels get dirty awful quick. Men's hands aren't always as clean as they might be.

COUNTY ATTORNEY. Ah, loyal to your sex, I see. But you and Mrs. Wright were neighbors. I suppose you were friends, too.

MRS. HALE. [*Shaking her head.*] I've not seen much of her of late years. I've not been in this house—it's more than a year.

COUNTY ATTORNEY. And why was that? You didn't like her?

MRS. HALE. I liked her all well enough. Farmers' wives have their hands full, Mr. Henderson. And then—

40 COUNTY ATTORNEY. Yes——? 40

MRS. HALE. [*Looking about.*] It never seemed a very cheerful place.

COUNTY ATTORNEY. No—it's not cheerful. I shouldn't say she had the homemaking instinct.

MRS. HALE. Well, I don't know as Wright had, either.

COUNTY ATTORNEY. You mean that they didn't get on very well?

45 MRS. HALE. No, I don't mean anything. But I don't think a place'd be 45 any cheerfuller for John Wright's being in it.

COUNTY ATTORNEY. I'd like to talk more of that a little later. I want to get the lay of things upstairs now.

[*He goes to the left, where three steps lead to a stair door.*]

SHERIFF. I Suppose anything Mrs. Peters does'll be all right. She was to take in some clothes for her, you know, and a few little things. We left in such a hurry yesterday.

COUNTY ATTORNEY. Yes, but I would like to see what you take, Mrs. Peters, and keep an eye out for anything that might be of use to us.

MRS. PETERS. Yes, Mr. Henderson.

[*The women listen to the men's steps on the stairs, then look about the kitchen.*]

50 MRS. HALE. I'd hate to have men coming into my kitchen, snooping 50 around and criticising.

[*She arranges the pans under sink which the* COUNTY ATTORNEY *had shoved out of place.*]

MRS. PETERS. Of course it's no more than their duty.

MRS. HALE. Duty's all right, but I guess that deputy sheriff that came out to make the fire might have got a little of this on. [*Gives the roller towel a pull.*] Wish I'd thought of that sooner. Seems mean to talk about her for not having things slicked up when she had to come away in such a hurry.

MRS. PETERS. [*Who has gone to a small table in the left rear corner of the room, and lifted one end of a towel that covers a pan.*] She had bread set.

[*Stands still.*]

MRS. HALE. [*Eyes fixed on a loaf of bread beside the breadbox, which is on a low shelf at the other side of the room. Moves slowly toward it.*] She was going to put this in there. [*Picks up loaf then abruptly drops it. In a manner of returning to familiar things.*] It's a shame about her fruit. I wonder if it's all gone. [*Gets up on the chair and looks.*] I think there's some here that's all right, Mrs. Peters. Yes— here; [*Holding it toward the window.*] this is cherries too. [*Looking again.*] I declare I believe that's the only one. [*Gets down, bottle in her hand. Goes to the sink and wipes it off on the outside.*] She'll feel awful bad after all her hard work in the hot weather. I remember the afternoon I put up my cherries last summer.

[*She puts the bottle on the big kitchen table, center of the room. With a sigh, is about to sit down in the rocking-chair. Before she is seated realizes what chair it is; with a slow look at it, steps back. The chair which she has touched rocks back and forth.*]

55 MRS. PETERS. Well, I must get those things from the front room 55 closet. [*She goes to the door at the right, but after looking into the other room, steps back.*] You coming with me, Mrs. Hale? You could help me carry them.

[*They go in the other room; reappear, MRS. PETERS carrying a dress and skirt, MRS. HALE following with a pair of shoes.*]

MRS. PETERS. My, it's cold in there.

[*She puts the clothes on the big table, and hurries to the stove.*]

MRS. HALE. [*Examining her skirt.*] Wright was close. I think maybe that's why she kept so much to herself. She didn't even belong to the Ladies Aid. I suppose she felt she couldn't do her part, and then you don't enjoy things when you feel shabby. She used to wear pretty clothes and be lively, when she was Minnie Foster, one of the town girls singing in the choir. But that—oh, that was thirty years ago. This all you was to take in?

MRS. PETERS. She said she wanted an apron. Funny thing to want, for there isn't much to get you dirty in jail, goodness knows. But I suppose just to make her feel more natural. She said they was in the top drawer in this cupboard. Yes, here. And then her little shawl that always hung behind the door. [*Opens stair door and looks.*] Yes, here it is.

[*Quickly shuts door leading upstairs.*]

MRS. HALE. [*Abruptly moving toward her.*] Mrs. Peters?

60 MRS. PETERS. Yes, Mrs. Hale? 60

MRS. HALE. Do you think she did it?

MRS. PETERS. [*In a frightened voice.*] Oh, I don't know.

MRS. HALE. Well, I don't think she did. Asking for an apron and her little shawl. Worrying about her fruit.

MRS. PETERS. [*Starts to speak, glances up, where footsteps are heard in the room above. In a low voice.*] Mr. Peters says it looks bad for her. Mr. Henderson is awful sarcastic in a speech and he'll make fun of her sayin' she didn't wake up.

65 MRS. HALE. Well, I guess John Wright didn't wake when they was slipping that rope under his neck.

MRS. PETERS. No, it's strange. It must have been done awful, crafty and still. They say it was such a—funny way to kill a man, rigging it all up like that.

MRS. HALE. That's just what Mr. Hale said. There was a gun in the house. He says that's what he can't understand.

MRS. PETERS. Mr. Henderson said coming out that what was needed for the case was a motive; something to show anger, or—sudden feeling.

MRS. HALE. [*Who is standing by the table.*] Well, I don't see any signs of anger around here. [*She puts her hand on the dish towel which lies on the table, stands looking down at table, one half of which is clean, the other half messy.*] It's wiped to here. [*Makes a move as if to finish work, then turns and looks at loaf of bread outside the breadbox. Drops towel. In that voice of coming back to familiar things.*] Wonder how they are finding things upstairs. I hope she had it a little more red-up up there. You know, it seems kind of *sneaking*. Locking her up in town and then coming out here and trying to get her own house to turn against her!

70 MRS. PETERS. But Mrs. Hale, the law is the law.

MRS. HALE. I s'pose 'tis. [*Unbuttoning her coat.*] Better loosen up your things, Mrs. Peters. You won't feel them when you go out.
[MRS. PETERS *takes off her fur tippet, goes to hang it on hook at back of room, stands looking at the under part of the small corner table.*]

MRS. PETERS. She was piecing a quilt.
[*She brings the large sewing basket and they look at the bright pieces.*]

MRS. HALE. It's log cabin pattern. Pretty, isn't it? I wonder if she was goin' to quilt it or just knot it?
[*Footsteps have been heard coming down the stairs. The* SHERIFF *enters followed by* HALE *and the* COUNTY ATTORNEY.]

SHERIFF. They wonder if she was going to quilt it or just knot it! [*The men laugh; the women look abashed.*]

75 COUNTY ATTORNEY. [*Rubbing his hands over the stove.*] Frank's fire   75
didn't do much up there, did it? Well, let's go out to the barn and
get that cleared up.
[*The men go outside.*]

MRS. HALE. [*Resentfully.*] I don't know as there's anything so strange,
our takin' up our time with little things while we're waiting for
them to get the evidence. [*She sits down at the big table smoothing
out a block with decision.*] I don't see as it's anything to laugh
about.

MRS. PETERS. [*Apologetically.*] Of course they've got awful important
things on their minds.
[*Pulls up a chair and joins* MRS. HALE *at the table.*]

MRS. HALE. [*Examining another block.*] Mrs. Peters, look at this one.
Here, this is the one she was working on, and look at the sewing!
All the rest of it has been so nice and even. And look at this! It's
all over the place! Why, it looks as if she didn't know what she was
about!
[*After she has said this they look at each other, then start to glance,
back at the door. After an instant* MRS. HALE *has pulled at a knot
and ripped the sewing.*]

MRS. PETERS. Oh, what are you doing, Mrs. Hale?

80 MRS. HALE. [*Mildly.*] Just pulling out a stitch or two that's not sewed   80
very good. [*Threading a needle.*] Bad sewing always made me fid-
gety.

MRS. PETERS. [*Nervously.*] I don't think we ought to touch things.

MRS. HALE. I'll just finish up this end. [*Suddenly stopping and leaning
forward.*] Mrs. Peters?

MRS. PETERS. Yes, Mrs. Hale?

MRS. HALE. What do you suppose she was so nervous about?

85 MRS. PETERS. Oh—I don't know. I don't know as she was nervous. I   85
sometimes sew awful queer when I'm just tired. [MRS. HALE *starts
to say something, looks at* MRS. PETERS, *then goes on sewing.*] Well,
I must get these things wrapped up. They may be through sooner
than we think. [*Putting apron and other things together.*] I wonder
where I can find a piece of paper, and string.

MRS. HALE. In that cupboard, maybe.

MRS. PETERS. [*Looking in cupboard.*] Why, here's a birdcage. [*Holds it
up.*] Did she have a bird, Mrs. Hale?

MRS. HALE. Why, I don't know whether she did or not—I've not been here for so long. There was a man around last year selling canaries cheap, but I don't know as she took one; maybe she did. She used to sing real pretty herself.

MRS. PETERS. [*Glancing around.*] Seems funny to think of a bird here. But she must have had one, or why would she have a cage? I wonder what happened to it.

90 MRS. HALE. I s'pose maybe the cat got it.

MRS. PETERS. No, she didn't have a cat. She's got that feeling some people have about cats—being afraid of them. My cat got in her room and she was real upset and asked me to take it out.

MRS. HALE. My sister Bessie was like that. Queer, ain't it?

MRS. PETERS. [*Examining the cage.*] Why, look at this door. It's broke. One hinge is pulled apart.

MRS. HALE. [*Looking too.*] Looks as if someone must have been rough with it.

95 MRS. PETERS. Why, yes. [*She brings the cage forward and puts it on the table.*]

MRS. HALE. I wish if they're going to find any evidence they'd be about it. I don't like this place.

MRS. PETERS. But I'm awful glad you came with me, Mrs. Hale. It would be lonesome for me sitting here alone.

MRS. HALE. It would, wouldn't it? [*Dropping her sewing.*] But I tell you what I do wish, Mrs. Peters. I wish I had come over sometimes when *she* was here. I—[*Looking around the room.*]—wish I had.

MRS. PETERS. But of course you were awful busy, Mrs. Hale—your house and your children.

100 MRS. HALE. I could've come. I stayed away because it weren't cheerful—and that's why I ought to have come. I—I've never liked this place. Maybe because it's down in a hollow and you don't see the road. I dunno what it is but it's a lonesome place and always was. I wish I had come over to see Minnie Foster sometimes. I can see now—[*Shakes her head.*]

MRS. PETERS. Well, you mustn't reproach yourself, Mrs. Hale. Somehow we just don't see how it is with other folks until—something comes up.

MRS. HALE. Not having children makes less work—but it makes a quiet house, and Wright out to work all day, and no company when he did come in. Did you know John Wright, Mrs. Peters?

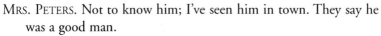

MRS. PETERS. Not to know him; I've seen him in town. They say he was a good man.

MRS. HALE. Yes—good; he didn't drink, and kept his word as well as most, I guess, and paid his debts. But he was a hard man, Mrs. Peters. Just to pass the time of day with him [*Shivers.*] Like a raw wind that gets to the bone. [*Pauses, her eye falling on the cage.*] I should think she would'a wanted a bird. But what do you suppose went with it?

105 MRS. PETERS. I don't know, unless it got sick and died. [*She reaches over and swings the broken door, swings it again. Both women watch it.*] 105

MRS. HALE. You weren't raised round here, were you? [MRS. PETERS *shakes her head.*] You didn't know—her?

MRS. PETERS. Not till they brought her yesterday.

MRS. HALE. She—come to think of it, she was kind of like a bird herself—real sweet and pretty, but kind of timid and—fluttery. How—she—did—change. [*Silence; then as if struck by a happy thought and relieved to get back to every day things.*] Tell you what, Mrs. Peters, why don't you take the quilt in with you? It might take up her mind.

MRS. PETERS. Why, I think that's a real nice idea, Mrs. Hale. There couldn't possibly be any objection to it, could there? Now, just what would I take? I wonder if her patches are in here—and her things.

[*They look in the sewing basket.*]

110 MRS. HALE. Here's some red. I expect this has got sewing things in it. [*Brings out a fancy box.*] What a pretty box. Looks like something somebody would give you. Maybe her scissors are in here. [*Opens box. Suddenly puts her hand to her nose.*] Why—[MRS. PETERS *bends nearer, then turns her face away.*] There's something wrapped up in this piece of silk. 110

MRS. PETERS. Why, this isn't her scissors.

MRS. HALE. [*Lifting the silk.*] Oh, Mrs. Peters—its—[MRS. PETERS *bends closer.*]

MRS. PETERS. It's the bird.

MRS. HALE. [*Jumping up.*] But, Mrs. Peters—look at it! Its neck! Look at its neck! It's all—other side *to.*

115 MRS. PETERS. Somebody—wrung—its—neck. 115

[*Their eyes meet. A look of growing comprehension, of horror. Steps are heard outside.* MRS. HALE *slips box under quilt pieces, and sinks into her chair. Enter* SHERIFF *and* COUNTY ATTORNEY. MRS. PETERS *rises.*]

COUNTY ATTORNEY. [*As one turning from serious things to little pleasantries.*] Well, ladies, have you decided whether she was going to quilt it or knot it?

MRS. PETERS. We think she was going to—knot it.

COUNTY ATTORNEY. Well, that's interesting, I'm sure. [*Seeing the birdcage.*] Has the bird flown?

MRS. HALE. [*Putting more quilt pieces over the box.*] We think the—cat got it.

120 COUNTY ATTORNEY. [*Preoccupied.*] Is there a cat?

[MRS. HALE *glances in a quick covert way at* MRS. PETERS.]

MRS. PETERS. Well, not *now*. They're superstitious, you know. They leave.

COUNTY ATTORNEY. [*To* SHERIFF PETERS, *continuing an interrupted conversation.*] No sign at all of anyone having come from the outside. Their own rope. Now let's go up again and go over it piece by piece. [*They start upstairs.*] It would have to have been someone who knew just the—[MRS. PETERS *sits down. The two women sit there not looking at one another, but as if peering into something and at the same time holding back. When they talk now it is in the manner of feeling their way over strange ground, as if afraid of what they are saying, but as if they can not help saying it.*]

MRS. HALE. She liked the bird. She was going to bury it in that pretty box.

MRS. PETERS. [*In a whisper.*] When *I* was a girl—my kitten—there was a boy took a hatchet, and before my eyes—and before I could get there—[*Covers her face an instant.*] If they hadn't held me back I would have—[*Catches herself, looks upstairs where steps are heard, falters weakly.*]—hurt him.

125 MRS. HALE. [*With a slow look around her.*] I wonder how it would seem never to have had any children around. [*Pause.*] No, Wright wouldn't like the bird—a thing that sang. She used to sing. He killed that, too.

MRS. PETERS. [*Moving uneasily.*] We don't know who killed the bird.

MRS. HALE. I knew John Wright.

MRS. PETERS. It was an awful thing was done in this house that night Mrs. Hale. Killing a man while he slept, slipping a rope around his neck that choked the life out of him.

MRS. HALE. His neck. Choked the life out of him. [*Her hand goes out and rests on the birdcage.*]

130 MRS. PETERS. [*With rising voice.*] We don't know who killed him. We don't *know.* 130

MRS. HALE. [*Her own feeling not interrupted.*] If there'd been years and years of nothing, then a bird to sing to you, it would be awful—still, after the bird was still.

MRS. PETERS. [*Something within her speaking.*] I know what stillness is. When we homesteaded in Dakota, and my first baby died—after he was two years old, and me with no other then—

MRS. HALE. [*Moving.*] How soon do you suppose they'll be through, looking for the evidence?

MRS. PETERS. I know what stillness is. [*Pulling herself back.*] The law has got to punish crime, Mrs. Hale.

135 MRS. HALE. [*Not as if answering that.*] I wish you'd seen Minnie Fos- 135 ter when she wore a white dress with blue ribbons and stood up there in the choir and sang. [A *look around the room.*] Oh, I *wish* I'd come over here once in a while! That was a crime! That was a crime! Who's going to punish that?

MRS. PETERS [*Looking upstairs.*] We mustn't—take on.

MRS. HALE. I might have known she needed help! I know how things can be—for women. I tell you, it's queer, Mrs. Peters. We live close together and we live far, apart. We all go through the same things—it's all just a different kind of the same thing. [*Brushes her eyes; noticing the bottle of fruit, reaches out for it.*] If I was you I wouldn't tell her her fruit was gone. Tell her it *ain't.* Tell her it's all right. Take this in to prove it to her. She—she may never know whether it was broke or not.

MRS. PETERS. [*Takes the bottle, looks about for something to wrap it in; takes petticoat from the clothes brought from the other room, very nervously begins, winding this around the bottle. In a false voice.*] My, it's a good thing the men couldn't hear us. Wouldn't they just laugh! Getting all stirred up over a little thing like a—dead canary. As if that could have anything to do with—with—wouldn't they *laugh!*

[*The men are heard coming down stairs.*]

MRS. HALE. [*Under her breath.*] Maybe they would—maybe they wouldn't.

140 COUNTY ATTORNEY. No, Peters, it's all perfectly clear except a reason 140 for doing it. But you know juries when it comes to women. If there was some definite thing. Something to show—something to make a story about—a thing that would connect up with this strange way of doing it—[*The women's eyes meet for an instant. Enter* HALE *from outer door.*]

HALE. Well, I've got the team around. Pretty cold out there.

COUNTY ATTORNEY. I'm going to stay here a while by myself. [*To the sheriff.*] You can send Frank out for me, can't you? I want to go over everything. I'm not satisfied that we can't do better.

SHERIFF. Do you want to see what Mrs. Peters is going to take in? [*The* COUNTY ATTORNEY *goes to the table, picks up the apron, laughs.*]

COUNTY ATTORNEY. Oh, I guess they're not very dangerous things the ladies have picked out. [*Moves a few things about, disturbing the quilt pieces which cover the box. Steps back.*] No, Mrs. Peters doesn't need supervising. For that matter, a sheriff's wife is married to the law. Ever think of it that way, Mrs. Peters? 146

145 MRS. PETERS. Not—just that way

SHERIFF. [*Chuckling.*] Married to the law. [*Moves toward the other room.*] I just want you to come in here a minute, George. We ought to take a look at these windows.

COUNTY ATTORNEY. [*Scoffingly.*] Oh, windows!

SHERIFF. We'll be right out, Mr. Hale.

[HALE *goes outside. The* SHERIFF *follows the* COUNTY ATTORNEY *into the other room. Then* MRS. HALE *rises, hands tight together, looking intensely at* MRS. PETERS, *whose eyes make a slow turn, finally meeting* MRS. HALE's. *A moment* MRS. HALE *holds her, then her own eyes point the way to where the box is concealed. Suddenly* MRS. PETERS *throws back quilt pieces and tries to put the box in the bag she is wearing. It is too big. She opens box, starts to take bird out, cannot touch it, goes to pieces, stands there helpless. Sound of a knob turning in the other room.* MRS. HALE *snatches the box and puts it in the pocket of her big coat. Enter* COUNTY ATTORNEY *and* SHERIFF.]

COUNTY ATTORNEY. [*Facetiously.*] Well, Henry, at least we found out that she was not going to quilt it. She was going to—what is it you call it, ladies?

150 MRS. HALE. [*Her hand against her pocket.*] We call it—knot it, Mr. 150
  Henderson.

CURTAIN

Questions on Meaning

1. Early in the play Glaspell reveals the male and female characters' attitudes toward each other. Find several passages in which the men comment upon their perceptions of women, and then the women's perceptions of men. How do these perceptions help to establish the tension in the play?

2. As the women begin to realize the truth, Mrs. Hale reproaches herself for not knowing how troubled Minnie Wright was, saying, "We live close together and we live far, apart." What does Mrs. Hale mean by this statement? What forces keep the women apart even though they are neighbors?

3. What does the County Attorney mean when he says that Mrs. Peters is "married to the law"? What is the significance of Mrs. Peters's response to his question?

Questions on Rhetorical Strategy and Style

1. How do the women persuade themselves that they are justified in withholding potential evidence? How valid do you consider their support for their position?

2. Identify the steps in the process that leads the women to their conclusion. What prevents the men from reaching the same conclusion?

3. Effective comparison & contrast requires a consistent basis for comparison. On what basis does Glaspell compare men and women? What conclusions does she seem to draw based on her comparison?

Writing Assignments

1. Susan Glaspell was a strong advocate for women's rights. Write an essay in which you analyze *Trifles* as an argument in favor of women's rights. Consider in your essay Glaspell's characterization of men and women as well as her focus on relationships between husbands and wives.

2. Read Glaspell's short-story version of this play, "A Jury of Her Peers." Write an essay analyzing the differences between the play and the story. Which version do you find more compelling? Why?

3. Domestic violence has been a prominent issue for the past decade or so. Investigate cases of abused women killing their batterers and write a report commenting on the nature of the defense offered for these women, the outcome of the cases, and the public's attitude toward their crimes.

COWBOYS ARE MY WEAKNESS

Pam Houston

Pam Houston (1962–) was born in New Jersey. She received a Ph.D. from the University of Utah and taught literature and creative writing at Denison University, her undergraduate alma mater. She is a river guide and has worked in many outdoor jobs, including working as a horse trainer and a ski instructor. Houston writes during the winter months; her work has appeared in Mirabella *and* Mademoiselle, *as well as in several literary magazines. Her first collection of short stories,* Cowboys Are My Weakness *(1992), attracted much critical attention. Her spare prose style is evident in the following selection, the title story from her book. In it she discusses male-female relationships with an honest perspective many readers have found refreshing.*

1   I have a picture in my mind of a tiny ranch on the edge of a stand of pine trees with some horses in the yard. There's a woman standing in the doorway in cutoffs and a blue chambray work shirt and she's just kissed her tall, bearded, and soft-spoken husband goodbye. There's laundry hanging outside and the morning sun is filtering through the tree branches like spiderwebs. It's the morning after a full moon, and behind the house the deer have eaten everything that was left in the garden.

If I were a painter, I'd paint that picture just to see if the girl in the doorway would turn out to be me. I've been out west ten years now, long enough to call it my home, long enough to know I'll be here forever, but I still don't know where that ranch is. And even though I've had plenty of men here, some of them tall and nearly all of them bearded, I still haven't met the man who has just walked out of the painting, who has just started his pickup truck, whose tire marks I can still see in the sandy soil of the drive.

The west isn't a place that gives itself up easily. Newcomers have to sink into it slowly, to descend through its layers, and I'm still descending. Like most easterners, I started out in the transitional zones, the big cities and the ski towns that outsiders have set up for their own comfort, the places so often referred to as "the best of both worlds." But I was bound to work my way back, through the land, into the small towns and beyond them. That's half the reason I wound up on a ranch near Grass Range, Montana; the other half is Homer.

I've always had this thing about cowboys, maybe because I was born in New Jersey. But a real cowboy is hard to find these days, even in the west. I thought I'd found one on several occasions, I even at one time thought Homer was a cowboy, and though I loved him like crazy for a while and in some ways always will, somewhere along the line I had to face the fact that even though Homer looked like a cowboy, he was just a capitalist with a Texas accent who owned a horse.

Homer's a wildlife specialist in charge of a whitetail deer management project on the ranch. He goes there every year to observe the deer from the start of the mating season in late October until its peak in mid-November. It's the time when the deer are most visible, when the bucks get so lusty they lose their normal caution, when the does run around in the middle of the day with their white tails in the air. When Homer talked me into coming with him, he said I'd love the ranch, and I did. It was sixty miles from the nearest paved road. All of the buildings were whitewashed and plain. One of them had been ordered from a 1916 Sears catalogue. The ranch hands still rode horses, and when the late-afternoon light swept the grainfields across from headquarters, I would watch them move the cattle in rows that looked like waves. There was a peace about the ranch that was uncanny and might have been complete if not for the eight or nine hungry barn cats that crawled up your legs if you even smelled like food, and the exotic chickens of almost every color that fought all day in their pens.

Homer has gone to the ranch every year for the last six, and he has a long history of stirring up trouble there. The ranch hands watch him sit on the hillside and hate him for the money he makes. He's slept with more than one or two of their wives and girlfriends. There was even some talk that he was the reason the ranch owner got divorced.

When he asked me to come with him I knew it would be me or somebody else and I'd heard good things about Montana so I went. There was a time when I was sure Homer was the man who belonged in my painting and I would have sold my soul to be his wife, or even his only girlfriend. I'd come close, in the spring, to losing my mind because of it, but I had finally learned that Homer would always be separate, even from himself, and by the time we got to Montana I was almost immune to him.

Homer and I live in Fort Collins, Colorado, most of the year, in houses that are exactly one mile apart. He's out of town as often as not, keeping track of fifteen whitetail deer herds all across the West. I go with him when he lets me, which is lately more and more. The herds Homer studies are isolated by geography, given plenty of food in bad winters, and protected from hunters and wolves. Homer is working on reproduction and genetics, trying to create, in the wild, super-bucks bigger and tougher than elk. The Montana herd has been his most successful, so he spends the long mating season there. Under his care the bucks have shown incredible increases in antler mass, in body weight, and in fertility.

The other scientists at the university that sponsors Homer respect him, not only for his success with the deer, but for his commitment to observation, for his relentless dedication to his hours in the field. They also think he is eccentric and a bit overzealous.

At first I thought he just liked to be outdoors, but when we got to the ranch his obsession with the deer made him even more like a stranger. He was gone every day from way before sunrise till long after dark. He would dress all in camouflage, even his gloves and socks, and sit on the hillsides above where the deer fed and watch, making notes a few times an hour, changing position every hour or two. If I went with him I wasn't allowed to move except when he did, and I was never allowed to talk. I'd try to save things up for later that I thought of during the day, but by the time we got back to our cabin they seemed unimportant and Homer liked to eat his dinner in front of the TV. By the time we got the dishes done it was way past Homer's bedtime. We were making love less and less, and when we did, it was always from behind.

The ranch owner's name was David, and he wasn't what you'd think a Montana ranch owner would be. He was a poet, and a vegetarian. He listened to Andreas Vollenweider and drank hot beverages with names like Suma and Morning Rain. He wouldn't let the ranch hands use pesticides or chemicals, he wouldn't hire them if they smoked cigarettes. He undergrazed the ranch by about fifty percent, so the organic grain was belly-high to a horse almost everywhere.

David had an idea about recreating on his forty thousand acres the Great Plains that only the Indians and the first settlers had seen. He wasn't making a lot of money ranching, but he was producing the fattest, healthiest, most organic Black Angus cattle in North America. He was sensitive, thoughtful, and kind. He was the kind of man I always knew I should fall in love with, but never did.

Homer and David ate exactly one dinner a week together, which I always volunteered to cook. Homer was always polite and full of incidental conversation and much too quick to laugh. David was quiet and sullen and so restrained that he was hard to recognize.

The irreconcilable differences between Homer and me had been revealing themselves one at a time since late summer. In early November I asked him what he wanted to do on Thanksgiving, and he said he'd like most of all to stay on the ranch and watch the does in heat.

15 Homer was only contracted to work on the ranch until the Sunday before Thanksgiving. When he asked me to come with him he told me we would leave the ranch in plenty of time to have the holidays at home.

I was the only child in a family that never did a lot of celebrating because my parents couldn't plan ahead. They were sun worshipers, and we spent every Thanksgiving in a plane on the way to Puerto Rico, every Christmas in a car on Highway 95, heading for Florida. What I remember most from those days is Casey Kasem's Christmas shows, the longdistance dedications, "'I'll be home for Christmas" from Bobby D. in Spokane to Linda S. in Decatur. We never had hotel reservations and the places we wound up in had no phones and plastic mattress covers and triple locks on the doors. Once we spent Christmas night parked under a fluorescent streetlight, sleeping in the car.

I've spent most of the holidays in my adult life making up for those road trips. I spend lots of money on hand-painted ornaments. I always cook a roast ten pounds bigger than anything we could possibly eat.

Homer thinks my enthusiasm about holidays is childish and self-serving. To prove it to me, last Christmas morning he set the alarm for six-thirty and went back to his house to stain a door. This year I wanted Thanksgiving in my own house. I wanted to cook a turkey we'd be eating for weeks.

I said, "Homer, you've been watching the deer for five weeks now. What else do you think they're gonna do?"

"You don't know anything about it," he said. "Thanksgiving is the premium time. Thanksgiving," he shook one finger in the air, "is the height of the rut."

David and I drank tea together, and every day took walks up into the canyon behind ranch headquarters. He talked about his ex-wife, Carmen, about the red flowers that covered the canyon walls in June, about imaging away nuclear weapons. He told me about the woman Homer was sleeping with on the ranch the year before, when I was back in Colorado counting days till he got home. She was the woman who took care of the chickens, and David said that when Homer left the ranch she wrote a hundred love songs and made David listen while she sang them all.

"She sent them on a tape to Homer," David said, "and when he didn't call or write, she went a little nuts. I finally told her to leave the ranch. I'm not a doctor, and we're a long way from anywhere out here."

From the top of the canyon we could see Homer's form blending with the trees on the ridge above the garden, where the deer ate organic potatoes by the hundreds of pounds.

"I understand if he wasn't interested anymore," David said. ""But I can't believe even he could ignore a gesture that huge."

We watched Homer crawl along the ridge from tree to tree. I could barely distinguish his movements from what the wind did to the tall grass. None of the deer below him even turned their heads.

"What is it about him?" David said, and I knew he was looking for an explanation about Carmen, but I'd never even met her and I didn't want to talk about myself.

"Homer's always wearing camouflage," I said. "Even when he's not."

The wind went suddenly still and we could hear, from headquarters, the sounds of cats fighting, a hen's frantic scream, and then, again, the cats.

David put his arm around me. "We're such good people," he said. "Why aren't we happy?"

30   One day when I got back from my walk with David, Homer was in the cabin in the middle of the day. He had on normal clothes and I could tell he'd shaved and showered. He took me into the bedroom and climbed on top of me frontwards, the way he did when we first met and I didn't even know what he did for a living.

Afterwards he said, "We didn't need a condom, did we?" I counted the days forward and backward and forward again. Homer always kept track of birth control and groceries and gas mileage and all the other things I couldn't keep my mind on. Still, it appeared to be exactly ten days before my next period.

"Yes," I said. "I think we did."

Homer has never done an uncalculated thing in his life, and for a moment I let myself entertain the possibility that his mistake meant that somewhere inside he wanted to have a baby with me, that he really wanted a family and love and security and the things I thought everybody wanted before I met Homer. On the other hand, I knew that one of the ways I had gotten in trouble with Homer, and with other men before him, was by inventing thoughts for them that they'd never had.

"Well," he said. "In that case we better get back to Colorado before they change the abortion laws."

35   Sometimes the most significant moments of your life reveal themselves to you even as they are happening, and I knew in that moment that I would never love Homer the same way again. It wasn't so much that not six months before, when I had asked Homer what we'd do if I got pregnant, he said we'd get married and have a family. It wasn't even that I was sure I wanted a baby. It wasn't even that I thought there was going to be a baby to want.

It all went back to the girl in the log cabin, and how the soft-spoken man would react if she thought she was going to have a baby. It would be winter now, and snowing outside the windows warm with yellow light. He might dance with the sheepdog on the living-room floor, he might sing the theme song from *Father Knows Best*, he might go out and do a swan dive into the snow.

I've been to a lot of school and read a lot of thick books, but at my very core there's a made-for-TV-movie mentality I don't think I'll ever shake. And although there's a lot of doubt in my mind about whether or not an ending as simple and happy as I want is possible anymore in the world, it was clear to me that afternoon that it wasn't possible with Homer.

Five o 'clock the next morning was the first time I saw the real cowboy. He was sitting in the cookhouse eating cereal and I couldn't make myself sleep next to Homer so I'd been up all night wandering around.

He was tall and thin and bearded. His hat was white and ratty and you could tell by looking at his stampede strap that it had been made around a campfire after lots of Jack Daniel's. I'd had my fingers in my hair for twelve hours and my face was breaking out from too much stress and too little sleep and I felt like such a greaseball that I didn't say hello. I poured myself some orange juice, drank it, rinsed the glass, and put it in the dish drainer. I took one more look at the cowboy, and walked back out the door, and went to find Homer in the field.

Homer's truck was parked by a culvert on the South Fork road, which meant he was walking the brush line below the cliffs that used to be the Blackfeet buffalo jumps. It was a boneyard down there, the place where hundreds of buffalo, chased by the Indians, had jumped five hundred feet to their death, and the soil was extremely fertile. The grass was thicker and sweeter there than anywhere on the ranch, and Homer said the deer sucked calcium out of the buffalo bones. I saw Homer crouched at the edge of a meadow I couldn't get to without being seen, so I went back and fell asleep in the bed of his truck.

It was hunting season, and later that morning Homer and I found a deer by the side of the road that had been poached but not taken. The poacher must have seen headlights or heard a truck engine and gotten scared.

I lifted the back end of the animal into the truck while Homer picked up the antlers. It was a young buck, two and a half at the oldest, but it would have been a monster in a few years, and I knew Homer was taking the loss pretty hard.

We took it down to the performance center, where they weigh the organic calves. Homer attached a meat hook to its antlers and hauled it into the air above the pickup.

"Try and keep it from swinging," he said. And I did my best, considering I wasn't quite tall enough to get a good hold, and its blood was bubbling out of the bullet hole and dripping down on me.

45 That's when the tall cowboy, the one from that morning, walked 45 out of the holding pen behind me, took a long slow look at me trying to steady the back end of the dead deer, and settled himself against the fence across the driveway. I stepped back from the deer and pushed the hair out of my eyes. He raised one finger to call me over. I walked slow and didn't look back at Homer.

"Nice buck," he said. "Did you shoot it?"

"It's a baby," I said. "'I don't shoot animals. A poacher got it last night."

"Who was the poacher?" he said, and tipped his hat just past my shoulder toward Homer.

"You're wrong," I said. "'You can say a lot of things about him, but he wouldn't poach a deer."

50 "My name's Montrose T. Coty," he said. "Everyone calls me 50 Monte."

I shook his hand. "Everyone calls you Homer's girlfriend," he said, "but I bet that's not your name."

"You're right," I said, "it's not."

I turned to look at Homer. He was taking measurements off the hanging deer: antler length, body length, width at its girth.

"Tonight's the Stockgrowers' Ball in Grass Range," Monte said. "'I thought you might want to go with me."

55 Homer was looking into the deer's hardened eyeballs. He had its 55 mouth open, and was pulling on its tongue.

"I have to cook dinner for Homer and David," I said. "I'm sorry. It sounds like fun."

In the car on the way back to the cabin, Homer said, "What was that all about?"

I said, "'Nothing," and then I said, "Monte asked me to the Stockgrowers' Ball."

"The Stockgrowers' Ball?" he said. "Sounds like a great time. What do stockgrowers do at a ball?" he said. ""Do they dance?"

60   I almost laughed with him until I remembered how much I loved   60
to dance. I'd been with Homer chasing whitetail so long that I'd forgotten that dancing, like holidays, was something I loved. And I
started to wonder just then what else being with Homer had made me
forget. Hadn't I, at one time, spent whole days listening to music?
Wasn't there a time when I wanted, more than anything, to buy a sail-
boat? And didn't I love to be able to go outdoors and walk anywhere
I wanted, and to make, if I wanted, all kinds of noise?

    I wanted to blame Homer, but I realized then it was more my fault
than his. Because even though I'd never let the woman in the chambray work shirt out of my mind I'd let her, in the last few years, become someone different, and she wasn't living, anymore, in my
painting. The painting she was living in, I saw, belonged to somebody
else.

    "So what did you tell him?" Homer said.

    "I told him I'd see if you'd cook dinner," I said.

    I tried to talk to Homer before I left. First I told him that it
wasn't a real date, that I didn't even know Monte, and really I was only
going because I didn't know if I'd ever have another chance to go to a
Stockgrowers' Ball. When he didn't answer at all I worked up to saying that maybe it was a good idea for me to start seeing other people.
That maybe we'd had two different ideas all along and we needed to
find two other people who would better meet our needs. I told him
that if he had any opinions I wished he'd express them to me, and he
thought for a few minutes and then he said,

65   "Well, I guess we have Jimmy Carter to thank for all the trouble   65
in Panama."

    I spent the rest of the day getting ready for the Stockgrowers' Ball.
All I'd brought with me was some of Homer's camouflage and blue
jeans, so I wound up borrowing a skirt that David's ex-wife had left
behind, some of the chicken woman's dress shoes that looked ridicu-
lous and made my feet huge, and a vest that David's grandfather had
been shot at in by the Plains Indians.

    Monte had to go into town early to pick up ranch supplies, so I
rode in with his friends Buck and Dawn, who spent the whole drive
telling me what a great guy Monte was, how he quit the rodeo circuit
to make a decent living for himself and his wife, how she'd left without saying goodbye not six months before.

They told me that he'd made two thousand dollars in one afternoon doing a Wrangler commercial. That he'd been in a laundromat on his day off and the director had seen him through the window, had gone in and said, "Hey, cowboy, you got an hour? You want to make two thousand bucks?"

"Ole Monte," Buck said. "He's the real thing."

70   After an hour and a half of washboard road we pulled into the dance hall just on our edge of town. I had debated about wearing the cowboy hat I'd bought especially for my trip to Montana, and was thankful I'd decided against it. It was clear, once inside, that only the men wore hats, and only dress hats at that. The women wore high heels and stockings and in almost every case hair curled away from their faces in great airy rolls.

We found Monte at a table in the corner, and the first thing he did was give me a corsage, a pink one, mostly roses that couldn't have clashed more with my rust-colored blouse. Dawn pinned it on me, and I blushed, I suppose, over my first corsage in ten years, and a little old woman in spike heels leaned over and said, "Somebody loves you!" just loud enough for Monte and Buck and Dawn to hear.

During dinner they showed a movie about a cattle drive. After dinner a young enthusiastic couple danced and sang for over an hour about cattle and ranch life and the Big Sky, a phrase which since I'd been in Montana had seemed perpetually on the tip of everybody's tongue.

After dinner the dancing started, and Monte asked me if I knew how to do the Montana two-step. He was more than a foot taller than me, and his hat added another several inches to that. When we stood on the dance floor my eyes came right to the place where his silk scarf disappeared into the shirt buttons on his chest. His big hands were strangely light on me and my feet went the right direction even though my mind couldn't remember the two-step's simple form.

"That's it," he said into the part in my hair. "Don't think. Just let yourself move with me."

75   And we were moving together, in turns that got tighter and tighter each time we circled the dance floor. The songs got faster and so did our motion until there wasn't time for anything but the picking up and putting down of feet, for the swirling colors of Carmen's ugly skirt, for breath and sweat and rhythm.

I was farther west than I'd ever imagined, and in the strange, nearly flawless synchronization on the dance floor I knew I could be a Montana ranch woman, and I knew I could make Monte my man. It had taken me ten years, and an incredible sequence of accidents, but that night I thought I'd finally gotten where I'd set out to go.

The band played till two and we danced till three to the jukebox. Then there was nothing left to do but get in the car and begin the two-hour drive home.

First we talked about our horses. It was the logical choice, the only thing we really had in common, but it only lasted twenty minutes.

I tried to get his opinion on music and sailing, but just like a cowboy, he was too polite for me to tell anything for sure.

80   Then we talked about the hole in my vest that the Indians shot,   80
which I was counting on, and half the reason I wore it.

The rest of the time we just looked at the stars.

I had spent a good portion of the night worrying about what I was going to say when Monte asked me to go to bed with him. When he pulled up between our two cabins he looked at me sideways and said, "I'd love to give you a great big kiss, but I've got a mouthful of chew."

I could hear Homer snoring before I got past the kitchen.

Partly because I didn't like the way Monte and Homer eyed each other, but mostly because I couldn't bear to spend Thanksgiving watching does in heat, I loaded my gear in my truck and got ready to go back to Colorado.

85   On the morning I left, Homer told me that he had decided that   85
I was the woman he wanted to spend the rest of his life with after all, and that he planned to go to town and buy a ring just as soon as the rut ended.

He was sweet on my last morning on the ranch, generous and attentive in a way I'd never seen. He packed me a sack lunch of chicken salad he mixed himself, and he went out to my car and dusted off the inch of snow that had fallen in our first brush with winter, overnight. He told me to call when I got to Fort Collins, he even said to call collect, but I suppose one of life's big tricks is to give us precisely the thing we want, two weeks after we've stopped wanting it, and I couldn't take Homer seriously, even when I tried.

When I went to say goodbye to David he hugged me hard, said I was welcome back on the ranch anytime. He said he enjoyed my company and appreciated my insight. Then he said he liked my perfume and I wondered where my taste in men had come from, I wondered whoever taught me to be so stupid about men.

I knew Monte was out riding the range, so I left a note on his car thanking him again for the dancing and saying I'd be back one day and we could dance again. I put my hat on, that Monte had never got to see, and rolled out of headquarters. It was the middle of the day, but I saw seven bucks in the first five miles, a couple of them giants, and when I slowed down they just stood and stared at the truck. It was the height of the rut and Homer said that's how they'd be, love-crazed and fearless as bears.

About a mile before the edge of ranch property, I saw something that looked like a lone antelope running across the skyline, but antelope are almost never alone, so I stopped the car to watch. As the figure came closer I saw it was a horse, a big chestnut, and it was carrying a rider at a full gallop, and it was coming right for the car.

90   I knew it could have been any one of fifty cowboys employed on   90
the ranch, and yet I've learned to expect more from life than that, and so in my heart I knew it was Monte. I got out of the car and waited, pleased that he'd see my hat most of all, wondering what he'd say when I said I was leaving.

He didn't get off his horse, which was sweating and shaking so hard I thought it might die while we talked.

"You on your way?" he said.

I smiled and nodded. His chaps were sweat-soaked, his leather gloves worn white.

"Will you write me a letter?" he said.

95   "Sure," I said.   95

"Think you'll be back this way?" he asked.

"If I come back," I said, "will you take me dancing?"

"Damn right," he said, and a smile that seemed like the smile I'd been waiting for my whole life spread wide across his face.

"Then it'll be sooner than later," I said.

100   He winked and touched the horse's flank with his spurs and it   100
hopped a little on the takeoff and then there was just dirt flying while the high grass swallowed the horse's legs. I leaned against the door of my pickup truck watching my new cowboy riding off toward where

the sun was already low in the sky and the grass shimmering like nothing I'd ever seen in the mountains. And for a minute I thought we were living inside my painting, but he was riding away too fast to tell. And I wondered then why I had always imagined my cowboy's truck as it was leaving. I wondered why I hadn't turned the truck around and painted my cowboy coming home.

There's a story—that isn't true—that I tell about myself when I first meet someone, about riding a mechanical bull in a bar. In the story, I stay on through the first eight levels of difficulty, getting thrown on level nine only after dislocating my thumb and winning my boyfriend, who was betting on me, a big pile of money. It was something I said in a bar one night, and I liked the way it sounded so much I kept telling it. I've been telling it for so many years now, and in such scrupulous detail, that it has become a memory and it's hard for me to remember that it isn't true. I can smell the smoke and beer-soaked carpets, I can hear the cheers of all the men. I can see the bar lights blur and spin, and I can feel the cold iron buck between my thighs, the painted saddle slam against my tailbone, the surprise and pain when my thumb extends too far and I let go. It's a good story, a story that holds my listeners' attention, and although I consider myself almost pathologically honest, I have somehow allowed myself this one small lie.

And watching Monte ride off through the long grains, I thought about the way we invent ourselves through our stories, and in a similar way, how the stories we tell put walls around our lives. And I think that may be true about cowboys. That there really isn't much truth in my saying cowboys are my weakness; maybe, after all this time, it's just something I've learned how to say.

I felt the hoofbeats in the ground long after Monte's white shirt and ratty hat melded with the sun. When I couldn't even pretend to feel them anymore, I got in the car and headed for the hard road.

I listened to country music the whole way to Cody, Wyoming. The men in the songs were all either brutal or inexpressive and always sorry later. The women were victims, every one. I started to think about coming back to the ranch to visit Monte, about another night dancing, about another night wanting the impossible love of a country song, and I thought:

This is not my happy ending.

This is not my story.

Questions on Meaning

1. What is the significance of the painting the narrator refers to? Notice that she talks about it twice. Where does it come up, and how does its meaning change?
2. Why does the narrator go to the ranch with Homer? How does this establish things about her character we need to understand?
3. In this story, Houston draws upon well-known myths about the American West. Which myths are being repeated, and how does she invent new ones?

Questions on Rhetorical Strategy and Style

1. In what ways do the main characters' actions progress within the story? What sort of tension is created by the way the story develops?
2. How would you define the story's point of view? What is the narrator's relationship to events and to her own life? How does that change?
3. What is your reaction to the story's ending? How does the narrator's realization reinforce the theme suggested in the title?

Writing Assignments

1. Create a portrait of an interesting character. To create a full picture of someone, you might include details about that person's temperament, mental facility, what he or she looks like, the person's language style, and the things the person likes to do.
2. Write a sketch of a place you find interesting. Provide details about the type of activity that takes place there, what it looks like, what people are saying, and what they are doing. While it is important to offer much detail, be selective. As you revise, consider how essential each element is to the success of the sketch. Keep only what needs to remain.

THE LOTTERY

Shirley Jackson

Shirley Hardie Jackson (1919-1965) was born in San Francisco. She received her B.A. from Syracuse University in 1940, then married literary critic Stanley Edgar Hyman, settling in North Bennington, Vermont, where they raised four children. Both parents continued vigorous literary careers. Jackson published the light and charming works Life among the Savages *(1953) and* Raising Demons *(1957) out of her experiences as a parent. At the same time, she was writing more disturbing works of horror and moral criticism,* The Lottery and Other Stories *(1949) and* The Haunting of Hill House *(1959). She said of "The Lottery" that she was hoping to force readers to see that their own lives contained inhumanity and cruelty.*

1   The morning of June 27th was clear and sunny, with the fresh warmth of a full-summer day; the flowers were blossoming profusely and the grass was richly green. The people of the village began to gather in the square, between the post office and the bank, around ten o'clock; in some towns there were so many people that the lottery took two days and had to be started on June 26th, but in this village, where there were only about three hundred people, the whole lottery took less than two hours, so it could begin at ten o'clock in the morning and still be through in time to allow the villagers to get home for noon dinner.

The children assembled first, of course. School was recently over for the summer, and the feeling of liberty sat uneasily on most of them; they tended to gather together quietly for a while before they broke into boisterous play, and their talk was still of the classroom and the teacher, of books and reprimands. Bobby Martin had already stuffed his pockets full of stones, and the other boys soon followed his example, selecting the smoothest and roundest stones; Bobby and Harry Jones and Dickie Delacroix—the villagers pronounced this name "Dellacroy"—eventually made a great pile of stones in one corner of the square and guarded it against the raids of the other boys. The girls stood aside, talking among themselves, looking over their shoulders at the boys, and the very small children rolled in the dust or clung to the hands of their older brothers or sisters.

Soon the men began to gather, surveying their own children, speaking of planting and rain, tractors and taxes. They stood together, away from the pile of stones in the corner, and their jokes were quiet and they smiled rather than laughed. The women, wearing faded house dresses and sweaters, came shortly after their menfolk. They greeted one another and exchanged bits of gossip as they went to join their husbands. Soon the women, standing by their husbands, began to call to their children, and the children came reluctantly, having to be called four or five times. Bobby Martin ducked under his mother's grasping hand and ran, laughing, back to the pile of stones. His father spoke up sharply, and Bobby came quickly and took his place between his father and his oldest brother.

The lottery was conducted—as were the square dances, the teenage club, the Halloween program—by Mr. Summers, who had time and energy to devote to civic activities. He was a round-faced, jovial man and he ran the coal business, and people were sorry for him, because he had no children and his wife was a scold. When he arrived in the square, carrying the black wooden box, there was a murmur of conversation among the villagers, and he waved and called, "Little late today, folks." The postmaster, Mr. Graves, followed him, carrying a three-legged stool, and the stool was put in the center of the square and Mr. Summers set the black box down on it. The villagers kept their distance, leaving a space between themselves and the stool, and when Mr. Summers said, "Some of you fellows want to give me a hand?" there was a hesitation before two men, Mr. Martin and his oldest son, Baxter, came forward to hold the box steady on the stool while Mr. Summers stirred up the papers inside it.

5   The original paraphernalia for the lottery had been lost long ago,   5
and the black box now resting on the stool had been put into use even
before Old Man Warner, the oldest man in town, was born. Mr. Summers spoke frequently to the villagers about making a new box, but
no one liked to upset even as much tradition as was represented by the
black box. There was a story that the present box had been made with
some pieces of the box that had preceded it, the one that had been
constructed when the first people settled down to make a village here.
Every year, after the lottery, Mr. Summers began talking again about
a new box, but every year the subject was allowed to fade off without
anything's being done. The black box grew shabbier each year; by now
it was no longer completely black but splintered badly along one side
to show the original wood color, and in some places faded or stained.

Mr. Martin and his oldest son, Baxter, held the black box securely
on the stool until Mr. Summers had stirred the papers thoroughly
with his hand. Because so much of the ritual had been forgotten or
discarded, Mr. Summers had been successful in having slips of paper
substituted for the chips of wood that had been used for generations.
Chips of wood, Mr. Summers had argued, had been all very well when
the village was tiny, but now that the population was more than three
hundred and likely to keep on growing, it was necessary to use something that would fit more easily into the black box. The night before
the lottery, Mr. Summers and Mr. Graves made up the slips of paper
and put them in the box, and it was then taken to the safe of Mr. Summers' coal company and locked up until Mr. Summers was ready to
take it to the square next morning. The rest of the year, the box was
put away, sometimes one place, sometimes another; it had spent one
year in Mr. Graves's barn and another year underfoot in the post office, and sometimes it was set on a shelf in the Martin grocery and left
there.

There was a great deal of fussing to be done before Mr. Summers
declared the lottery open. There were the lists to make up—of heads
of families, heads of households in each family, members of each
household in each family. There was the proper swearing-in of Mr.
Summers by the postmaster, as the official of the lottery; at one time,
some people remembered, there had been a recital of some sort, per-
formed by the official of the lottery, a perfunctory, tuneless chant that
had been rattled off duly each year; some people believed that the official of the lottery used to stand just so when he said or sang it, oth-

ers believed that he was supposed to walk among the people, but years and years ago this part of the ritual had been allowed to lapse. There had been, also, a ritual salute, which the official of the lottery had had to use in addressing each person who came up to draw from the box, but this also had changed with time, until now it was felt necessary only for the official to speak to each person approaching. Mr. Summers was very good at all this; in his clean white shirt and blue jeans, with one hand resting carelessly on the black box, he seemed very proper and important as he talked interminably to Mr. Graves and the Martins.

Just as Mr. Summers finally left off talking and turned to the assembled villagers, Mrs. Hutchinson came hurriedly along the path to the square, her sweater thrown over her shoulders, and slid into place in the back of the crowd. "Clean forgot what day it was," she said to Mrs. Delacroix, who stood next to her, and they both laughed softly. "Thought my old man was out back stacking wood," Mrs. Hutchinson went on, "and then I looked out the window and the kids were gone, and then I remembered it was the twentyseventh and came a-running." She dried her hands on her apron, and Mrs. Delacroix said, "You're in time, though. They're still talking away up there."

Mrs. Hutchinson craned her neck to see through the crowd and found her husband and children standing near the front. She tapped Mrs. Delacroix on the arm as a farewell and began to make her way through the crowd. The people separated good-humoredly to let her through; two or three people said, in voices just loud enough to be heard across the crowd, "Here comes your Missus, Hutchinson," and "Bill, she made it after all." Mrs. Hutchinson reached her husband, and Mr. Summers, who had been waiting, said cheerfully, "Thought we were going to have to get on without you, Tessie." Mrs. Hutchinson said, grinning, "Wouldn't have me leave m'dishes in the sink, now, would you, Joe?" and soft laughter ran through the crowd as the people stirred back into position after Mrs. Hutchinson's arrival.

10   "Well, now," Mr. Summers said soberly, "guess we better get   10 started, get this over with, so's we can go back to work. Anybody ain't here?"

"Dunbar," several people said. "Dunbar, Dunbar."

Mr. Summers consulted his list. "Clyde Dunbar," he said. "That's right. He's broke his leg, hasn't he? Who's drawing for him?"

"Me, I guess," a woman said, and Mr. Summers turned to look at her. "Wife draws for her husband," Mr. Summers said. "Don't you have a grown boy to do it for you, Janey?" Although Mr. Summers and everyone else in the village knew the answer perfectly well, it was the business of the official of the lottery to ask such questions formally. Mr. Summers waited with an expression of polite interest while Mrs. Dunbar answered.

"Horace's not but sixteen yet," Mrs. Dunbar said regretfully. "Guess I gotta fill in for the old man this year."

15 "Right," Mr. Summers said. He made a note on the list he was 15 holding. Then he asked, "Watson boy drawing this year?"

A tall boy in the crowd raised his hand. "Here," he said. "I'm drawing for m'mother and me." He blinked his eyes nervously and ducked his head as several voices in the crowd said things like "Good fellow, Jack," and "Glad to see your mother's got a man to do it."

"Well," Mr. Summers said, "guess that's everyone. Old Man Warner make it?"

"Here," a voice said, and Mr. Summers nodded.

A sudden hush fell on the crowd as Mr. Summers cleared his throat and looked at the list. "All ready?" he called. "Now, I'll read the names—heads of families first—and the men come up and take a paper out of the box. Keep the paper folded in your hand without looking at it until everyone has had a turn. Everything clear?"

20 The people had done it so many times that they only half listened 20 to the directions; most of them were quiet, wetting their lips, not looking around. Then Mr. Summers raised one hand high and said, "Adams." A man disengaged himself from the crowd and came forward. "Hi, Steve," Mr. Summers said, and Mr. Adams said, "Hi, Joe." They grinned at one another humorlessly and nervously. Then Mr. Adams reached into the black box and took out a folded paper. He held it firmly by one corner as he turned and went hastily back to his place in the crowd, where he stood a little apart from his family, not looking down at his hand.

"Allen," Mr. Summers said. "Anderson . . . Bentham."

"Seems like there's no time at all between lotteries any more," Mrs. Delacroix said to Mrs. Graves in the back row. "Seems like we got through with the last one only last week."

"Time sure goes fast," Mrs. Graves said.

"Clark . . . Delacroix."

25 "There goes my old man," Mrs. Delacroix said. She held her 25
breath while her husband went forward.

"Dunbar," Mr. Summers said, and Mrs. Dunbar went steadily to
the box while one of the women said, "Go on, Janey," and another
said, "There she goes."

"We're next," Mrs. Graves said. She watched while Mr. Graves
came around from the side of the box, greeted Mr. Summers gravely,
and selected a slip of paper from the box. By now, all through the
crowd there were men holding the small folded papers in their large
hands, turning them over and over nervously. Mrs. Dunbar and her
two sons stood together, Mrs. Dunbar holding the slip of paper.

"Harburt . . . Hutchinson."

"Get up there, Bill," Mrs. Hutchinson said, and the people near
her laughed.

30 "Jones." 30

"They do say," Mr. Adams said to Old Man Warner, who stood
next to him, "that over in the north village they're talking of giving up
the lottery."

Old Man Warner snorted. "Pack of crazy fools," he said. "Listening to the young folks, nothing's good enough for *them*. Next thing
you know, they'll be wanting to go back to living in caves, nobody
work any more, live *that* way for a while. Used to be a saying about
'Lottery in June, corn be heavy soon.' First thing you know, we'd all
be eating stewed chickweed and acorns. There's *always* been a lottery,"
he added petulantly. "Bad enough to see young Joe Summers up there
joking with everybody."

"Some places have already quit lotteries," Mrs. Adams said.

"Nothing but trouble in *that*," Old Man Warner said stoutly.
"Pack of young fools."

35 "Martin." And Bobby Martin watched his father go forward. 35
"Overdyke . . . Percy."

"I wish they'd hurry," Mrs. Dunbar said to her older son. "I wish
they'd hurry."

"They're almost through," her son said.

"You get ready to run tell Dad," Mrs. Dunbar said.

Mr. Summers called his own name and then stepped forward precisely and selected a slip from the box. Then he called, "Warner."

40 "Seventy-seventh year I been in the lottery," Old Man Warner 40
said as he went through the crowd. "Seventy-seventh time."

"Watson." The tall boy came awkwardly through the crowd. Someone said, "Don't be nervous, Jack," and Mr. Summers said, "Take your time, son."

"Zanini."

After that, there was a long pause, a breathless pause, until Mr. Summers, holding his slip of paper in the air, said, "All right, fellows." For a minute, no one moved, and then all the slips of paper were opened. Suddenly, all the women began to speak at once, saying, "Who is it?" "Who's got it?" "Is it the Dunbars?" "Is it the Watsons?" Then the voices began to say, "It's Hutchinson. It's Bill," "Bill Hutchinson's got it."

"Go tell your father," Mrs. Dunbar said to her older son.

45   People began to look around to see the Hutchinsons. Bill 45 Hutchinson was standing quiet, staring down at the paper in his hand. Suddenly, Tessie Hutchinson shouted to Mr. Summers, "You didn't give him time enough to take any paper he wanted. I saw you. It wasn't fair."

"Be a good sport, Tessie," Mrs. Delacroix called, and Mrs. Graves said, "All of us took the same chance."

"Shut up, Tessie," Bill Hutchinson said.

"Well, everyone," Mr. Summers said, "that was done pretty fast, and now we've got to be hurrying a little more to get done in time." He consulted his next list. "Bill," he said, "you draw for the Hutchinson family. You got any other households in the Hutchinsons?"

"There's Don and Eva," Mrs. Hutchinson yelled. "Make them take their chance!"

50   "Daughters draw with their husbands' families, Tessie," Mr. Sum- 50 mers said gently. "You know that as well as anyone else."

"It wasn't *fair*," Tessie said.

"I guess not, Joe," Bill Hutchinson said regretfully. "My daughter draws with her husband's family, that's only fair. And I've got no other family except the kids."

"Then, as far as drawing for families is concerned, it's you." Mr. Summers said in explanation, "and as far as drawing for households is concerned, that's you, too. Right?"

"Right," Bill Hutchinson said.

55   "How many kids, Bill?" Mr. Summers asked formally. 55

"Three," Bill Hutchinson said. "There's Bill, Jr., and Nancy, and little Dave. And Tessie and me."

"All right, then," Mr. Summers said. "Harry, you got their tickets back?"

Mr. Graves nodded and held up the slips of paper. "Put them in the box, then," Mr. Summers directed. "Take Bill's and put it in."

"I think we ought to start over," Mrs. Hutchinson said, as quietly as she could. "I tell you it wasn't *fair*. You didn't give him time enough to choose. *Every*body saw that."

60 Mr. Graves had selected the five slips and put them in the box, 60 and he dropped all the papers but those onto the ground, where the breeze caught them and lifted them off.

"Listen, everybody," Mrs. Hutchinson was saying to the people around her.

"Ready, Bill?" Mr. Summers asked, and Bill Hutchinson, with one quick glance around at his wife and children, nodded.

"Remember," Mr. Summers said, "take the slips and keep them folded until each person has taken one. Harry, you help little Dave." Mr. Graves took the hand of the little boy, who came willingly with him up to the box. "Take a paper out of the box, Davy," Mr. Summers said. Davy put his hand into the box and laughed. "Take just *one* paper," Mr. Summers said. "Harry, you hold it for him." Mr. Graves took the child's hand and removed the folded paper from the tight fist and held it while little Dave stood next to him and looked up at him wonderingly.

"Nancy next," Mr. Summers said. Nancy was twelve, and her school friends breathed heavily as she went forward, switching her skirt, and took a slip daintily from the box. "Bill, Jr.," Mr. Summers said, and Billy, his face red and his feet over-large, nearly knocked the box over as he got a paper out. "Tessie," Mr. Summers said. She hesitated for a minute, looking around defiantly, and then set her lips and went up to the box. She snatched a paper out and held it behind her.

65 "Bill," Mr. Summers said, and Bill Hutchinson reached into the 65 box and felt around, bringing his hand out at last with the slip of paper in it.

The crowd was quiet. A girl whispered, "I hope it's not Nancy," and the sound of the whisper reached the edges of the crowd.

"It's not the way it used to be," Old Man Warner said clearly. "People ain't the way they used to be."

"All right," Mr. Summers said. "Open the papers. Harry, you open little Dave's."

Mr. Graves opened the slip of paper and there was a general sigh through the crowd as he held it up and everyone could see that it was blank. Nancy and Bill, Jr., opened theirs at the same time, and both beamed and laughed, turning around to the crowd and holding their slips of paper above their heads.

70   "Tessie," Mr. Summers said. There was a pause, and then Mr. Summers looked at Bill Hutchinson, and Bill unfolded his paper and showed it. It was blank.

"It's Tessie," Mr. Summers said, and his voice was hushed. "Show us her paper, Bill."

Bill Hutchinson went over to his wife and forced the slip of paper out of her hand. It had a black spot on it, the black spot Mr. Summers had made the night before with the heavy pencil in the coal-company office. Bill Hutchinson held it up, and there was a stir in the crowd.

"All right, folks," Mr. Summers said. "Let's finish quickly."

Although the villagers had forgotten the ritual and lost the original black box, they still remembered to use stones. The pile of stones the boys had made earlier was ready; there were stones on the ground with the blowing scraps of paper that had come out of the box. Mrs. Delacroix selected a stone so large she had to pick it up with both hands and turned, to Mrs. Dunbar. "Come on," she said. "Hurry up."

Mrs. Dunbar had small stones in both hands, and she said, gasping for breath, "I can't run at all. You'll have to go ahead and I'll catch up with you."

75   The children had stones already, and someone gave little Davy Hutchinson a few pebbles.

Tessie Hutchinson was in the center of a cleared space by now, and she held her hands out despertely as the villagers moved in on her. "It isn't fair," she said. A stone hit her on the side of the head.

Old Man Warner was saying, "Come on, come on, everyone." Steve Adams was in the front of the crowd of villagers, with Mrs. Graves beside him.

"It isn't fair, it isn't right," Mrs. Hutchinson screamed, and then they were upon her.

Questions on Meaning

1. Why does the story begin with the children, and why does it end with the little boy being given a few stones?
2. Tessie Hutchinson becomes a scapegoat for the community. Look up the word "scapegoat" to see exactly what it means and where it originated.
3. Is this story possible? Could people act so casually about such a horrifying prospect as killing a friend or neighbor? Discuss the possibilities of such behavior.

Questions on Rhetorical Strategy and Style

1. At what point in the story does the reader know that something horrible is about to happen? How does the mood of the whole story lead to that moment? Or does it?
2. The families are divided into prescribed groupings, daughters with husbands' families, children with parents until a certain age. Why do we classify and divide groups of people in these ways? What is to be gained from family groupings? What is lost?
3. A news reporter recently described villagers he had met in Rwanda, where the Tutsi massacres took place. He said that the people told him that they must conform to everyone else's behavior, or they too would be killed. Discuss this kind of argument for military and civil violence. Do you believe it to be a sound argument for any occasion?

Writing Assignments

1. A famous German minister, Diedrich Bonhoeffer, said of the Nazis, "When they came for the Jews, I said nothing; when they came for the Communists, I said nothing; when they came for the Catholics, I said nothing; so when they came for me, there was no one to speak." What does such a statement show about our responsibility for others?
2. Traditions can be good for a society or culture, but they can also cause great damage. Choose a holiday or event and discuss the pros and cons of the traditional approaches to the occasion.
3. The story revolves around an election. Why are elections surrounded with so much ceremony? We have election judges, election officials, and election rules and regulations. Does the right to vote deserve so much time and ceremony? Why or why not?

ARABY

James Joyce

James Augustine Aloysius Joyce (1882-1941) was born in Dublin, a city he once called "the center of paralysis." He attended Clongowes Wood College but his parents fell on hard times and he had to leave the school; he later attended Belevedere College on a scholarship. He describes these early years in his short story collection Dubliners *(1914) and in his semi-autobiographical novel* Portrait of the Artist as a Young Man *(1914-15). Ultimately Joyce took a degree in modern languages from University College, Dublin, in 1902. He met his lifetime companion, Nora Barnacle, two years later. They moved to Paris and then to Trieste, where their son, Giorgio, and daughter, Lucia, were born. Their travels took them from Zurich and then back to Paris, where Joyce completed* Ulysses *and* Finnegan's Wake, *his two most famous and ambitious novels. The German occupation of Paris in World War II forced Joyce and his family to leave for Zurich, where they lived until Joyce's death in 1941. "Araby" is the third story in* Dubliners.

1   North Richmond Street, being blind, was a quiet street except at the hour when the Christian Brothers' School set the boys free. An uninhabited house of two storeys stood at the blind end, detached from its neighbours in a square ground. The other houses of the street, conscious of decent lives within them, gazed at one another with brown imperturbable faces.

The former tenant of our house, a priest, had died in the back drawing room. Air, musty from having long been enclosed, hung in all the rooms, and the waste room behind the kitchen was littered with old useless papers. Among these I found a few paper-covered books, the pages of which were curled and damp: *The Abbott*, by Walter Scott, *The Devout Communicant* and *The Memoirs of Vidocq*. I liked the last best because its leaves were yellow. The wild garden behind the house contained a central apple-tree and a few straggling bushes under one of which I found the late tenant's rusty bicycle-pump. He had been a very charitable priest; in his will he had left all his money to institutions and the furniture of his house to his sister.

When the short days of winter came dusk fell before we had well eaten our dinners. When we met in the street the houses had grown sombre. The space of sky above us was the colour of ever-changing violet and towards it the lamps of the street lifted their feeble lanterns. The cold air stung us and we played till our bodies glowed. Our shouts echoed in the silent street. The career of our play brought us through the dark muddy lanes behind the houses where we ran the gauntlet of the rough tribes from the cottages, to the back doors of the dark dripping gardens where odours arose from the ashpits, to the dark odorous stables where a coachman smoothed and combed the horse or shook music from the buckled harness. When we returned to the street light from the kitchen windows had filled the areas. If my uncle was seen turning the corner we hid in the shadow until we had seen him safely housed. Or if Mangan's sister came out on the doorstep to call her brother in to his tea we watched her from our shadow peer up and down the street. We waited to see whether she would remain or go in and, if she remained, we left our shadow and walked up to Mangan's steps resignedly. She was waiting for us, her figure defined by the light from the half-opened door. Her brother always teased her before he obeyed and I stood by the railings looking at her. Her dress swung as she moved her body and the soft rope of her hair tossed from side to side.

Every morning I lay on the floor in the front parlor watching her door. The blind was pulled down within an inch of the sash so that I could not be seen. When she came out on the doorstep my heart leaped. I ran to the hall, seized my books and followed her. I kept her brown figure always in my eye and, when we came near the point at which our ways diverged, I quickened my pace and passed her. This happened morning after morning. I had never spoken to her, except for a few casual words, and yet her name was like a summons to all my foolish blood.

5   Her image accompanied me even in places the most hostile to romance. On Saturday evenings when my aunt went marketing I had to go to carry some of the parcels. We walked through the flaring street, jostled by drunken men and bargaining women, amid the curses of

labourers, the shrill litanies of shop-boys who stood on guard by the barrels of pigs' cheeks, the nasal chanting of street singers, who sang a *come-all-you* about O'Donovan Rossa, or a ballad about the troubles in our native land. These noises converged in a single sensation of life for me: I imagined that I bore my chalice safely through the throng of foes. Her name sprang to my lips at moments in strange prayers and praises which I myself did not understand. My eyes were often full of tears (I could not tell why) and at times a flood from my heart seemed to pour itself out into my bosom. I thought little of the future. I did not know whether I would ever speak to her or not or, if I spoke to her, how I could tell her of my confused adoration. But my body was like a harp and her words and gestures were like fingers running upon the wires.

One evening I went into the back drawing-room in which the priest had died. It was a dark rainy evening and there was no sound in the house. Through one of the broken panes I heard the rain impinge upon the earth, the fine incessant needles of water playing in the sodden beds. Some distant lamp or lighted window gleamed below me. I was thankful that I could see so little. All my senses seemed to desire to veil themselves and, feeling that I was about to slip from them, I pressed the palms of my hands together until they trembled, murmuring: "*O love! O love!*" many times.

At last she spoke to me. When she addressed the first words to me I was so confused that I did not know what to answer. She asked me was I going to *Araby*. I forget whether I answered yes or no. It would be a splendid bazaar, she said; she would love to go.

—And why can't you? I asked.

While she spoke she turned a silver bracelet round and round her wrist. She could not go, she said, because there would be a retreat that week in her convent. Her brother and two other boys were fighting for their caps and I was alone at the railings. She held one of the spikes, bowing her head towards me. The light from the lamp opposite our door caught the white curve of her neck, lit up her hair that rested there and, falling, lit up the hand upon the railing. It fell over one side of her dress and caught the white border of a petticoat, just visible as she stood at ease.

10   —It's well for you, she said.

—If I go, I said, I will bring you something.

What innumerable follies laid waste my waking and sleeping thoughts after that evening! I wished to annihilate the tedious intervening days. I chafed against the work of school. At night in my bedroom and by day in the classroom her image came between me and the page I strove to read. The syllables of the word *Araby* were called to me through the silence in which my soul luxuriated and cast an Eastern enchantment over me. I asked for leave to go to the bazaar on Saturday night. My aunt was surprised and hoped it was not some Freemason affair. I answered few questions in class. I watched my master's face pass from amiability to sternness; he hoped I was not beginning to idle. I could not call my wandering thoughts together. I had hardly any patience with the serious work of life which, now that it stood between me and my desire, seemed to me child's play, ugly monotonous child's play.

On Saturday morning I reminded my uncle that I wished to go to the bazaar in the evening. He was fussing at the hallstand, looking for the hatbrush, and answered me curtly:

—Yes, boy, I know.

As he was in the hall I could not go into the front parlour and lie at the window. I left the house in bad humour and walked slowly towards the school. The air was pitilessly raw and already my heart misgave me.

When I came home to dinner my uncle had not yet been home. Still, it was early. I sat staring at the clock for some time and, when its ticking began to irritate me, I left the room. I mounted the staircase and gained the upper part of the house. The high cold empty gloomy rooms liberated me and I went from room to room singing. From the front window I saw my companions playing below in the street. Their cries reached me weakened and indistinct and, leaning my forehead against the cool glass, I looked over at the dark house where she lived. I may have stood there for an hour, seeing nothing but the brown-clad figure cast by my imagination, touched discreetly by the lamplight at the curved neck, at the hand upon the railing and at the border below the dress.

When I came downstairs again I found Mrs. Mercer sitting at the fire. She was an old garrulous woman, a pawnbroker's widow, who collected used stamps for some pious purpose. I had to endure the gossip of the tea-table. The meal was prolonged beyond an hour and still my uncle did not come. Mrs. Mercer stood up to go: she was sorry she

15

15

couldn't wait any longer, but it was after eight o'clock and she did not like to be out late, as the night air was bad for her. When she had gone I began to walk up and down the room, clenching my fists. My aunt said:

—I'm afraid you may put off your bazaar for this night of Our Lord.

At nine o'clock I heard my uncle's latchkey in the halldoor. I heard him talking to himself and heard the hallstand rocking when it had received the weight of his overcoat. I could interpret these signs. When he was midway through his dinner I asked him to give me the money to go to the bazaar. He had forgotten.

20
—The people are in bed and after their first sleep now, he said. 20

I did not smile. My aunt said to him energetically:

—Can't you give him the money and let him go? You've kept him late enough as it is.

My uncle said he was very sorry he had forgotten. He said he believed in the old saying: "All work and no play makes Jack a dull boy." He asked me where I was going and, when I had told him a second time he asked me did I know *The Arab's Farewell to his Steed*. When I left the kitchen he was about to recite the opening lines of the piece to my aunt.

I held a florin tightly in my hand as I strode down Buckingham Street towards the station. The sight of the streets thronged with buyers and glaring with gas recalled to me the purpose of my journey. I took my seat in a third-class carriage of a deserted train. After an intolerable delay the train moved out of the station slowly. It crept onward among ruinous houses and over the twinkling river. At Westland Row Station a crowd of people pressed to the carriage doors; but the porters moved them back, saying that it was a special train for the bazaar. I remained alone in the bare carriage. In a few minutes the train drew up beside an improvised wooden platform. I passed out on to the road and saw by the lighted dial of a clock that it was ten minutes to ten. In front of me was a large building which displayed the magical name.

25
I could not find any sixpenny entrance and, fearing that the 25 bazaar would be closed, I passed in quickly through a turnstile, handing a shilling to a weary-looking man. I found myself in a big hall girdled at half its height by a gallery. Nearly all the stalls were closed and the greater part of the hall was in darkness. I recognized a silence like

that which pervades a church after a service. I walked into the centre of the bazaar timidly. A few people were gathered about the stalls which were still open. Before a curtain, over which the words *Café Chantant* were written in coloured lamps, two men were counting money on a salver. I listened to the fall of the coins.

Remembering with difficulty why I had come I went over to one of the stalls and examined porcelain vases and flowered tea-sets. At the door of the stall a young lady was talking and laughing with two young gentlemen. I remarked their English accents and listened vaguely to their conversation.

—O, I never said such a thing!

—O, but you did!

—O, but I didn't!

—Didn't she say that?

—Yes I heard her.

—O, there's a. . . fib!

Observing me the young lady came over and asked me did I wish to buy anything. The tone in her voice was not encouraging; she seemed to have spoken to me out of a sense of duty. I looked humbly at the great jars that stood like eastern guards at either side of the dark entrance to the stall and murmured:

—No, thank you.

The young lady changed the position of one of the vases and went back to the two young men. They began to talk of the same subject. Once or twice the young lady glanced at me over her shoulder.

I lingered before her stall, though I knew my stay was useless, to make my interest in her wares seem the more real. Then I turned away slowly and walked down the middle of the bazaar. I allowed the two pennies to fall against the sixpence in my pocket. I heard a voice call from one end of the gallery that the light was out. The upper part of the hall was now completely dark.

Gazing up into the darkness I saw myself as a creature driven and derided by vanity; and my eyes burned with anguish and anger.

Questions on Meaning

1. Joyce became angry and disaffected with the Catholic church, though his religious education strongly influences all his writings. What does he mean at the beginning of the story when he says that the priest who had owned his family's house was a generous man who "in his will left all his money to institutions and the furniture of his house to his sister"?
2. The narrator in the story falls madly in love with his friend Mangan's sister. What happens to his physical health and to his concentration at school? What is Joyce saying about love?
3. Why does the boy go to the bazaar? Why does he fail to accomplish his goal?

Questions on Rhetorical Strategy and Style

1. The descriptions of Mangan's sister are quite vivid and yet they never really tell the reader what she looks like. She twists her silver bracelets and moves her head gracefully. Why doesn't Joyce tell more about her looks?
2. *Araby* is the name for a local bazaar or carnival in the story; the dictionary defines it as a poetic word for Arabia. What feelings and images does the name evoke? How do these feelings contrast with the description of the narrator's home?
3. How does the reader know that the aunt and uncle in the story are short of money? What does the money in the story suggest about the boy's hopes and values?

Writing Assignments

1. Describe your "first love," that is, the first time you had a crush on someone. Why does the experience usually seem so hopeless and desperate?
2. The girls at the bazaar, who talk in English accents, are barely polite to the boy. What kinds of politics existed between the English and the Irish at the time of this story? Discuss how a social or political situation can affect someone's personal life.
3. The story begins by describing the street as "blind," or a dead-end. Draw a map of a street where you lived as a child. Then write about some incident that happened there.

❧ GIRL ❧

Jamaica Kincaid

Born Elaine Potter Richardson in St. John's, Antigua, in the West Indies, Jamaica Kincaid (1949-) left Antigua for New York when she was seventeen, took classes at a community college, studied photography at the New School for Social Research, and attended Franconia College. She has been a staff writer for The New Yorker *and has published her work in* Rolling Stone, The Village Voice, *and* The Paris Review. *Her first book,* At the Bottom of the River *(1983) won an award from the American Academy and Institute of Arts and Letters. Her more recent works include* The Autobiography of My Mother *(1996) and* My Brother *(1997). The following selection originally appeared in* The New Yorker *and was included in* At the Bottom of the River. *It vividly narrates a relationship between a powerful mother and her young daughter and confronts us with the advice the daughter must listen to.*

Wash the white clothes on Monday and put them on the stone heap; wash the color clothes on Tuesday and put them on the clothesline to dry; don't walk barehead in the hot sun; cook pumpkin fritters in very hot sweet oil; soak your little clothes right after you take them off; when buying cotton to make yourself a nice blouse, be sure that it doesn't have gum on it, because that way it won't hold up well after a wash; soak salt fish overnight before you cook it; is it true that you sing benna in Sunday school?; always eat your food in such a way that it won't turn someone else's stomach; on Sundays try to walk like a lady and not like the slut you are so bent on becoming; don't sing benna in Sunday school; you mustn't speak to wharf-rat boys, not even to give directions; don't eat fruits on the street—flies will follow you; *but I don't sing benna on Sundays at all and never in Sunday school*; this is how to sew on a button; this is how to make a buttonhole for the button you have just sewed on; this is how to hem a dress when you see the hem coming down and so to prevent yourself from looking like the slut I know you are so bent on becoming; this is how you iron your father's khaki shirt so that it doesn't have a crease; this is how you iron your father's khaki pants so that they don't have a crease; this is how you grow okra—far from the house, because okra tree harbors red ants; when you are growing dasheen, make sure it gets plenty of water or else it makes your throat itch when you are eating it; this is how you sweep a corner; this is how you sweep a whole house; this is how you sweep a yard; this is how you smile to someone you don't like too much; this how you smile to someone you don't like at all; this is how you smile to someone you like completely; this is how you set a table for tea; this is how you set a table for dinner; this is how you set a table for dinner with an important guest; this is how you set a table for lunch; this is how you set a table for breakfast; this is how to behave in the presence of men who don't know you very well, and this way they won't recognize immediately the slut I have warned you against becoming; be sure to wash every day, even if it is with your own spit; don't squat down to play marbles—you are not a boy, you know; don't pick people's flowers—you might catch something; don't throw stones at blackbirds, because it might not be a blackbird at all; this is how to make a bread pudding; this is how to make doukona; this is how to make pepper pot; this is how to make a good medicine for a cold; this is how to make a good medicine to throw away a child before it even becomes a child; this is how to catch a fish; this is how to throw back a fish you don't like, and that way something bad won't fall on you; this is how to bully a man; this is how a man bullies you; this is how to love a man, and if this doesn't work there are other ways, and if they don't work don't feel too bad about giving up; this is how to spit up in the air if you feel like it and this is how to move quick so that it doesn't fall on you; this is how to make ends meet; always squeeze bread to make sure it's fresh; *but what if the baker won't let me feel the bread?*; you mean to say that after all you are really going to be the kind of woman who the baker won't let near the bread?

Questions on Meaning

1. In this short piece, Kincaid gives us a glimpse into the relationship between a mother and daughter. How would you describe that relationship?
2. How would you characterize the advice offered by the mother in this story? What information about her community and its assumptions regarding gender roles can you infer from it?

Questions on Rhetorical Strategy and Style

1. What is this story's texture? How does it make you feel? Why do you think Kincaid chose to present it as a brief monologue?
2. Kincaid doesn't describe the physical setting of "Girl" directly, but provides clues in the content of the mother's advice. Go through the story and find as many details about place as you can, then write a description of the characters' home and neighborhood.
3. "Girl" makes an interesting use of example: Kincaid strings together a barrage of examples to tell her reader something about the characters, but doesn't explain precisely what they're meant to illustrate. What point do you think she is trying to make with them?

Writing Assignments

1. Write a short narrative piece about a time when someone with authority over you gave you advice. What kind of advice was it? How did you feel about receiving it? What was your response? In your narrative, try to convey a sense of the mood surrounding the exchange by the way you describe the things around you.
2. Write an essay about your relationship with one of your parents. Recount in detail significant moments you spent together. Your purpose is to convey something about the understandings you share.

BALTHAZAR'S MARVELOUS AFTERNOON

Gabriel García Márquez

Gabriel García Márquez was born in 1928 in Aracataca, Colombia. He was the eldest child of a poor family and was reared by his maternal grandparents. He began writing in childhood and, after a period studying law, took up writing as a profession with very little success. His breakthrough novel One Hundred Years of Solitude *(1967), written in a creative burst that lasted eighteen months, drove him deeply into debt, and nearly ruined his health. He won the Nobel Prize for Literature in 1982. In this story, he describes the life of an artist and the drives that motivate and sometimes obsess the imaginative person who must be creative.*

1 The cage was finished. Balthazar hung it under the eave, from force of habit, and when he finished lunch everyone was already saying that it was the most beautiful cage in the world. So many people came to see it that a crowd formed in front of the house, and Balthazar had to take it down and close the shop.

"You have to shave," Ursula, his wife, told him. "You look like a Capuchin."

"It's bad to shave after lunch," said Balthazar.

He had two weeks' growth, short, hard, and bristly hair like the mane of a mule, and the general expression of a frightened boy. But it was a false expression. In February he was thirty; he had been living with Ursula for four years, without marrying her and without having children, and life had given him many reasons to be on guard but none to be frightened. He did not even know that for some people the cage he had just made was the most beautiful one in the world. For him, accustomed to making cages since childhood, it had been hardly any more difficult than the others.

"Then rest for a while," said the woman. "With that beard you can't show yourself anywhere."

While he was resting, he had to get out of his hammock several times to show the cage to the neighbors. Ursula had paid little attention to it until then. She was annoyed because her husband had neglected the work of his carpenter's shop to devote himself entirely to the cage, and for two weeks had slept poorly, turning over and muttering incoherencies, and he hadn't thought of shaving. But her annoyance dissolved in the face of the finished cage. When Balthazar woke up from his nap, she had ironed his pants and a shirt; she had put them on a chair near the hammock and had carried the cage to the dining table. She regarded it in silence.

"How much will you charge?" she asked.

"I don't know," Balthazar answered. "I'm going to ask for thirty pesos to see if they'll give me twenty."

"Ask for fifty," said Ursula. "You've lost a lot of sleep in these two weeks. Furthermore, it's rather large. I think it's the biggest cage I've ever seen in my life."

Balthazar began to shave.

"Do you think they'll give me fifty pesos?"

"That's nothing for Mr. Chepe Montiel, and the cage is worth it," said Ursula. "You should ask for sixty."

The house lay in the stifling shadow. It was the first week of April and the heat seemed less bearable because of the chirping of the cicadas. When he finished dressing. Balthazar opened the door to the patio to cool off the house, and a group of children entered the dining room.

The news had spread. Dr. Octavio Giraldo, an old physician, happy with life but tired of his profession, thought about Balthazar's cage while he was eating lunch with his invalid wife. On the inside terrace, where they put the table on hot days, there were many flowerpots and two cages with canaries. His wife liked birds, and she liked them so much that she hated cats because they could eat them up. Thinking about her, Dr. Giraldo went to see a patient that afternoon, and when he returned he went by Balthazar's house to inspect the cage.

15   There were a lot of people in the dining room. The cage was on display on the table: with its enormous dome of wire, three stories inside, with passageways and compartments especially for eating and sleeping and swings in the space set aside for the birds' recreation, it seemed like a small-scale model of a gigantic ice factory. The doctor inspected it carefully, without touching it, thinking that in effect the cage was better than its reputation, and much more beautiful than any he had ever dreamed of for his wife.

"This is a flight of the imagination," he said. He sought out Balthazar among the group of people and, fixing his maternal eyes on him, added, "You would have been an extraordinary architect."

Balthazar blushed.

"Thank you," he said.

"It's true," said the doctor. He was smoothly and delicately fat, like a woman who had been beautiful in her youth, and he had delicate hands. His voice seemed like that of a priest speaking Latin. "You wouldn't even need to put birds in it," he said, making the cage turn in front of the audience's eyes as if he were auctioning it off, "It would be enough to hang it in the trees so it could sing by itself." He put it back on the table, thought a moment, looking at the cage, and said:

20   "Fine, then I'll take it."

"It's sold," said Ursula.

"It belongs to the son of Mr. Chepe Montiel," said Balthazar. "He ordered it specially."

The doctor adopted a respectful attitude.

"Did he give you the design?"

25   "No," said Balthazar. "He said he wanted a large cage, like this one, for a pair of troupials."

The doctor looked at the cage.

"But this isn't for troupials."

"Of course it is, Doctor," said Balthazar, approaching the table. The children surrounded him. "The measurements are carefully calculated," he said, pointing to the different compartments with his forefinger. Then he struck the dome with his knuckles, and the cage filled with resonant chords.

"It's the strongest wire you can find, and each joint is soldered outside and in," he said.

30   "It's even big enough for a parrot," interrupted one of the children.   30

"That it is," said Balthazar.

The doctor turned his head.

"Fine, but he didn't give you the design," he said. "He gave you no exact specifications, aside from making it a cage big enough for troupials. Isn't that right?"

"That's right," said Balthazar.

35   "Then there's no problem," said the doctor. "One thing is a cage   35 big enough for troupials, and another is this cage. There's no proof that this one is the one you were asked to make."

"It's this very one," said Balthazar, confused. "That's why I made it."

The doctor made an impatient gesture.

"You could make another one," said Ursula, looking at her husband. And then, to the doctor: "You're not in any hurry."

"I promised it to my wife for this afternoon," said the doctor.

40   "I'm very sorry, Doctor," said Balthazar, "but I can't sell you something that's sold already."   40

The doctor shrugged his shoulders. Drying the sweat from his neck with a handkerchief, he contemplated the cage silently with the fixed, unfocused gaze of one who looks at a ship which is sailing away.

"How much did they pay you for it?"

Balthazar sought out Ursula's eyes without replying.

"Sixty pesos," she said.

45   The doctor kept looking at the cage. "It's very pretty." He sighed.   45 "Extremely pretty." Then, moving toward the door, he began to fan himself energetically, smiling, and the trace of that episode disappeared forever from his memory.

"Montiel is very rich," he said.

In truth, José Montiel was not as rich as he seemed, but he would have been capable of doing anything to become so. A few blocks from there, in a house crammed with equipment, where no one had ever smelled a smell that couldn't be sold, he remained indifferent to the news of the cage. His wife, tortured by an obsession with death, closed the doors and windows after lunch and lay for two hours with her eyes opened to the shadow of the room, while José Montiel took his siesta. The clamor of many voices surprised her there. Then she opened the door to the living room and found a crowd in front of the house, and

Balthazar with the cage in the middle of the crowd, dressed in white, freshly shaved, with that expression of decorous candor with which the poor approach the houses of the wealthy.

"What a marvelous thing!" José Montiel's wife exclaimed, with a radiant expression, leading Balthazar inside. "I've never seen anything like it in my life," she said, and added, annoyed by the crowd which piled up at the door:

"But bring it inside before they turn the living room into a grandstand."

Balthazar was no stranger to José Montiel's house. On different occasions, because of his skill and forthright way of dealing, he had been called in to do minor carpentry jobs. But he never felt at ease among the rich. He used to think about them, about their ugly and argumentative wives, about their tremendous surgical operations, and he always experienced a feeling of pity. When he entered their houses, he couldn't move without dragging his feet.

"Is Pepe home?" he asked.

He had put the cage on the dining-room table.

"He's at school," said José Montiel's wife. "But he shouldn't be long," and she added, "Montiel is taking a bath."

In reality, José Montiel had not had time to bathe. He was giving himself an urgent alcohol rub, in order to come out and see what was going on. He was such a cautious man that he slept without an electric fan so he could watch over the noises of the house while he slept.

"Adelaide!" he shouted. "What's going on?"

"Come and see what a marvelous thing!" his wife shouted.

José Montiel, obese and hairy, his towel draped around his neck, appeared at the bedroom window.

"What is that?"

"Pepe's cage," said Balthazar.

His wife looked at him perplexedly.

"Whose?"

"Pepe's," replied Balthazar. And then, turning toward José Montiel, "Pepe ordered it."

Nothing happened at that instant, but Balthazar felt as if someone had just opened the bathroom door on him. José Montiel came out of the bedroom in his underwear.

"Pepe!" he shouted.

"He's not back," whispered his wife, motionless.

189

Pepe appeared in the doorway. He was about twelve, and had the same curved eyelashes and was as quietly pathetic as his mother.

"Come here," José Montiel said to him. "Did you order this?"

The child lowered his head. Grabbing him by the hair, José Montiel forced Pepe to look him in the eye.

"Answer me."

70 The child bit his lip without replying. 70

"Montiel," whispered his wife.

José Montiel let the child go and turned toward Balthazar in a fury. "I'm very sorry, Balthazar," he said. "But you should have consulted me before going on. Only to you would it occur to contract with a minor." As he spoke, his face recovered its serenity. He lifted the cage without looking at it and gave it to Balthazar.

"Take it away at once, and try to sell it to whomever you can," he said. "Above all, I beg you not to argue with me." He patted him on the back and explained, "The doctor has forbidden me to get angry."

The child had remained motionless, without blinking, until Balthazar looked at him uncertainly with the cage in his hand. Then he emitted a gutteral sound, like a dog's growl, and threw himself on the floor screaming.

75 José Montiel looked at him, unmoved, while the mother tried to 75
pacify him. "Don't even pick him up," he said. "Let him break his head on the floor, and then put salt and lemon on it so he can rage to his heart's content." The child was shrieking tearlessly while his mother held him by the wrists.

"Leave him alone," José Montiel insisted.

Balthazar observed the child as he would have observed the death throes of a rabid animal. It was almost four o'clock. At that hour, at his house, Ursula was singing a very old song and cutting slices of onion.

"Pepe," said Balthazar.

He approached the child, smiling, and held the cage out to him. The child jumped up, embraced the cage which was almost as big as he was, and stood looking at Balthazar through the wirework without knowing what to say. He hadn't shed one tear.

80 "Balthazar," said José Montiel softly. "I told you already to take it 80
away."

"Give it back," the woman ordered the child.

"Keep it," said Balthazar. And then, to José Montiel: "After all, that's what I made it for."

José Montiel followed him into the living room.

"Don't be foolish, Balthazar," he was saying, blocking his path. "Take your piece of furniture home and don't be silly. I have no intention of paying you a cent."

85   "It doesn't matter," said Balthazar. "I made it expressly as a gift for   85
Pepe. I didn't expect to charge anything for it."

As Balthazar made his way through the spectators who were blocking the door, José Montiel was shouting in the middle of the living room. He was very pale and his eyes were beginning to get red.

"Idiot!" he was shouting. "Take your trinket out of here. The last thing we need is for some nobody to give orders in my house. Son of a bitch!"

In the pool hall, Balthazar was received with an ovation. Until that moment, he thought that he had made a better cage than ever before, that he'd had to give it to the son of José Montiel so he wouldn't keep crying, and that none of these things was particularly important. But then he realized that all of this had a certain importance for many people, and he felt a little excited.

"So they give you fifty pesos for the cage."

90   "Sixty," said Balthazar.   90

"Score one for you," someone said. "You're the only one who has managed to get such a pile of money out of Mr. Chepe Montiel. We have to celebrate."

They bought him a beer, and Balthazar responded with a round for everybody. Since it was the first time he had ever been out drinking, by dusk he was completely drunk, and he was talking about a fabulous project of a thousand cages, at sixty pesos each, and then of a million cages, till he had sixty million pesos. "We have to make a lot of things to sell to the rich before they die," he was saying, blind drunk. "All of them are sick, and they're going to die. They're so screwed up they can't even get angry any more." For two hours he was paying for the jukebox, which played without interruption. Everybody toasted Balthazar's health, good luck, and fortune, and the death of the rich, but at mealtime they left him alone in the pool hall.

Ursula had waited for him until eight, with a dish of fried meat covered with slices of onion. Someone told her that her husband was in the pool hall, delirious with happiness, buying beer for everyone, but she didn't believe it, because Balthazar had never got drunk. When she went to bed, almost at midnight, Balthazar was in a lighted room where there were little tables, each with four chairs, and an outdoor dance floor, where the plovers were walking around. His face was smeared with rouge, and since he couldn't take one more step, he thought he wanted to lie down with two women in the same bed. He had spent so much that he had had to leave his watch in pawn, with the promise to pay the next day. A moment later, spread-eagled in the street, he realized that his shoes were being taken off, but he didn't want to abandon the happiest dream of his life. The women who passed on their way to five-o'clock mass didn't dare look at him, thinking he was dead.

Questions on Meaning

1. Why did Balthazar refuse to take money for his work?
2. Explain the title. Assuming that the title is not ironic, what were the events that made the afternoon marvelous?
3. Look up the name Balthazar in a Biblical concordance. What do you make of the Biblical precedent?
4. Why do you think that Márquez chose to base the story around the idea of a beautiful bird cage? What meanings do we attach to birds? To cages? And what about creating one that is so beautiful that everyone wants it?

Questions on Rhetorical Strategy and Style

1. The world Márquez creates is realistic, yet with overtones of magic. What events or details convey the impression that Balthazar's reality is not quite ordinary?
2. Find the term *surrealism* in a reference book on artistic techniques. Explain how "Balthazar's Marvelous Afternoon" exemplifies surrealism as a technique.

Writing Assignments

1. Write an essay that tells the story of a time when you did work just for the joy of it, or a time when you participated in a skilled performance that brought you great satisfaction.
2. Look up the word *hero* in a dictionary. What are the circumstances required to produce a hero? Do the circumstances of this story warrant our calling Balthazar a hero? Why? If he is not a hero, what is he? Write an essay that defines the concept of hero through several examples.

A MOVING DAY

Susan Nunes

Born in Hawaii to a family of mixed ethnic heritage (Japanese and Portuguese), Susan Nunes has written children's books, short stories, and novels. Her works include A Small Obligation and Other Stories of Hilo *(1982),* Coyote Dreams *(1988), and* The Last Dragon *(1994). "A Moving Day" was first published in 1990, in a collection edited by Sylvia Watanabe and Carol Bruchac titled* Home to Stay: Asian American Women's Fiction. *The story recalls not only personal reminiscences, but also the shameful memory of the internment of Japanese-Americans during World War II. The recollection of the betrayal of so many loyal citizens, many of them native born, by their own country haunts the work of many Japanese-American writers. In this story, the internment hovers over the narrator's tale as she ponders saying farewell to her childhood home.*

1   Across the street, the bulldozer roars to life. Distracted, my mother looks up from the pile of linen that she has been sorting. She is seventy, tiny and fragile, the flesh burned off her shrinking frame. Her hair is grey now—she has never dyed it—and she wears it cut no-nonsense short with the nape shaved. She still has a beautiful neck, in another life, perfect for kimono. She has taken a liking to jeans, cotton smocks, baggy sweaters, and running shoes. When I was a child she wouldn't leave the house without nylons.

Her hands, large-jointed with arthritis, return with a vengeance to the pile of linen. I have always been wary of her energy. Now she is making two stacks, the larger one for us, the smaller for her to keep.

There is a finality in the way she places things in the larger pile, as if to say that's it. For her, it's all over, all over but this last accounting. She does not look forward to what is coming. Strangers. Schedules. The regulated activities of those considered too old to regulate themselves. But at least, at the *very* least, she'll not be a burden. She sorts through the possessions of a lifetime, she and her three daughters. It's time she passed most of this on. Dreams are lumber. She can't *wait* to be rid of them.

My two sisters and I present a contrast. There is nothing purposeful or systematic about the way we move. In fact, we don't know where we're going. We know there is a message in all this activity, but we don't know what it is. Still, we search for it in the odd carton, between layers of tissue paper and silk. We open drawers, peer into the recess of cupboards, rummage through the depths of closets. We lift, untuck, unwrap, and set aside. The message is there, we know. But what is it? Perhaps if we knew, then we wouldn't have to puzzle out our mother's righteous determination to shed the past.

There is a photograph of my mother taken on the porch of my grandparents' house when she was in her twenties. She is wearing a floral print dress with a square, lace-edged collar and a graceful skirt that shows off her slim body. Her shoulder length hair has been permed. It is dark and thick and worn parted on the side to fall over her right cheek. She is very fair; "one pound powder," her friends called her. She is smiling almost reluctantly, as if she meant to appear serious but the photographer has said something amusing. One arm rests lightly on the railing, the other, which is at her side, holds a handkerchief. They were her special pleasure, handkerchiefs of hand-embroidered linen as fine as ricepaper. Most were gifts (she used to say that when she was a girl, people gave one another little things—a handkerchief, a pincushion, pencils, hair ribbons), and she washed and starched them by hand, ironed them, taking care with the rolled hems, and stored them in a silk bag from Japan.

5 There is something expectant in her stance, as if she were waiting for something to happen. She says, your father took this photograph in 1940, before we were married. She lowers her voice confidentially and adds, now he cannot remember taking it. My father sits on the balcony, an open book on his lap, peacefully smoking his pipe. The bulldozer tears into the foundations of the Kitamura house.

What about this? My youngest sister has found a fishing boat carved of tortoise shell.

Hold it in your hand and look at it. Every plank on the hull is visible. Run your fingers along the sides, you can feel the joints. The two masts, about six inches high, are from the darkest part of the shell. I broke one of the sails many years ago. The remaining one is quite remarkable, so thin that the light comes through it in places. It is ribbed to give the effect of cloth pushed gently by the wind.

My mother reaches for a sheet of tissue paper and takes the boat from my sister. She says, it was a gift from Mr. Oizumi. He bought it from an artisan in Kamakura.

Stories cling to the thing, haunt it like unrestful spirits. They are part of the object. They have been there since we were children. In 1932, Mr. Oizumi visits Japan. He crosses the Pacific by steamer, and when he arrives he is hosted by relatives eager to hear of his good fortune. But Mr. Oizumi soon tires of their questions. He wants to see what has become of the country It will be arranged, he is told. Mr. Oizumi is a meticulous man. Maps are his passion. A trail of neat X's marks the steps of his journey. On his map of China, he notes each military outpost in Manchuria and appends a brief description of what he sees. Notes invade the margins, march over the blank spaces. The characters are written in a beautiful hand, precise, disciplined, orderly. Eventually, their trail leads to the back of the map. After Pearl Harbor, however, Mr. Oizumi is forced to burn his entire collection. The U.S. Army has decreed that enemy aliens caught with seditious material will be arrested. He does it secretly in the shed behind his home, his wife standing guard. They scatter the ashes in the garden among the pumpkin vines.

10 My grandfather's library does not escape the flames either. After 10 the Army requisitions the Japanese school for wartime headquarters, they give my mother's parents twenty-four hours to vacate the premises, including the boarding house where they lived with about twenty students from the plantation camps outside Hilo. There is no time to save the books. Her father decides to nail wooden planks over the shelves that line the classrooms. After the Army moves in, they rip open the planks, confiscate the books, and store them in the basement of the post office. Later, the authorities burn everything. Histories, children's stories, primers, biographies, language texts, everything, even a set of Encyclopaedia Brittanica. My grandfather is shipped to

Oahu and imprisoned on Sand Island. A few months later, he is released after three prominent Caucasians vouch for his character. It is a humiliation he doesn't speak of, ever.

All of this was part of the boat. After I broke the sail, she gathered the pieces and said, I'm not sure we can fix this. It was not a toy. Why can't you leave my things alone?

For years the broken boat sat on our bookshelf, a reminder of the brutality of the next generation.

Now she wants to give everything away. We have to beg her to keep things. Dishes from Japan, lacquerware, photographs, embroidery, letters. She says, I have no room. You take them, here, *take* them. Take them or I'll get rid of them.

They're piled around her, they fill storage chests, they fall out of open drawers and cupboards. She wants only to keep a few things—her books, some photographs, three carved wooden figures from Korea that belonged to her father, a few of her mother's dishes, perhaps one futon.

15   My sister holds a porcelain teapot by its bamboo handle. Four   15
white cranes edged in black and gold fly around it. She asks, Mama, can't you hang on to this? If you keep it, I can borrow it later.

My mother shakes her head. She is adamant. And what would I do with it? I don't want any of this. Really.

My sister turns to me. She sighs. The situation is hopeless. You take it, she says. It'll only get broken at my place. The kids.

It had begun slowly, this shedding of the past, a plate here, a dish there, a handkerchief, a doily, a teacup, a few photographs, one of Grandfather's block prints. Nothing big. But then the odd gesture became a pattern; it got so we never left the house empty-handed. At first we were amused. After all, when we were children she had to fend us off her things. Threaten. We were always *at* them. She had made each one so ripe with memories that we found them impossible to resist. We snuck them outside, showed them to our friends, told and retold the stories. They bear the scars of all this handling, even her most personal possessions. A chip here, a crack there. Casualties. Like the music box her brother brought home from Italy after the war. It played a Brahms lullaby. First we broke the spring, then we lost the winding key, and for years it sat mutely on her dresser.

She would say again and again, it's impossible to keep anything nice with you children. And we'd retreat, wounded, for a while. The problem with children is they can wipe out your history. It's a miracle that anything survives this onslaught.

20   There's a photograph of my mother standing on the pier in Honolulu in 1932, the year she left Hawaii to attend the University of California. She's loaded to the ears with leis. She's wearing a fedora pulled smartly to the side. She's not smiling. Of my mother's two years there, my grandmother recalled that she received good grades and never wore kimono again. My second cousin, with whom my mother stayed when she first arrived, said she was surprisingly sophisticated—she liked hats. My mother said that she was homesick. Her favorite class was biology and she entertained thoughts of becoming a scientist. Her father, however, wanted her to become a teacher, and his wishes prevailed, even though he would not have forced them upon her. She was a dutiful daughter.

During her second year, she lived near campus with a mathematics professor and his wife. In exchange for room and board she cleaned house, ironed, and helped prepare meals. One of the things that survives from this period is a black composition book entitled, *Recipes of California.* As a child, I read it like a book of mysteries for clues to a life both alien and familiar. Some entries she had copied by hand; others she cut out of magazines and pasted on the page, sometimes with a picture or drawing. The margins contained her cryptic comments: "'Saturday bridge club," "From Mary G. Do not give away," underlined, "chopped suet by hand, wretched task, bed at 2 a.m., exhausted." I remember looking up "'artichoke" in the dictionary and asking Mr. Okinaga, the vegetable vendor, if he had any edible thistles. I never ate one until I was twenty.

That book holds part of the answer to why our family rituals didn't fit the norm of either our relatives or the larger community in which we grew up. At home, we ate in fear of the glass of spilled milk, the stray elbow on the table, the boarding house reach. At my grandparents', we slurped our chasuke. We wore tailored dresses, white cotton pinafores, and Buster Brown shoes with white socks; however, what we longed for were the lacy dresses in the National Dollar Store that the Puerto Rican girls wore to church on Sunday. For six years, I marched to Japanese language school after my regular classes; however, we only spoke English at home. We talked too loudly and all at once, which mortified my mother, but she was always complaining about Japanese indirectness. I know that she smarted under a system in which the older son is the center of the familial universe, but at thirteen I had a fit of jealous rage over her fawning attention to our only male cousin.

My sister has found a photograph of my mother, a round faced and serious twelve or thirteen, dressed in kimono and seated, on her knees, on the tatami floor. She is playing the koto. According to my mother, girls were expected to learn this difficult stringed instrument because it was thought to teach discipline. Of course, everything Japanese was a lesson in discipline—flower arranging, calligraphy, judo, brush painting, embroidery, everything. One summer my sister and I had to take ikebana, the art of flower arrangement, at Grandfather's school. The course was taught by Mrs. Oshima, a diminutive, softspoken, terrifying woman, and my supplies were provided by my grandmother, whose tastes ran to the oversized. I remember little of that class and its principles. What I remember most clearly is having to walk home carrying one of our creations, which, more often than not, towered above our heads.

How do we choose among what we experience, what we are taught, what we run into by chance, or what is forced upon us? What is the principle of selection? My sisters and I are not bound by any of our mother's obligations, nor do we follow the rituals that seemed so important. My sister once asked, do you realize that when she's gone that's *it*? She was talking about how to make sushi, but it was a profound question nonetheless.

I remember, after we moved to Honolulu and my mother stopped teaching and began working long hours in administration, she was less vigilant about the many little things that once consumed her attention. While we didn't slide into savagery, we economized in more ways than one. She would often say, there's simply no time anymore to do things right.

I didn't understand then why she looked so sad, but somehow I knew the comment applied to us.

So how do I put her wish, whatever it was, into perspective? It is hidden in layers of silk, sheathed in the folds of an old kimono that no one knows how to wear any more. I don't understand why we carry out this fruitless search. Whatever it is we are looking for, we're not going to find it. My sister tries to lift a box filled with record albums, old seventy-eights, gives up, and sets it down again. My mother says, there are people who collect these things. Imagine.

Right, just imagine.

I think about my mother bathing me and singing, "The snow is snowing, the wind is blowing, but I will weather the storm." And I think of her story of a country boy carried by the Tengu on a fantastic flight over the cities of Japan, but who chooses in the end to return to the unchanging world of his village. So much for questions which have no answers, why we look among objects for meanings which have somehow escaped us in the growing up and growing old.

30   However, my mother is a determined woman. She will take noth-   30
ing with her if she can help it. It is all ours. And on the balcony my father knocks the ashes of his pipe into a porcelain ashtray, and the bulldozer is finally silent.

Questions on Meaning

1. The story opens with the sound of a bulldozer. What is the significance of this image? How does it influence the reader's perception of the action in the story?
2. What does the narrator mean when she says, "The problem with children is they can wipe out your history"? What other forces in the story wipe out history?
3. Why do you think the mother is ready to give away all of her things? Why are the daughters unable to understand her wishes?

Questions on Rhetorical Strategy and Style

1. Effective narrative must have a point. What do you think the point of this story is? What features of the story lead to this point?
2. This story presents a number of contrasts: between parents and children, between Americans and Japanese, between the images in photographs, as well as other contrasts. Choose two of these contrasts and explain how they contribute to the effect of the story.
3. The tortoise shell fishing boat serves as an example of the importance of objects to a family's history. Explain how the stories associated with the boat illustrate the narrator's feelings about preserving the past.

Writing Assignments

1. Choose an object in your home that holds particular meaning for you or your family. Write an essay describing the object and explaining its significance.
2. Read historical accounts of the internment of Japanese Americans during World War II; then read accounts written by those interned. Write a report exploring the complexity of the issue, focusing on the government's rationale for the internment, the prevalence of anti-Japanese sentiment, and the impact of internment on Japanese Americans.

I STAND HERE IRONING

Tillie Olsen

Tillie Olsen (1913–) was born in Nebraska in a working class family. She has worked at jobs involving manual labor much of her life, educating herself by reading on her own. She published a few short pieces in the 1930s but stopped writing when she married and began raising her four children. More than two decades later she returned to writing and published a collection of stories entitled Tell Me a Riddle *(1956), in which the story "I Stand Here Ironing" was published. In 1984 as editor Olsen published* Mother to Daughter, Daughter to Mother: Mothers on Mothering, *a collection of writings on themes of mother-hood. Olsen has received several fellowships and has held visiting professorships at major universities, where she works to help younger writers develop.*

I stand here ironing, and what you asked me moves tormented back and forth with the iron.

"I wish you would manage the time to come in and talk with me about your daughter. I'm sure you can help me understand her. She's a youngster who needs help and whom I'm deeply interested in helping."

"Who needs help." . . . Even if I came, what good would it do? You think because I am her mother I have a key, or that in some way you could use me as a key? She has lived for nineteen years. There is all that life that has happened outside of me, beyond me.

And when is there time to remember, to sift, to weigh, to estimate, to total? I will start and there will be an interruption and I will have to gather it all together again. Or I will become engulfed with all I did or did not do, with what should have been and what cannot be helped.

From *Tell Me a Riddle.* Published by Delacorte Press/Seymour Laurence, a division of Bantam Doubleday Dell Publishing Group, Inc. Copyright © 1956, 1957, 1960, 1961 by Tillie Olsen.

5 She was a beautiful baby. The first and only one of our five that 5
was beautiful at birth. You do not guess how new and uneasy her ten-
ancy in her now-loveliness. You did not know her all those years she
was thought homely, or see her poring over her baby pictures, making
me tell her over and over how beautiful she had been—and would be,
I would tell her—and was now, to the seeing eye. But the seeing eyes
were few or nonexistent. Including mine.

I nursed her. They feel that's important nowadays. I nursed all the
children, but with her, with all the fierce rigidity of first motherhood,
I did like the books then said. Though her cries battered me to trembling and my breasts ached with swollenness, I waited till the clock
decreed.

Why do I put that first? I do not even know if it matters, or if it
explains anything.

She was a beautiful baby. She blew shining bubbles of sound. She
loved motion, loved light, loved color and music and textures. She
would lie on the floor in her blue overalls patting the surface so hard
in ecstasy her hands and feet would blur. She was a miracle to me, but
when she was eight months old I had to leave her daytimes with the
woman downstairs to whom she was no miracle at all, for I worked or
looked for work and for Emily's father, who "could no longer endure"
(he wrote in his good-bye note) "sharing want with us."

I was nineteen. It was the pre-relief, pre-WPA world of the depression. I would start running as soon as I got off the streetcar, running up the stairs, the place smelling sour, and awake or asleep to
startle awake, when she saw me she would break into a clogged weeping that could not be comforted, a weeping I can hear yet.

10 After a while I found a job hashing at night so I could be with her 10
days, and it was better. But it came to where I had to bring her to his
family and leave her.

It took a long time to raise the money for her fare back. Then she
got chicken pox and I had to wait longer. When she finally came, I
hardly knew her, walking quick and nervous like her father, looking
like her father, thin, and dressed in a shoddy red that yellowed her skin
and glared at the pockmarks. All the baby loveliness gone.

She was two. Old enough for nursery school they said, and I did
not know then what I know now—the fatigue of the long day, and the
lacerations of group life in the kinds of nurseries that are only park-
ing places for children.

Except that it would have made no difference if I had known. It was the only place there was. It was the only way we could be together, the only way I could hold a job.

And even without knowing, I knew. I knew the teacher that was evil because all these years it has curdled into my memory, the little boy hunched in the corner, her rasp, "why aren't you outside, because Alvin hits you? That's no reason, go out, scaredy." I knew Emily hated it even if she did not clutch and implore "don't go Mommy" like the other children, mornings.

15   She always had a reason why we should stay home. Momma, you look sick. Momma, I feel sick. Momma, the teachers aren't there today, they're sick. Momma, we can't go, there was a fire there last night. Momma, it's a holiday today, no school, they told me.

But never a direct protest, never rebellion. I think of our others in their three-, four-year-oldness—the explosions, the tempers, the denunciations, the demands—and I feel suddenly ill. I put the iron down. What in me demanded that goodness in her? And what was the cost, the cost to her of such goodness?

The old man living in the back once said in his gentle way: "You should smile at Emily more when you look at her." What *was* in my face when I looked at her? I loved her. There were all the acts of love.

It was only with the others I remembered what he said, and it was the face of joy, and not of care or tightness or worry I turned to them—too late for Emily. She does not smile easily, let alone almost always as her brothers and sisters do. Her face is closed and sombre, but when she wants, how fluid. You must have seen it in her pantomimes, you spoke of her rare gift for comedy on the stage that rouses a laughter out of the audience so dear they applaud and applaud and do not want to let her go.

Where does it come from, that comedy? There was none of it in her when she came back to me that second time, after I had had to send her away again. She had a new daddy now to learn to love, and I think perhaps it was a better time.

20   Except when we left her alone nights, telling ourselves she was old enough.

"Can't you go some other time, Mommy, like tomorrow?" she would ask. "Will it be just a little while you'll be gone? Do you promise?"

The time we came back, the front door open, the clock on the floor in the hall. She rigid awake. "It wasn't just a little while. I didn't cry. Three times I called you, just three times, and then I ran down-stairs to open the door so you could come faster. The clock talked loud. I threw it away, it scared me what it talked."

She said the clock talked loud again that night I went to the hospital to have Susan. She was delirious with the fever that comes before red measles, but she was fully conscious all the week I was gone and the week after we were home when she could not come near the new baby or me.

She did not get well. She stayed skeleton thin, not wanting to eat, and night after night she had nightmares. She would call for me, and I would rouse from exhaustion to sleepily call back: "You're all right, darling, go to sleep, it's just a dream," and if she still called, in a sterner voice, "now go to sleep, Emily, there's nothing to hurt you." Twice, only twice, when I had to get up for Susan anyhow, I went in to sit with her.

25   Now when it is too late (as if she would let me hold and comfort   25
her like I do the others) I get up and go to her at once at her moan or restless stirring. "Are you awake, Emily? Can I get you something?" And the answer is always the same: "No, I'm all right, go back to sleep, Mother."

They persuaded me at the clinic to send her away to a convalescent home in the country where "she can have the kind of food and care you can't manage for her, and you'll be free to concentrate on the new baby." They still send children to that place. I see pictures on the society page of sleek young women planning affairs to raise money for it, or dancing at the affairs, or decorating Easter eggs or filling Christmas stockings for the children.

They never have a picture of the children so I do not know if the girls still wear those gigantic red bows and the ravaged looks on the every other Sunday when parents can come to visit "unless otherwise notified"—as we were notified the first six weeks.

Oh it is a handsome place, green lawns and tall trees and fluted flower beds. High up on the balconies of each cottage the children stand, the girls in their red bows and white dresses, the boys in white suits and giant red ties. The parents stand below shrieking up to be heard and the children shriek down to be heard, and between them the invisible wall "Not To Be Contaminated by Parental Germs or Physical Affection."

There was a tiny girl who always stood hand in hand with Emily. Her parents never came. One visit she was gone. "They moved her to

Rose Cottage," Emily shouted in explanation. "They don't like you to love anybody here."

30   She wrote once a week, the labored writing of a seven-year-old. "I am fine. How is the baby. If I write my leter nicly I will have a star. Love" There never was a star. We wrote every other day, letters she could never hold or keep but only hear read—once. "We simply do not have room for children to keep any personal possessions," they patiently explained when we pieced one Sunday's shrieking together to plead how much it would mean to Emily, who loved so to keep things, to be allowed to keep her letters and cards.

Each visit she looked frailer. "She isn't eating," they told us.

(They had runny eggs for breakfast or mush with lumps, Emily said later, I'd hold it in my mouth and not swallow. Nothing ever tasted good, just when they had chicken.)

It took us eight months to get her released home, and only the fact that she gained back so little of her seven lost pounds convinced the social worker.

I used to try to hold and love her after she came back, but her body would stay stiff, and after a while she'd push away. She ate little. Food sickened her, and I think much of life too. Oh she had physical lightness and brightness, twinkling by on skates, bouncing like a ball up and down up and down over the jump rope, skimming over the hill; but these were momentary.

35   She fretted about her appearance, thin and dark and foreign-looking at a time when every little girl was supposed to look or thought she should look a chubby blonde replica of Shirley Temple. The doorbell sometimes rang for her, but no one seemed to come and play in the house or be a best friend. Maybe because we moved so much.

There was a boy she loved painfully through two school semesters. Months later she told me how she had taken pennies from my purse to buy him candy. "Licorice was his favorite and I brought him some every day, but he still liked Jennifer better'n me. Why, Mommy?" The kind of question for which there is no answer.

School was a worry to her. She was not glib or quick in a world where glibness and quickness were easily confused with ability to learn. To her overworked and exasperated teachers she was an over-conscientious "slow learner" who kept trying to catch up and was absent entirely too often.

I let her be absent, though sometimes the illness was imaginary. How different from my now-strictness about attendance with the others. I wasn't working. We had a new baby, I was home anyhow. Sometimes, after Susan grew old enough, I would keep her home from school, too, to have them all together.

Mostly Emily had asthma, and her breathing, harsh and labored, would fill the house with a curiously tranquil sound. I would bring the two old dresser mirrors and her boxes of collections to her bed. She would select beads and single earrings, bottle tops and shells, dried flowers and pebbles, old postcards and scraps, all sorts of oddments; then she and Susan would play Kingdom, setting up landscapes and furniture, peopling them with action.

40 Those were the only times of peaceful companionship between 40 her and Susan. I have edged away from it, that poisonous feeling between them, that terrible balancing of hurts and needs I had to do between the two, and did so badly, those earlier years.

Oh there are conflicts between the others too, each one human, needing, demanding, hurting, taking—but only between Emily and Susan, no, Emily toward Susan that corroding resentment. It seems so obvious on the surface, yet it is not obvious. Susan, the second child, Susan, golden- and curly-haired and chubby, quick and articulate and assured, everything in appearance and manner Emily was not; Susan, not able to resist Emily's precious things, losing or sometimes clumsily breaking them; Susan telling jokes and riddles to company for applause while Emily sat silent (to say to me later: that was *my* riddle, Mother, I told it to Susan); Susan, who for all the five years' difference in age was just a year behind Emily in developing physically.

I am glad for that slow physical development that widened the difference between her and her contemporaries, though she suffered over it. She was too vulnerable for that terrible world of youthful competition, of preening and parading, of constant measuring of yourself against every other, of envy, "If I had that copper hair," "If I had that skin. . . ." She tormented herself enough about not looking like the others, there was enough of the unsureness, the having to be conscious of words before you speak, the constant caring—what are they thinking of me? without having it all magnified by the merciless physical drives.

Ronnie is calling. He is wet and I change him. It is rare there is such a cry now. That time of motherhood is almost behind me when the ear is not one's own but must always be racked and listening for the child cry, the child call. We sit for a while and I hold him, looking out over the city spread in charcoal with its soft aisles of light.

"*Shoogily*," he breathes and curls closer. I carry him back to bed, asleep. *Shoogily*. A funny word, a family word, inherited from Emily, invented by her to say: *comfort*.

In this and other ways she leaves her seal, I say aloud. And startle at my saying it. What do I mean? What did I start to gather together, to try and make coherent? I was at the terrible, growing years. War years. I do not remember them well. I was working, there were four smaller ones now, there was not time for her. She had to help be a mother, and housekeeper, and shopper. She had to set her seal. Mornings of crisis and near hysteria trying to get lunches packed, hair combed, coats and shoes found, everyone to school or Child Care on time, the baby ready for transportation. And always the paper scribbled on by a smaller one, the book looked at by Susan then mislaid, the homework not done. Running out to that huge school where she was one, she was lost, she was a drop; suffering over the unpreparedness, stammering and unsure of her classes.

45 There was so little time left at night after the kids were bedded 45 down. She would struggle over books, always eating (it was in those years she developed her enormous appetite that is legendary in our family) and I would be ironing, or preparing food for the next day, or writing V-mail to Bill, or tending the baby. Sometimes, to make me laugh, or out of her despair, she would imitate happenings or types at school.

I think I said once: "Why don't you do something like this in the school amateur show?" One morning she phoned me at work, hardly understandable through the weeping: "Mother, I did it. I won, I won; they gave me first prize; they clapped and clapped and wouldn't let me go."

Now suddenly she was Somebody, and as imprisoned in her difference as she had been in anonymity.

She began to be asked to perform at other high schools, even in colleges, then at city and statewide affairs. The first one we went to, I only recognized her that first moment when thin, shy, she almost drowned herself into the curtains. Then: Was this Emily? The control, the command, the convulsing and deadly clowning, the spell, then the roaring, stamping audience, unwilling to let this rare and precious laughter out of their lives.

Afterwards: You ought to do something about her with a gift like that—but without money or knowing how, what does one do? We have left it all to her, and the gift has as often eddied inside, clogged and clotted, as been used and growing.

50   She is coming. She runs up the stairs two at a time with her light graceful step, and I know she is happy tonight. Whatever it was that occasioned your call did not happen today.

"Aren't you ever going to finish the ironing, Mother? Whistler painted his mother in a rocker. I'd have to paint mine standing over an ironing board." This is one of her communicative nights and she tells me everything and nothing as she fixes herself a plate of food out of the icebox.

She is so lovely. Why did you want me to come in at all? Why were you concerned? She will find her way.

She starts up the stairs to bed. "Don't get me up with the rest in the morning." "But I thought you were having midterms." "Oh, those," she comes back in, kisses me, and says quite lightly, "in a couple of years when we'll all be atom-dead they won't matter a bit."

She has said it before. She *believes* it. But because I have been dredging the past, and all that compounds a human being is so heavy and meaningful in me, I cannot endure it tonight.

55   I will never total it all. I will never come in to say: She was a child seldom smiled at. Her father left me before she was a year old. I had to work her first six years when there was work, or I sent her home and to his relatives. There were years she had care she hated. She was dark and thin and foreign-looking in a world where the prestige went to blondeness and curly hair and dimples, she was slow where glibness was prized. She was a child of anxious, not proud, love. We were poor and could not afford for her the soil of easy growth. I was a young mother, I was a distracted mother. There were the other children pushing up, demanding. Her younger sister seemed all that she was not. There were years she did not want me to touch her. She kept too much in herself, her life was such she had to keep too much in herself. My wisdom came too late. She has much to her and probably little will come of it. She is a child of her age, of depression, of war, of fear.

Let her be. So all that is in her will not bloom—but in how many does it? There is still enough left to live by. Only help her to know—help make it so there is cause for her to know—that she is more than this dress on the ironing board, helpless before the iron.

Questions on Meaning

1. Who is the "you" the narrator in this story is addressing? How much can you put together from references in the story to fill in the situation that has occasioned the narrator's thoughts on this day?
2. At the end of the story the narrator concludes her daughter Emily is "a child of her age, of depression, of war, of fear." How fully does this explain what Emily is like? What other factors, if any, must be considered?
3. How do you react to the story's ending, the mother's acceptance that there is much in her daughter that will not bloom and this is true of most people? Does the story suggest the mother is being realistic or defeatist in this attitude? Support your answer with details from the story.

Questions on Rhetorical Strategy and Style

1. The story is shaped around a series of memories and thoughts that come to the narrator as she irons and thinks about how someone could understand her daughter. Chart how the story moves repeatedly back and forth between past and present. What effect is gained by this structure?
2. After first showing us the mother's thoughts about Emily throughout the story, the author allows us near the end to see Emily briefly in the present. How do you react when you see and hear her? What effect does the story achieve by contrasting what her mother has been thinking with what we finally actually see?

Writing Assignments

1. The narrator worries near the end of the story that "I will never total it all" to completely understand her daughter. Consider what this means—can we ever total up everything that makes us who we are? If yes, how? If no, why not?
2. Are you a "child of your age"? Write an essay that examines the extent to which the world in which you lived as a child shaped who you are today.

THE CASK OF AMONTILLADO

Edgar Allan Poe

Edgar Allan Poe was born in 1809 in Boston. The son of poor traveling actors, he was orphaned at age three and taken in as a foster child by a tobacco merchant. They traveled to England, where Poe began an education that was later continued at the University of Virginia. Given Poe's childhood, it is not surprising that the rest of his life was a melodrama: He quarreled with his foster father, ran up gambling debts, was dismissed from West Point, married his thirteen-year-old cousin, wrote three unsuccessful volumes of poetry, was addicted to drugs and alcohol his whole life, and died in poverty after the death of his wife. However, he also acquired fame based on the carefully crafted short stories that continue to keep him among the foremost writers in American literature. In The Cask of Amontillado, *Poe uses an eerie carnival setting to tell the story of a long-standing grudge that leads a man of questionable sanity to exact a chilling revenge upon his perceived enemy.*

1 The thousand injuries of Fortunato I had borne as I best could; but when he ventured upon insult, I vowed revenge. You, who so well know the nature of my soul, will not suppose, however, that I gave utterance to a threat. *At length* I would be avenged; this was a point definitely settled—but the very definitiveness with which it was resolved, precluded the idea of risk. I must not only punish, but punish with impunity. A wrong is unredressed when retribution over-

takes its redresser. It is equally unredressed when the avenger fails to make himself felt as such to him who has done the wrong.

It must be understood, that neither by word nor deed had I given Fortunato cause to doubt my good-will. I continued, as was my wont, to smile in his face, and he did not perceive that my smile *now* was at the thought of his immolation.

He had a weak point—this Fortunato—although in other regards he was a man to be respected and even feared. He prided himself on his connoisseurship in wine. Few Italians have the true virtuoso spirit. For the most part their enthusiasm is adopted to suit the time and opportunity—to practice imposture upon the British and Austrian *millionaires*. In painting and gemmary, Fortunato, like his countrymen, was quack—but in the matter of old wines he was sincere. In this respect I did not differ from him materially: I was skilful in the Italian vintages myself, and bought largely whenever I could.

It was about dusk, one evening during the supreme madness of the carnival season, that I encountered my friend. He accosted me with excessive warmth, for he had been drinking much. The man wore motley. He had on a tight-fitting parti-striped dress, and his head was surmounted by the conical cap and bells. I was so pleased to see him, that I thought I should never have done wringing his hand.

5   I said to him: "My dear Fortunato, you are luckily met. How remarkably well you are looking to-day! But I have received a pipe of what passes for Amontillado, and I have my doubts."

"How?" said he. "Amontillado? A pipe? Impossible! And in the middle of the carnival!"

"I have my doubts," I replied; "and I was silly enough to pay the full Amontillado price without consulting you in the matter. You were not to be found, and I was fearful of losing a bargain."

"Amontillado!"

"I have my doubts."

10   "Amontillado!"

"And I must satisfy them."

"Amontillado!"

"As you are engaged, I am on my way to Luchesi. If any one has a critical turn it is he: He will tell me—"

"Luchesi cannot tell Amontillado from Sherry."

15   "And yet some fools will have it that his taste is a match for your own."

"Come, let us go."

"Whither?"

"To your vaults."

"My friend, no; I will not impose upon your good nature. I perceive you have an engagement. Luchesi—"

"I have no engagement;—come."

"My friend, no. It is not the engagement, but the severe cold with which I perceive you are afflicted. The vaults are insufferably damp. They are encrusted with nitre."

"Let us go, nevertheless. The cold is merely nothing. Amontillado! You have been imposed upon. And as for Luchesi, he cannot distinguish Sherry from Amontillado."

Thus speaking, Fortunato possessed himself of my arm. Putting on a mask of black silk, and drawing a *roquelaire* closely about my person, I suffered him to hurry me to my palazzo.

There were no attendants at home; they had absconded to make merry in honor of the time. I had told them that I should not return until the morning, and had given them explicit orders not to stir from the house. These orders were sufficient, I well knew, to insure their immediate disappearance, one and all, as soon as my back was turned.

I took from their sconces two flambeaux, and giving one to Fortunato, bowed him through several suites of rooms to the archway that led into the vaults. I passed down a long and winding staircase, requesting him to be cautious as he followed. We came at length to the foot of the descent, and stood together upon the damp ground of the catacombs of the Montresors.

The gait of my friend was unsteady, and the bells upon his cap jingled as he strode.

"The pipe?" said he.

"It is farther on," said I; "but observe the white web-work which gleams from these cavern walls."

He turned towards me, and looked into my eyes with two filmy orbs that distilled the rheum of intoxication.

"Nitre?" he asked, at length.

"Nitre," I replied. "How long have you had that cough?"

"Ugh! ugh! ugh!—ugh! ugh! ugh!—ugh! ugh! ugh!—ugh! ugh! ugh!—ugh! ugh! ugh!"

My poor friend found it impossible to reply for many minutes.

"It is nothing," he said, at last.

35 "Come," I said, with decision, "we will go back; your health is 35
precious. You are rich, respected, admired, beloved; you are happy, as
once I was. You are a man to be missed. For me it is no matter. We
will go back; you will be ill, and I cannot be responsible. Besides there
is Luchesi—"

"Enough," he said; "the cough is a mere nothing; it will not kill
me. I shall not die of a cough."

"True—true," I replied; "and, indeed, I had no intention of 35
alarming you unnecessarily; but you should use all proper caution. A
draught of this Medoc will defend us from the damps."

Here I knocked off the neck of a bottle which I drew from a long
row of its fellows that lay upon the mould.

"Drink," I said, presenting him the wine.

40 He raised it to his lips with a leer. He paused and nodded to me 40
familiarly, while his bells jingled.

"I drink," he said, "to the buried that repose around us."

"And I to your long life."

He again took my arm, and we proceeded.

"These vaults," he said, "are extensive."

45 "The Montresors," I replied, "were a great and numerous family." 45

"I forget your arms."

"A huge human foot d'or, in a field azure; the foot crushes a ser-
pent rampant whose fangs are imbedded in the heel."

"And the motto?"

"Nemo me impune lacessit."

50 "Good!" he said. 50

The wine sparkled in his eyes and the bells jingled. My own fancy
grew warm with the Medoc. We had passed through long walls of
piled bones, with casks and puncheons intermingling, into the inmost
recesses of the catacombs. I paused again, and this time I made bold
to seize Fortunato by an arm above the elbow.

"The nitre!" I said; "see, it increases. It hangs like moss upon the
vaults. We are below the river's bed. The drops of moisture trickle
among the bones. Come, we will go back ere it is too late. Your
cough—"

"It is nothing," he said; "let us go on. But first, another draught
of the Medoc."

I broke and reached him a flagon of De Grâve. He emptied it at a breath. His eyes flashed with a fierce light. He laughed and threw the bottle upward with a gesticulation I did not understand.

55   I looked at him in surprise. He repeated the movement—a grotesque one.

"You do not comprehend?" he said.

"Not I," I replied.

"Then you are not of the brotherhood."

"How?"

60   "You are not of the masons."

"Yes, yes," I said; "yes, yes."

"You? Impossible! A mason?"

"A mason," I replied.

"A sign," he said.

65   "It is this," I answered, producing a trowel from beneath the folds of my *roquelaire.*

"You jest," he exclaimed, recoiling a few paces. "But let us proceed to the Amontillado."

"Be it so," I said, replacing the tool beneath the cloak, and again offering him my arm. He leaned upon it heavily. We continued our route in search of the Amontillado. We passed through a range of low arches, descended, passed on, and descending again, arrived at a deep crypt, in which the foulness of the air caused our flambeaux rather to glow than flame.

At the most remote end of the crypt there appeared another less spacious. Its walls had been lined with human remains, piled to the vault overhead, in the fashion of the great catacombs of Paris. Three sides of this interior crypt were still ornamented in this manner. From the fourth the bones had been thrown down, and lay promiscuously upon the earth, forming at one point a mound of some size. Within the wall thus exposed by the displacing of the bones, we perceived a still interior recess, in depth about four feet, in width three, in height six or seven. It seemed to have been constructed for no especial use within itself, but formed merely the interval between two of the colossal supports of the roof of the catacombs, and was backed by one of their circumscribing walls of solid granite.

It was in vain that Fortunato, uplifting his dull torch, endeavored to pry into the depth of the recess. Its termination the feeble light did not enable us to see.

70 "Proceed," I said; "herein is the Amontillado. As for Luchesi—" 70

"He is an ignoramus," interrupted my friend, as he stepped unsteadily forward, while I followed immediately at his heels. In an instant he had reached the extremity of the niche, and finding his progress arrested by the rock, stood stupidly bewildered. A moment more and I had fettered him to the granite. In its surface were two iron staples, distant from each other about two feet, horizontally. From one of these depended a short chain, from the other a padlock. Throwing the links about his waist, it was but the work of a few seconds to secure it. He was too much astounded to resist. Withdrawing the key I stepped back from the recess.

"Pass your hand," I said, "over the wall; you cannot help feeling the nitre. Indeed, it is *very* damp. Once more let me *implore* you to return. No? Then I must positively leave you. But I must first render you all the little attentions in my power."

"The Amontillado!" ejaculated my friend, not yet recovered from his astonishment.

"True," I replied; "the Amontillado."

75 As I said these words I busied myself among the pile of bones of 75 which I have before spoken. Throwing them aside, I soon uncovered a quantity of building stone and mortar. With these materials and with the aid of my trowel, I began vigorously to wall up the entrance of the niche.

I had scarcely laid the first tier of the masonry when I discovered that the intoxication of Fortunato had in a great measure worn off. The earliest indication I had of this was a low moaning cry from the depths of the recess. It was *not* the cry of a drunken man. There was then a long and obstinate silence. I laid the second tier, and the third, and the fourth; and then I heard the furious vibrations of the chain. The noise lasted for several minutes, during which, that I might hearken to it with the more satisfaction, I ceased my labors and sat down upon the bones. When at last the clanking subsided, I resumed the trowel, and finished without interruption the fifth, the sixth, and the seventh tier. The wall was now nearly upon a level with my breast. I again paused, and holding the flambeaux over the mason-work, threw a few feeble rays upon the figure within.

A succession of loud and shrill screams, bursting suddenly from the throat of the chained form, seemed to thrust me violently back. For a brief moment I hesitated—I trembled. Unsheathing my rapier,

I began to grope with it about the recess; but the thought of an instant reassured me. I placed my hand upon the solid fabric of the catacombs, and felt satisfied. I reapproached the wall. I replied to the yells of him who clamoured. I re-echoed—I aided—I surpassed them in volume and in strength. I did this, and the clamourer grew still.

It was now midnight, and my task was drawing to a close. I had completed the eighth, the ninth and the tenth tier. I had finished a portion of the last and the eleventh; there remained but a single stone to be fitted and plastered in. I struggled with its weight; I placed it partially in its destined position. But now there came from out the niche a low laugh that erected the hairs upon my head. It was succeeded by a sad voice, which I had difficulty in recognizing as that of the noble Fortunato. The voice said—

"Ha! ha! ha!—he! he!—a very good joke indeed—an excellent jest. We will have many a rich laugh about it at the palazzo—he! he! he!—over our wine—he! he! he!"

80   "The Amontillado!" I said.   80

"He! ha! he!—he! he! he!—yes, the Amontillado. But is it not getting late? Will not they be awaiting us at the palazzo, the Lady Fortunato and the rest? Let us be gone."

"Yes," I said, "let us be gone."

"For the love of God, Montresor!"

"Yes," I said, "for the love of God."

85   But to these words I hearkened in vain for a reply. I grew impatient. I called aloud: 85

"Fortunato!"

No answer. I called again:

"Fortunato!"

No answer still. I thrust a torch through the remaining aperture and let it fall within. There came forth in return only a tingling of the bells. My heart grew sick—on account of the dampness of the catacombs. I hastened to make an end of my labour. I forced the last stone into its position; I plastered it up. Against the new masonry I re-erected the old rampart of bones. For the half of a century no mortal has disturbed them. *In pace requiescat!*

Questions on Meaning

1. What does Montresor tell us about the nature of the insult he has suffered? What does this tell us about Montresor?
2. Why does Montresor continue to suggest that the pair leave the vaults? What impact do his protestations have on Fortunato?
3. Why do you think Montresor waits fifty years to tell his story? What does his ability to wait this long tell us about his character?

Questions on Rhetorical Strategy and Style

1. Our perceptions of the narrator influence the way we respond to a narrative. How would you characterize Montresor, the narrator of this story? How does this characterization affect your reading of the story?
2. Montresor uses vivid details in describing Fortunato and the vaults. Choose several specific details and explain their significance to the story.
3. List the steps in the process of luring Fortunato into the crypt. To what purpose does Montresor take these steps? Why doesn't he use a more straightforward process?

Writing Assignments

1. Tell this story from the point of view of Fortunato as he watches the last stone being put into place. Consider his relationship with Montresor, his vanity, and his apparent ignorance of the perceived insult that leads to his doom.
2. Analyze the character of Montresor. What indications do we have of his grasp of reality? What does his family crest and motto say about his character? What do the details he provides of his revenge tell us about him?

⥲ LULLABY ⥲

Leslie Marmon Silko

Leslie Marmon Silko (1948–), who has Pueblo and La-
guna Indian, Mexican, and white ancestors, was born in
Albuquerque, New Mexico. She grew up on the Laguna
Pueblo reservation and attended both Indian school and
public school in Albuquerque. She graduated from the
University of New Mexico (1969) and attended law school
for a short time before turning to writing and teaching. In
1981 she received a MacArthur Foundation grant. Silko's
books include Laguna Woman: Poems *(1974),* Ceremony *(1977),* Storyteller *(1981),* Delicacy and the
Strength of Lace: Letters *(1986),* Almanac of the Dead
(1991), Sacred Water Narratives and Pictures *(1993),*
Yellow Woman *(1993), and* Yellow Woman and a
Beauty of the Spirit *(1996). The story that follows, cho-*
sen to appear in Martha Foley's Best Short Stories of
1975, *reveals how the invasion of white culture affected the*
life of a Navajo family.

1   The sun had gone down but the snow in the wind gave off its   1
own light. It came in thick tufts like new wool—washed before the weaver spins it. Ayah reached out for it like her own
babies had, and she smiled when she remembered how she had
laughed at them. She was an old woman now, and her life had become
memories. She sat down with her back against the wide cottonwood
tree, feeling the rough bark on her back bones; she faced east and listened to the wind and snow sing a high-pitched Yeibechei song. Out
of the wind she felt warmer, and she could watch the wide, fluffy snow
fill in her tracks, steadily, until the direction she had come from was
gone. By the light of the snow she could see the dark outline of the big

arroyo a few feet away. She was sitting on the edge of Cebolleta Creek, where in the springtime the thin cows would graze on grass already chewed flat to the ground. In the wide, deep creek bed where only a trickle of water flowed in the summer, the skinny cows would wander, looking for new grass along winding paths splashed with manure.

Ayah pulled the old Army blanket over her head like a shawl. Jimmie's blanket—the one he had sent to her. That was a long time ago and the green wool was faded, and it was unraveling on the edges. She did not want to think about Jimmie. So she thought about the weaving and the way her mother had done it. On the tall wooden loom set into the sand under a tamarack tree for shade. She could see it clearly. She had been only a little girl when her grandma gave her the wooden combs to pull the twigs and burrs from the raw, freshly washed wool. And while she combed the wool, her grandma sat beside her spinning a silvery strand of yarn around the smooth cedar spindle. Her mother worked at the loom with yarns dyed bright yellow and red and gold. She watched them dye the yarn in boiling black pots full of beeweed petals, juniper berries, and sage. The blankets her mother made were soft and woven so tight that rain rolled off them like birds' feathers. Ayah remembered sleeping warmly on cold windy nights, wrapped in her mother's blankets on the hogan's sandy floor.

The snow drifted now, with the northwest wind hurling it in gusts. It drifted up around her black overshoes—old ones with little metal buckles. She smiled at the snow which was trying to cover her little by little. She could remember when they had no black rubber overshoes; only the high buckskin leggings that they wrapped over their elkhide moccasins. If the snow was dry or frozen, a person could walk all day and not get wet; and in the evenings the beams of the ceiling would hang with lengths of pale buckskin leggings drying out slowly.

She felt peaceful remembering. She didn't feel cold any more. Jimmie's blanket seemed warmer than it had ever been. And she could remember the morning he was born. She could remember whispering to her mother, who was sleeping on the other side of the hogan, to tell her it was time now. She did not want to wake the others. The second time she called to her, her mother stood up and pulled on her shoes; she knew. They walked to the old stone hogan together, Ayah walking a step behind her mother. She waited alone learning the rhythms of the pains while her mother went to call the old woman to help them. The morning was already warm even before dawn and Ayah smelled the bee flowers blooming and the young willow growing at the springs. She could remember that so clearly, but his birth merged into the births of the other children and to her it became all the same birth. They named him for the summer morning and in English they called him Jimmie.

It wasn't like Jimmie died. He just never came back, and one day a dark blue sedan with white writing on its doors pulled up in front of the boxcar shack where the rancher let the Indians live. A man in a khaki uniform trimmed in gold gave them a yellow piece of paper and told them that Jimmie was dead. He said the Army would try to get the body back and then it would be shipped to them; but it wasn't likely because the helicopter had burned after it crashed. All of this was told to Chato because he could understand English. She stood inside the doorway holding the baby while Chato listened. Chato spoke English like a white man and he spoke Spanish too. He was taller than the white man and he stood straighter too. Chato didn't explain why; he just told the military man they could keep the body if they found it. The white man looked bewildered; he nodded his head and left. Then Chato looked at her and shook his head, and then he told her, "Jimmie isn't coming home anymore," and when he spoke, he used the words to speak of the dead. She didn't cry then, but she hurt inside with anger. And she mourned him as the years passed, when a horse fell with Chato and broke his leg, and the white rancher told them he wouldn't pay Chato until he could work again. She mourned Jimmie because he would have worked for his father then; he would have saddled the big bay horse and ridden the fence lines each day, with wire cutters and heavy gloves, fixing the breaks in the barbed wire and putting the stray cattle back inside again.

She mourned him after the white doctors came to take Danny and Ella away. She was at the shack alone that day they came. It was back in the days before they hired Navajo women to go with them as interpreters. She recognized one of the doctors. She had seen him at the children's clinic at Cañoncito about a month ago. They were wearing khaki uniforms and they waved papers at her and a black ball-point pen, trying to make her understand their English words. She was frightened by the way they looked at the children, like the lizard watches the fly. Danny was swinging on the tire swing on the elm tree behind the rancher's house, and Ella was toddling around the front door, dragging the broomstick horse Chato made for her. Ayah could see they wanted her to sign the papers, and Chato had taught her to sign her name. It was something she was proud of. She only wanted them to go, and to take their eyes away from her children.

She took the pen from the man without looking at his face and she signed the papers in three different places he pointed to. She stared at the ground by their feet and waited for them to leave. But they stood there and began to point and gesture at the children. Danny stopped swinging. Ayah could see his fear. She moved suddenly and grabbed Ella into her arms; the child squirmed, trying to get back to her toys. Ayah ran with the baby toward Danny; she screamed for him to run and then she grabbed him around his chest and carried him too. She ran south into the foothills of juniper trees and black lava rock. Behind her she heard the doctors running, but they had been taken by surprise, and as the hills became steeper and the cholla cactus were thicker, they stopped. When she reached the top of the hill, she stopped to listen in case they were circling around her. But in a few minutes she heard a car engine start and they drove away. The children had been too surprised to cry while she ran with them. Danny was shaking and Ella's little fingers were gripping Ayah's blouse.

She stayed up in the hills for the rest of the day, sitting on a black lava boulder in the sunshine where she could see for miles all around her. The sky was light blue and cloudless, and it was warm for late April. The sun warmth relaxed her and took the fear and anger away. She lay back on the rock and watched the sky. It seemed to her that she could walk into the sky, stepping through clouds endlessly. Danny played with little pebbles and stones, pretending they were birds' eggs and then little rabbits. Ella sat at her feet and dropped fistfuls of dirt into the breeze, watching the dust and particles of sand intently. Ayah watched a hawk soar high above them, dark wings gliding; hunting or only watching, she did not know. The hawk was patient and he circled all afternoon before he disappeared around the high volcanic peak the Mexicans called Guadalupe.

Late in the afternoon, Ayah looked down at the gray boxcar shack with the paint all peeled from the wood: the stove pipe on the roof was rusted and crooked. The fire she had built that morning in the oil drum stove had burned out. Ella was asleep in her lap now and Danny sat close to her, complaining that he was hungry; he asked when they would go to the house. "We will stay up here until your father comes," she told him, "because those white men were chasing us." The boy remembered then and he nodded at her silently.

If Jimmie had been there he could have read those papers and explained to her what they said. Ayah would have known then, never to sign them. The doctors came back the next day and they brought a BIA policeman with them. They told Chato they had her signature and that was all they needed. Except for the kids. She listened to Chato sullenly; she hated him when he told her it was the old woman who died in the winter, spitting blood; it was her old grandma who had given the children this disease. "They don't spit blood," she said coldly. "The whites lie." She held Ella and Danny, close to her, ready to run to the hills again. "I want a medicine man first," she said to Chato, not looking at him. He shook his head. "It's too late now. The policeman is with them. You signed the paper." His voice was gentle.

It was worse than if they had died: to lose the children and to know that somewhere, in a place called Colorado, in a place full of sick and dying strangers, her children were without her. There had been babies that died soon after they were born, and one that died before he could walk. She had carried them herself, up to the boulders and great pieces of the cliff that long ago crashed down from Long Mesa; she laid them in the crevices of sandstone and buried them in fine brown sand with round quartz pebbles that washed down the hills in the rain. She had endured it because they had been with her. But she could not bear this pain. She did not sleep for a long time after they took her children. She stayed on the hill where they had fled the first time, and she slept rolled up in the blanket Jimmie had sent her. She carried the pain in her belly and it was fed by everything she saw: the blue sky of their last day together and the dust and pebbles they played with; the swing in the elm tree and broomstick horse choked life from her. The pain filled her stomach and there was no room for food or for her lungs to fill with air. The air and the food would have been theirs.

She hated Chato, not because he let the policeman and doctors put the screaming children in the government car, but because he had taught her to sign her name. Because it was like the old ones always told her about learning their language or any of their ways: It endangers you. She slept alone on the hill until the middle of November when the first snows came. Then she made a bed for herself where the children had slept. She did not lie down beside Chato again until many years later, when he was sick and shivering and only her body could keep him warm. The illness came after the white rancher told Chato he was too old to work for him anymore, and Chato and his old woman should be out of the shack by the next afternoon because the rancher had hired new people to work there. That had satisfied her. To see how the white man repaid Chato's years of loyalty and work. All of Chato's fine-sounding English talk didn't change things.

It snowed steadily and the luminous light from the snow gradually diminished into the darkness. Somewhere in Ceboletta a dog barked and other village dogs joined with it. Ayah looked in the direction she had come, from the bar where Chato was buying the wine. Sometimes he told her to go on ahead and wait; and then he never came. And when she finally went back looking for him, she would find him passed out at the bottom of the wooden steps to Azzie's Bar. All the wine would be gone and most of the money too, from the pale blue check that came to them once a month in a government envelope. It was then that she would look at his face and his hands, scarred by ropes and the barbed wire of all those years, and she would think, this man is a stranger; for forty years she had smiled at him and cooked his food, but he remained a stranger. She stood up again, with the snow almost to her knees, and she walked back to find Chato.

It was hard to walk in the deep snow and she felt the air burn in her lungs. She stopped a short distance from the bar to rest and readjust the blanket. But this time he wasn't waiting for her at the bottom step with his old Stetson hat pulled down and his shoulders hunched up in his long wool overcoat.

She was careful not to slip on the wooden steps. When she pushed the door open, warm air and cigarette smoke hit her face. She looked around slowly and deliberately, in every corner, in every dark place that the old man might find to sleep. The bar owner didn't like Indians in there, especially Navajos, but he let Chato come in because he could talk Spanish like he was one of them. The men at the bar stared at her, and the bartender saw that she left the door open wide. Snowflakes were flying inside like moths and melting into a puddle on the oiled wood floor. He motioned to her to close the door, but she did not see him. She held herself straight and walked across the room slowly, searching the room with every step. The snow in her hair melted and she could feel it on her forehead. At the far corner of the room, she saw red flames at the mica window of the old stove door; she looked behind the stove just to make sure. The bar got quiet except for the Spanish polka music playing on the jukebox. She stood by the stove and shook the snow from her blanket and held it near the stove to dry. The wet wool smell reminded her of newborn goats in early March, brought inside to warm near the fire. She felt calm.

In past years they would have told her to get out. But her hair was white now and her face was wrinkled. They looked at her like she was a spider crawling slowly across the room. They were afraid; she could feel the fear. She looked at their faces steadily. They reminded her of the first time the white people brought her children back to her that winter. Danny had been shy and hid behind the thin white woman who brought them. And the baby had not known her until Ayah took her into her arms, and then Ella had nuzzled close to her as she had when she was nursing. The blonde woman was nervous and kept looking at a dainty gold watch on her wrist. She sat on the bench near the small window and watched the dark snow clouds gather around the mountains; she was worrying about the unpaved road. She was frightened by what she saw inside too: the strips of venison drying on a rope across the ceiling and the children jabbering excitedly in a language she did not know. So they stayed for only a few hours. Ayah watched the government car disappear down the road and she knew they were already being weaned from these lava hills and from this sky. The last time they came was in early June, and Ella stared at her the way the men in the bar were now staring. Ayah did not try to pick her up; she smiled at her instead and spoke cheerfully to Danny. When he tried to answer her, he could not seem to remember and he spoke English words with the Navajo. But he gave her a scrap of paper that he had found somewhere and carried in his pocket; it was folded in half, and he shyly looked up at her and said it was a bird. She asked Chato if they were home for good this time. He spoke to the white woman and she shook her head. "How much longer?" he asked, and she said she didn't know; but Chato saw how she stared at the boxcar shack. Ayah turned away then. She did not say good-bye.

She felt satisfied that the men in the bar feared her. Maybe it was her face and the way she held her mouth with teeth clenched tight, like there was nothing anyone could do to her now. She walked north down the road, searching for the old man. She did this because she had the blanket, and there would be no place for him except with her and the blanket in the old adobe barn near the arroyo. They always slept there when they came to Cebolleta. If the money and the wine were gone, she would be relieved because then they could go home again; back to the old hogan with a dirt roof and rock walls where she herself had been born. And the next day the old man could go back to the few sheep they still had, to follow along behind them, guiding them, into dry sandy arroyos where sparse grass grew. She knew he did not like walking behind old ewes when for so many years he rode big quarter horses and worked with cattle. But she wasn't sorry for him; he should have known all along what would happen.

There had not been enough rain for their garden in five years; and that was when Chato finally hitched a ride into the town and brought back brown boxes of rice and sugar and big tin cans of welfare peaches. After that, at the first of the month they went to Ceboletta to ask the postmaster for the check; and then Chato would go to the bar and cash it. They did this as they planted the garden every May, not because anything would survive the summer dust, but because it was time to do this. The journey passed the days that smelled silent and dry like the caves above the canyon with yellow painted buffaloes on their walls.

He was walking along the pavement when she found him. He did not stop or turn around when he heard her behind him. She walked beside him and she noticed how slowly he moved now. He smelled strong of woodsmoke and urine. Lately he had been forgetting. Sometimes he called her by his sister's name and she had been gone for a long time. Once she had found him wandering on the road to the white man's ranch, and she asked him why he was going that way; he laughed at her and said, "You know they can't run that ranch without me," and he walked on determined, limping on the leg that had been crushed many years before. Now he looked at her curiously, as if for the first time, but he kept shuffling along, moving slowly along the side of the highway. His gray hair had grown long and spread out on the shoulders of the long overcoat. He wore the old felt hat pulled down over his ears. His boots were worn out at the toes and he had stuffed pieces of an old red shirt in the holes. The rags made his feet look like little animals up to their ears in snow. She laughed at his feet; the snow muffled the sound of her laugh. He stopped and looked at her again. The wind had quit blowing and the snow was falling straight down; the southeast sky was beginning to clear and Ayah could see a star.

"Let's rest awhile," she said to him. They walked away from the road and up the slope to the giant boulders that had tumbled down from the red sandrock mesa throughout the centuries of rainstorms and earth tremors. In a place where the boulders shut out the wind, they sat down with their backs against the rock. She offered half of the blanket to him and they sat wrapped together.

The storm passed swiftly. The clouds moved east. They were massive and full, crowding together across the sky. She watched them with the feeling of horses—steely blue-gray horses startled across the sky. The powerful haunches pushed into the distances and the tail hairs streamed white mist behind them. The sky cleared. Ayah saw that there was nothing between her and the stars. The light was crystalline. There was no shimmer, no distortion through earth haze. She breathed the clarity of the night sky; she smelled the purity of the half moon and the stars. He was lying on his side with his knees pulled up near his belly for warmth. His eyes were closed now, and in the light from the stars and the moon, he looked young again.

She could see it descend out of the night sky: an icy stillness from the edge of the thin moon. She recognized the freezing. It came gradually, sinking snowflake by snowflake until the crust was heavy and deep. It had the strength of the stars in Orion, and its journey was endless. Ayah knew that with the wine he would sleep. He would not feel it. She tucked the blanket around him, remembering how it was when Ella had been with her; and she felt the rush so big inside her heart for the babies. And she sang the only song she knew to sing for babies. She could not remember if she had ever sung it to her children, but she knew that her grandmother had sung it and her mother had sung it:

> The earth is your mother,
>   she holds you.
> The sky is your father,
>   he protects you.
> Sleep,
> sleep.
> Rainbow, is your sister,
>   she loves you.
> The winds are your brothers,
>   they sing to you.
> Sleep,
> sleep.
> We are together always
> We are together always
> There never was a time
> when this
> was not so.

Questions on Meaning

1. Silko reveals through Ayah's memories the profound changes in her world. In one rumination, Ayah is helping her grandmother and mother comb, dye, and weave the wool for their blankets under a tamarack tree; in another, buying boxes of rice and cans of welfare peaches with government checks cashed at a bar. What are her best memories? What are her worst? How did white man and white culture affect these changes?

2. Silko says that Ayah came to hate Chato because he taught her to sign her name. Why would he have taught her? How did that ability—which she once held proudly—eventually confirm for her what the elders had said about "learning their language or any of their ways"?

3. What was different about Ella and Danny the last time they were taken back to their boxcar home? Why did Ayah not say goodbye to her children this last time they visited? What alternatives do you think she had for seeing her children again or for having them returned to her?

Questions on Rhetorical Strategy and Style

1. The stories from cultures with a rich oral history—such as Native American cultures—typically are quite involute, stories within stories within stories. Find examples of where Silko breaks off from the main story to explore a tangential story, and another, and then finally wends her way back to the original tale about Ayah as an old woman.

2. Silko's intimate knowledge of the lifestyle and geography of her subjects and her eye for descriptive detail tantalize the reader's senses. Reread her description of the young Ayah on a lava boulder in the hills with her children after escaping from the white doctors, and her description of the old Ayah at Azzie's Bar looking for Chato. How does she appeal to our senses of sight, smell, hearing, and touch? Find other examples of this multidimensional imagery.

3. Locate where Silko uses a cause and effect writing strategy to explain Ayah's distrust for white men and white culture. In what ways did the white man control the Indian's destiny? Why did the whites not attempt to communicate with the Indians in their own language?

Writing Assignments

1. Learn about conditions on Indian reservations today and the opportunities for Native Americans in today's society. What percentage of Native Americans complete high school versus whites, blacks, Hispanics, and Asians? What percentage graduate from college? What institutional prejudices still work against American Indians? What do you think needs to be done to improve opportunities for Native Americans?

2. By treaty, Indian tribes are considered "sovereign nations." In governmental relations, tribes are neither subordinate to state government nor at the level of state government, but rather are considered to be at the level of the federal government. Research how this status affects tribes in terms of using tribal lands and recovering natural resources on (or under) tribal lands. Who makes decisions about controversial uses of tribal land (such as gambling casinos and radioactive waste dumps)? What are the various benefits and detriments to Native Americans of lucrative, yet potentially dangerous, land use?

3. Perhaps the most painful memory to Ayah was having her children forcefully taken away from her. Unfortunately, for many different reasons, children in our culture are still separated from their parents against their parents' will. Write an essay describing the conditions under which you feel it is justifiable—or perhaps necessary—to take children from their parents. How should they be removed? What efforts must be made to reunite them? What doublechecks can be built into the system to ensure that children do not fall through bureaucratic loopholes?

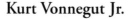 HARRISON BERGERON

Kurt Vonnegut Jr.

Kurt Vonnegut was born in 1922 in Indianapolis, Indiana. He was educated at Cornell, Carnegie-Mellon, and the University of Chicago, where his master's thesis was unanimously rejected by the department of anthropology. He served in the Army in World War II and was a prisoner of war in Dresden, Germany, during the Allied fire bombing of that city. He has worked as a police reporter, a public relations writer, a Saab dealer, and a teacher. Vonnegut is that rarity, a popular writer who also has considerable standing among critics and intellectuals. The novels he wrote during the sixties, especially Cat's Cradle *(1963), found a cult following among students.* Slaughterhouse Five *(1969), perhaps his best, depicted the destruction by fire-bombing of Dresden. The satire and absurdity that are the trademarks of his novels occur also in "Harrison Bergeron," where Vonnegut sides with the non-conformist, the rule-breaker, the person who stands outside the narrow moral universe of conventional society.*

The year was 2081, and everybody was finally equal. They weren't only equal before God and the law. They were equal every which way. Nobody was smarter than anybody else. Nobody was better looking than anybody else. Nobody was stronger or quicker than anybody else. All this equality was due to the 211th, 212th, and 213th Amendments to the Constitution, and to the unceasing vigilance of agents of the United States Handicapper General.

Some things about living still weren't quite right, though. April, for instance, still drove people crazy by not being springtime. And it was in that clammy month that the H-G men took George and Hazel Bergeron's fourteen-year-old son, Harrison, away.

It was tragic, all right, but George and Hazel couldn't think about it very hard. Hazel had a perfectly average intelligence, which meant she couldn't think about anything except in short bursts. And George, while his intelligence was way above normal, had a little mental handicap radio in his ear. He was required by law to wear it at all times. It was tuned to a government transmitter. Every twenty seconds or so, the transmitter would send out some sharp noise to keep people like George from taking unfair advantage of their brains.

George and Hazel were watching television. There were tears on Hazel's cheeks, but she'd forgotten for the moment what they were about.

5   On the television screen were ballerinas.   5

A buzzer sounded in George's head. His thoughts fled in panic, like bandits from a burglar alarm.

"That was a real pretty dance, that dance they just did," said Hazel.

"Huh?" said George.

"That dance—it was nice," said Hazel.

"Yup," said George. He tried to think a little about the ballerinas. 10 They weren't really very good—no better than anybody else would   10 have been, anyway. They were burdened with sashweights and bags of birdshot, and their faces were masked, so that no one, seeing a free and graceful gesture or a pretty face, would feel like something the cat drug in. George was toying with the vague notion that maybe dancers shouldn't be handicapped. But he didn't get very far with it before another noise in his ear radio scattered his thoughts.

George winced. So did two out of the eight ballerinas.

Hazel saw him wince. Having no mental handicap herself, she had to ask George what the latest sound had been.

"Sounded like somebody hitting a milk bottle with a ball peen hammer," said George

"I'd think it would be real interesting, hearing all the different sounds," said Hazel, a little envious. "All the things they think up."

15   "Um," said George.   15

"Only, if I was Handicapper General, you know what I would do?" said Hazel. Hazel, as a matter of fact, bore a strong resemblance to the Handicapper General, a woman named Diana Moon Glampers. "If I was Diana Moon Glampers," said Hazel, "I'd have chimes on Sunday—just chimes. Kind of in honor of religion."

"I could think, if it was just chimes," said George.

"Well—maybe make 'em real loud," said Hazel. "I think I'd make a good Handicapper General."

"Good as anybody else," said George.

20 "Who knows better'n I do what normal is?" said Hazel. 20

"Right," said George. He began to think glimmeringly about his abnormal son who was now in jail, about Harrison, but a twenty-one-gun salute in his head stopped that.

"Boy!" said Hazel, "that was a doozy, wasn't it?"

It was such a doozy that George was white and trembling, and tears stood on the rims of his red eyes. Two of the eight ballerinas had collapsed to the studio floor, [and] were holding their temples.

"All of a sudden you look so tired," said Hazel. "Why don't you stretch out on the sofa, so's you can rest your handicap bag on the pillows, honeybunch." She was referring to the forty-seven pounds of birdshot in a canvas bag, which was padlocked around George's neck. "Go on and rest the bag for a little while," she said. "I don't care if you're not equal to me for a while."

25 George weighed the bag with his hands. "I don't mind it," he said. 25 "I don't notice it any more. It's just a part of me."

"You been so tired lately—kind of wore out," said Hazel. "if there was just some way we could make a little hole in the bottom of the bag, and just take out a few of them lead balls. Just a few."

"Two years in prison and two thousand dollars fine for every ball I took out," said George. "I don't call that a bargain."

"If you could just take a few out when you came home from work," said Hazel. "I mean—you don't compete with anybody around here. You just set around."

"If I tried to get away with it, said George, then other people'd get away with it—and pretty soon we'd be right back to the dark ages again, with everybody competing against everybody else. You wouldn't like that, would you?"

30 "I'd hate it," said Hazel. 30

"There you are," said George. "The minute people start cheating on laws, what do you think happens to society?"

If Hazel hadn't been able to come up with an answer to this question George couldn't have supplied one. A siren was going off in his head.

"Reckon it'd fall all apart," said Hazel.

"What would?" said George blankly.

35 "Society," said Hazel uncertainly. "Wasn't that what you just 35 said?"

"Who knows?" said George.

The television program was suddenly interrupted for a news bulletin. It wasn't clear at first as to what the bulletin was about, since the announcer, like all announcers, had a serious speech impediment. For about half a minute, and in a state of high excitement, the announcer tried to say, "Ladies and gentlemen—"

He finally gave up, handed the bulletin to a ballerina to read.

"That's all right—" Hazel said of the announcer, "he tried. That's the big thing. He tried to do the best he could with what God gave him. He should get a nice raise for trying so hard."

40 "Ladies and gentlemen—" said the ballerina, reading the bulletin. 40 She must have been extraordinarily beautiful, because the mask she wore was hideous. And it was easy to see that she was the strongest and most graceful of all the dancers, for her handicap bags were as big as those worn by two-hundred-pound men.

And she had to apologize at once for her voice, which was a very unfair voice for a woman to use. Her voice was a warm, luminous, timeless melody. "Excuse me—" she said, and she began again, making her voice absolutely uncompetitive.

"Harrison Bergeron, age fourteen," she said in a grackle squawk, "has just escaped from jail, where he was held on suspicion of plotting to overthrow the government. He is a genius and an athlete, is under-handicapped, and should be regarded as extremely dangerous."

A police photograph of Harrison Bergeron was flashed on the screen upside down, then sideways, upside down again, then right side up. The picture showed the full length of Harrison against a background calibrated in feet and inches. He was exactly seven feet tall.

The rest of Harrison's appearance was Halloween and hardware. Nobody had ever borne heavier handicaps. He had outgrown hindrances faster than the H-G men could think them up. Instead of a little ear radio for a mental handicap, he wore a tremendous pair of earphones, and spectacles with thick wavy lenses. The spectacles were intended to make him not only half blind, but to give him whanging headaches besides.

Scrap metal was hung all over him. Ordinarily, there was a certain symmetry, a military neatness to the handicaps issued to strong people, but Harrison looked like a walking junkyard. In the race of life, Harrison carried three hundred pounds.

And to offset his good looks, the H-G men required that he wear at all times a red rubber ball for a nose, keep his eyebrows shaved off, and cover his even white teeth with black caps at snaggle-tooth random.

"If you see this boy," said the ballerina, "do not—I repeat, do not—try to reason with him."

There was the shriek of a door being torn from its hinges.

Screams and barking cries of consternation came from the television set. The photograph of Harrison Bergeron on the screen jumped again and again, as though dancing to the tune of an earthquake.

George Bergeron correctly identified the earthquake, and well he might have—for many was the time his own home had danced to the same crashing tune. "My God—" said George, "that must be Harrison!"

The realization was blasted from his mind instantly by the sound of an automobile collision in his head.

When George could open his eyes again, the photograph of Harrison was gone. A living, breathing Harrison filled the screen.

Clanking, clownish, and huge, Harrison stood in the center of the studio. The knob of the uprooted studio door was still in his hand. Ballerinas, technicians, musicians, and announcers cowered on their knees before him, expecting to die.

"I am the Emperor!" cried Harrison. "Do you hear? I am the Emperor! Everybody must do what I say at once!" He stamped his foot and the studio shook.

"Even as I stand here——" he bellowed, "crippled, hobbled, sickened—I am a greater ruler than any man who ever lived. Now watch me become what I *can* become!"

Harrison tore the straps of his handicap harness like wet tissue paper, tore straps guaranteed to support five thousand pounds.

Harrison's scrap-iron handicaps crashed to the floor.

Harrison thrust his thumbs under the bar of the padlock that secured his head harness. The bar snapped like celery. Harrison smashed his headphones and spectacles against the wall.

He flung away his rubber-ball nose, revealed a man that would have awed Thor, the god of thunder.

60 "I shall now select my Empress!" he said, looking down on the cowering people. "Let the first woman who dares rise to her feet claim her mate and her throne!"

A moment passed, and then a ballerina arose swaying like a willow.

Harrison plucked the mental handicap from her ear, snapped off her physical handicaps with marvelous delicacy. Last of all, he removed her mask.

She was blindingly beautiful.

"Now—" said Harrison, taking her hand, "shall we show the peo-
65 ple the meaning of the word dance? Music!" he commanded.

The musicians scrambled back into their chairs, and Harrison stripped them of their handicaps, too. "Play your best," he told them, "and I'll make you barons and dukes and earls."

The music began. It was normal at first—cheap, silly, false. But Harrison snatched two musicians from their chairs, waved them like batons as he sang the music as he wanted it played. He slammed them back into their chairs.

The music began again and was much improved.

Harrison and his Empress merely listened to the music for a while—listened gravely, as though synchronizing their heartbeats with it.

They shifted their weights to their toes.

70 Harrison placed his big hands on the girl's tiny waist, letting her sense the weightlessness that would soon be hers.

And then, in an explosion of joy and grace, into the air they sprang!

Not only were the laws of the land abandoned, but the law of gravity and the laws of motion as well.

They reeled, whirled, swiveled, flounced, capered, gamboled, and spun.

They leaped like deer on the moon.

75 The studio ceiling was thirty feet high, but each leap brought the dancers nearer to it.

It became their obvious intention to kiss the ceiling.

They kissed it.

And then, neutralizing gravity with love and pure will, they remained suspended in air inches below the ceiling, and they kissed each other for a long, long time.

It was then that Diana Moon Glampers, the Handicapper General, came into the studio with a double-barreled ten-gauge shotgun. She fired twice and the Emperor and the Empress were dead before they hit the floor.

80 Diana Moon Glampers loaded the gun again. She aimed it at the musicians and told them they had ten seconds to get their handicaps back on.

It was then that the Bergerons' television tube burned out. Hazel turned to comment about the blackout to George. But George had gone out into the kitchen for a can of beer.

George came back in with the beer, paused while a handicap signal shook him up. And then he sat down again.

"You been crying?" he said to Hazel.

"Yup," she said.

85 "What about?" he said.

"I forget," she said. "Something real sad on television."

"What was it?" he said.

"It's all kind of mixed up in my mind," said Hazel.

"Forget sad things," said George.

90 "I always do," said Hazel.

"That's my girl," said George. He winced. There was the sound of a riveting gun in his head.

"Gee— I could tell that one was a doozy," said Hazel.

"You can say that again," said George.

"Gee—" said Hazel, "I could tell that one was a doozy."

Questions on Meaning

1. What has caused the world of "Harrison Bergeron" to be filled with handicaps for the best and the brightest people?
2. Vonnegut's story is not "politically correct"; that is, the attitudes expressed and implied do not fall in line with liberal political values. List the politically incorrect attitudes found in "Harrison Bergeron," and point to the characters, events, or situations that represent the attitudes.

Questions on Rhetorical Strategy and Style

1. Vonnegut seems to be suggesting a cause/effect relationship between basic American values (such as Equal Rights) and Mediocrity. Explain the thinking that leads to that conclusion.
2. Is Vonnegut merely criticizing democracies or is he arguing for a return to some kind of aristocracy or fascism? Explain.

Writing Assignments

1. Do you agree with the politics expressed in "Harrison Bergeron"? Use your personal experience, observation of others, or reading to write an essay on the benefits or the dangers of competition.
2. Research the history of affirmative action legislation. Write an essay that describes the measures the American government has taken to promote equal access to employment or education.
3. This story is a kind of fiction describing "dystopias," that is, alternate realities that are horrifying to our sensibilities. Two famous novels—George Orwell's *1984* and Aldous Huxley's *Brave New World*—describe similar dystopias. Read one of them and write an essay comparing the political attitudes of that author with the political attitudes of Vonnegut.
4. Research the history of business monopolies in the United States. Describe the measures the government has taken to restrict unfair competition.

⤙ A WORN PATH ⤚

Eudora Welty

Born in Jackson, Mississippi, Eudora Welty (1909-) attended Mississippi State College for Women and was graduated from the University of Wisconsin in 1929. She lived briefly in New York, where she worked in an advertising firm, but returned to her native Mississippi during the Great Depression to help her family and to write. Welty has published three novels and many stories and articles; she won the O. Henry short fiction award, the Pulitzer Prize for her novel The Optimist's Daughter *(1972), the National Medal for Literature, and the Presidential Medal of Freedom, thus becoming one of the most honored and admired writers of the century. Welty captures the life of the South and the lives of the people she knew and loved. That tenderness is clearly demonstrated in "A Worn Path."*

1 It was December—a bright frozen day in the early morning. Far out in the country there was an old Negro woman with her head tied in a red rag, coming along a path through the pinewoods. Her name was Phoenix Jackson. She was very old and small and she walked, slowly in the dark pine shadows, moving a little from side to side in her steps, with the balanced heaviness and lightness of a pendulum in a grandfather clock. She carried a thin, small cane made from an umbrella, and with this she kept tapping the frozen earth in front of her. This made a grave and persistent noise in the still air, that seemed meditative, like the chirping of a solitary little bird.

She wore a dark striped dress reaching down to her shoetops, and an equally long apron of bleached sugar sacks, with a full pocket; all, neat and tidy, but every time she took a step she might have fallen over her shoelaces, which dragged from her unlaced shoes. She looked straight ahead. Her eyes were blue with age. Her skin had a pattern all its own of numberless branching wrinkles and as though a whole little tree stood in the middle of her forehead, but a golden color ran underneath, and the two knobs of her cheeks were illuminated by a yellow burning under the dark. Under the red rag her hair came down on her neck in the frailest of ringlets, still black, and with an odor like copper.

Now and then there was a quivering in the thicket. Old Phoenix said, "Out of my way, all you foxes, owls, beetles, jack rabbits, coons, and wild animals! . . . Keep out from under these feet, little bobwhites. . . . Keep the big wild hogs out of my path. Don't let none of those come running in my direction. I got a long way." Under her small black-freckled hand her cane, limber as a buggy whip, would switch at the brush as if to rouse up any hiding things.

On she went. The woods were deep and still. The sun made the pine needles almost too bright to look at, up where the wind rocked. The cones dropped as light as feathers. Down in the hollow was the mourning dove—it was not too late for him.

5   The path ran up a hill. "Seem like there is chains about my feet,   5
time I get this far," she said, in the voice of argument old people keep to use with themselves. "Something always take a hold on this hill—pleads I should stay."

After she got to the top she turned and gave a full, severe look behind her where she had come. "Up through pines," she said at length. "Now down through oaks."

Her eyes opened their widest and she started down gently. But before she got to the bottom of the hill a bush caught her dress.

Her fingers were busy and intent, but her skirts were full and long, so that before she could pull them free in one place they were caught in another. It was not possible to allow the dress to tear. "I in the thorny bush," she said. "Thorns, you doing your appointed work. Never want to let folks past—no sir. Old eyes thought you was a pretty little *green* bush."

Finally, trembling all over, she stood free, and after a moment dared to stoop for her cane.

10   "Sun so high!" she cried, leaning back and looking, while the   10
thick tears went over her eyes. "The time getting all gone here."

At the foot of this hill was a place where a log was laid across the creek.

"Now comes the trial," said Phoenix.

Putting her right foot out, she mounted the log and shut her eyes. Lifting her skirt, leveling her cane fiercely before her, like a festival figure in some parade, she began to march across. Then she opened her eyes and she was safe on the other side.

"I wasn't as old as I thought," she said.

15   But she sat down to rest. She spread her skirts on the bank around   15 her and folded her hands over her knees. Up above her was a tree in a pearly cloud of mistletoe. She did not dare to close her eyes, and when a little boy brought her a little plate with a slice of marble-cake on it she spoke to him. "That would be acceptable," she said. But when she went to take it there was just her own hand in the air.

So she left that tree, and had to go through a barbed-wire fence. There she had to creep and crawl, spreading her knees and stretching her fingers like a baby trying to climb the steps. But she talked loudly to herself: she could not let her dress be torn now, so late in the day, and she could not pay for having her arm or leg sawed off if she got caught fast where she was.

At last she was safe through the fence and risen up out in the clearing. Big dead trees, like black men with one arm, were standing in the purple stalks of the withered cotton field. There sat a buzzard.

"Who you watching?"

In the furrow she made her way along

20   "Glad this not the season for bulls," she said, looking sideways,   20 "and the good Lord made his snakes to curl up and sleep in the winter. A pleasure I don't see no two-headed snake coming around that tree, where it come once. It took a while to get by him, back in the summer."

She passed through the old cotton and went into a field of dead corn. It whispered and shook, and was taller than her head. "Through the maze now," she said, for there was no path.

Then there was something tall, black, and skinny there, moving before her.

At first she took it for a man. It could have been a man dancing in the field. But she stood still and listened, and it did not make a sound. It was as silent as a ghost.

"Ghost," she said sharply, "who be you the ghost of? For I have heard of nary death close by."

But there was no answer, only the ragged dancing in the wind.

She shut her eyes, reached out her hand, and touched a sleeve. She found a coat and inside that an emptiness, cold as ice.

"You scarecrow," she said. Her face lighted. "I ought to be shut up for good," she said with laughter. "My senses is gone. I too old. I the oldest people I ever know. Dance, old scarecrow," she said, "while I dancing with you."

She kicked her foot over the furrow, and with mouth drawn down shook her head once or twice in a little strutting way. Some husks blew down and whirled in streamers about her skirts.

Then she went on, parting her way from side to side with the cane, through the whispering field. At last she came to the end, to a wagon track, where the silver grass blew between the red ruts. The quail were walking around like pullets, seeming all dainty and unseen.

"Walk pretty," she said. "This the easy place. This the easy going."

She followed the track, swaying through the quiet bare fields, through the little strings of trees silver in their dead leaves, past cabins silver from weather, with the doors and windows boarded shut, all like old women under a spell sitting there. "I walking in their sleep," she said, nodding her head vigorously.

In a ravine she went where a spring was silently flowing through a hollow log. Old Phoenix bent and drank. "Sweetgum makes the water sweet," she said, and drank more. "Nobody knows who made this well, for it was here when I was born."

The track crossed a swampy part where the moss hung as white as lace from every limb. "Sleep on, alligators, and blow your bubbles." Then the track went into the road.

Deep, deep the road went down between the high green-colored banks. Overhead the live-oaks met, and it was as dark as a cave.

A black dog with a lolling tongue came up out of the weeds by the ditch. She was meditating, and not ready, and when he came at her she only hit him a little with her cane. Over she went in the ditch, like a little puff of milk-weed.

Down there, her senses drifted away. A dream visited her, and she reached her hand up, but nothing reached down and gave her a pull. So she lay there and presently went to talking. "Old woman," she said to herself, "that black dog come up out of the weeds to stall you off, and now there he sitting on his fine tail, smiling at you."

A white man finally came along and found her—a hunter, a young man, with his dog on a chain.

"Well, Granny!" he laughed. "What are you doing there?"

"Lying on my back like a June-bug waiting to be turned over, mister," she said, reaching up her hand.

40 He lifted her up, gave her a swing in the air, and set her down. 40 "Anything broken, Granny?"

"No, sir, them old dead weeds is springy enough," said Phoenix, when she had got her breath. "I thank you for your trouble."

"Where do you live, Granny?" he asked, while the two dogs were growling at each other.

"Away back yonder, sir, behind that ridge. You can't even see it from here."

"On your way home?"

45 "No, sir, I going to town." 45

"Why that's too far! That's as far as I walk when I come out myself, and I get something for my trouble." He patted the stuffed bag he carried, and there hung down a little closed claw. It was one of the bobwhites, with its beak hooked bitterly to show it was dead. "Now you go on home, Granny!"

"I bound to go to town, mister," said Phoenix. "The time come around."

He gave another laugh, filling the whole landscape. "I know you colored people! Wouldn't miss going to town to see Santa Claus!"

But something held Old Phoenix very still. The deep lines in her face went into a fierce and different radiation. Without warning she had seen with her own eyes a flashing nickel fall out of the man's pocket on to the ground.

50 "How old are you, Granny?" he was saying. 50

"There is no telling, mister," she said, "no telling."

Then she gave a little cry and clapped her hands, and said, "Git on away from here, dog! Look! Look at that dog!" She laughed as if in admiration. "He ain't scared of nobody. He a big black dog." She whispered, "Sick him!"

"Watch me get rid of that cur," said the man. "Sick him, Pete! Sick him!"

Phoenix heard the dogs fighting and heard the man running and throwing sticks. She even heard a gunshot. But she was slowly bending forward by that time, further and further forward, the lids stretched down over her eyes, as if she were doing this in her sleep. Her chin was lowered almost to her knees. The yellow palm of her hand came out from the fold of her apron. Her fingers slid down and along the ground under the piece of money with the grace and care they would have in lifting an egg from under a sitting hen. Then she slowly straightened up, she stood erect, and the nickel was in her apron pocket. A bird flew by. Her lips moved. "God watching me the whole time. I come to stealing."

55   The man came back, and his own dog panted about them. "Well, 55 I scared him off that time," he said, and then he laughed and lifted his gun and pointed it at Phoenix.

She stood straight and faced him.

"Doesn't the gun scare you?" he said, still pointing it.

"No, sir, I seen plenty go off closer by, in my day, and for less what I done," she said, holding utterly still.

He smiled, and shouldered the gun. "Well, Granny," he said, "you must be a hundred years old, and scared of nothing. I'd give you a dime if I had any money with me. But you take my advice and stay home, and nothing will happen to you."

60   "I bound to go on my way, mister," said Phoenix. She inclined her 60 head in the red rag. Then they went in different directions, but she could hear the gun shooting again and again over the hill.

She walked on. The shadows hung from the oak trees to the road like curtains. Then she smelled wood-smoke, and smelled the river, and she saw a steeple and the cabins on their steep steps. Dozens of little black children whirled around her. There ahead was Natchez shining. Bells were ringing. She walked on.

In the paved city it was Christmas time. There were red and green electric lights strung and crisscrossed everywhere, and all turned on in the daytime. Old Phoenix would have been lost if she had not distrusted her eyesight and depended on her feet to know where to take her.

She paused quietly on the sidewalk, where people were passing by. A lady came along in the crowd, carrying an armful of red-, green-, and silver-wrapped presents; she gave off perfume like the red roses in hot summer, and Phoenix stopped her.

"Please, missy, will you lace up my shoe?" She held up her foot.

65 "What do you want, Grandma?"

"See my shoe," said Phoenix. "Do all right for out in the country, but wouldn't look right to go in a big building."

"Stand still then, Grandma," said the lady. She put her packages down carefully on the sidewalk beside her and laced and tied both shoes tightly.

"Can't lace 'em with a cane," said Phoenix. "Thank you, missy. I doesn't mind asking a nice lady to tie up my shoe when I gets out on the street."

Moving slowly and from side to side, she went into the stone building and into a tower of steps, where she walked up and around and around until her feet knew to stop.

70 She entered a door, and there she saw nailed up on the wall the document that had been stamped with the gold seal and framed in the gold frame which matched the dream that was hung up in her head.

"Here I be," she said. There was a fixed and ceremonial stiffness over her body.

"A charity case, I suppose," said an attendant who sat at the desk before her.

But Phoenix only looked above her head. There was sweat on her face; the wrinkles shone like a bright net.

"Speak up, Grandma" the woman said. "What's your name? We must have your history, you know. Have you been here before? What seems to be the trouble with you?"

75 Old Phoenix only gave a twitch to her face as if a fly were bothering her.

"Are you deaf?" cried the attendant.

But then the nurse came in.

"Oh, that's just old Aunt Phoenix," she said. "She doesn't come for herself—she has a little grandson. She makes these trips just as regular as clockwork. She lives away back off the Old Natchez Trace." She bent down. "Well, Aunt Phoenix, why don't you just take a seat? We won't keep you standing after your long trip." She pointed.

The old woman sat down, bolt upright in the chair.

"Now, how is the boy?" asked the nurse.

80 Old Phoenix did not speak.

"I said, how is the boy?"

But Phoenix only waited and stared straight ahead, her face very solemn and withdrawn into rigidity.

"Is his throat any better?" asked the nurse. "Aunt Phoenix, don't you hear me? Is your grandson's throat any better since the last time you came for the medicine?"

85   With her hand on her knees, the old woman waited, silent, erect,   85 and motionless, just as if she were in armor.

"You mustn't take up our time this way, Aunt Phoenix," the nurse said. "Tell us quickly about your grandson, and get it over. He isn't dead, is he?"

At last there came a flicker and then a flame of comprehension across her face, and she spoke.

"My grandson. It was my memory had left me. There I sat and forgot why I made my long trip."

"Forgot?" The nurse frowned. "After you came so far?"

90   Then Phoenix was like an old woman begging a dignified for-   90 giveness for waking up frightened in the night. "I never did go to school—I was too old at the Surrender," she said in a soft voice. "I'm an old woman without an education. It was my memory fail me. My little grandson, he is just the same, and I forgot it in the coming."

"Throat never heals, does it?" said the nurse, speaking in a loud, sure voice to Old Phoenix. By now she had a card with something written on it, a little list. "Yes, Swallowed lye. When was it—January—two—three years ago—"

Phoenix spoke unasked now. "No, missy, he not dead, he just the same. Every little while his throat begin to close up again, and he not able to swallow. He not get his breath. He not able to help himself. So the time come around, and I go on another trip for soothing medicine."

"All right. The doctor said as long as you came to get it you could have it," said the nurse. "But it's an obstinate case."

"My little grandson, he sit up there in the house all wrapped up, waiting by himself," Phoenix went on. "We is the only two left in the world. He suffer and it don't seem to put him back at all. He got a sweet look. He going to last. He wear a little patch quilt and peep out, holding his mouth open like a little bird. I remembers so plain now. I not going to forget him again, no, the whole enduring time. I could tell him from all the others in creation."

95   "All right." The nurse was trying to hush her now. She brought   95
her a bottle of medicine. "Charity," she said, making a check mark in
a book.

Old Phoenix held the bottle close to her eyes and then carefully
put it into her pocket.

"I thank you," she said.

"It's Christmas time, Grandma," said the attendant. "Could I give
you a few pennies out of my purse?"

"Five pennies is a nickel," said Phoenix stiffly.

100   "Here's a nickel," said the attendant.   100

Phoenix rose carefully and held out her hand. She received the
nickel and then fished the other nickel out of her pocket and laid it
beside the new one. She stared at her palm closely, with her head on
one side.

Then she gave a tap with her cane on the floor.

"This is what come to me to do," she said. "I going to the store
and buy my child a little windmill they sells, make out of paper. He
going to find it hard to believe there such a thing in the world. I'll
march myself back where he waiting, holding it straight up in this
hand."

She lifted her free hand, gave a little nod, turned round, and
walked out of the doctor's office. Then her slow step began on the
stairs, going down.

Questions on Meaning

1. Phoenix Jackson is contrasted to the hunter who talks to her in the wood. What does Welty achieve by contrasting her to this bold young man with a gun?
2. Phoenix says that she was "too old at the Surrender" to have learned to read. She is a woman who knew slavery. What kind of education did she gain from her experience, and how does that learning differ from schooling?
3. The ailing grandson for whom Phoenix walks so far almost seems to be a dream of the old woman's imagination. He is her only family, and in the end she goes to buy him a toy with her two nickels. Why doesn't she buy food or more medicine for the next month? What does the windmill represent in her relationship with the child?

Questions on Rhetorical Strategy and Style

1. Welty said that she wrote this tale after having seen an old woman walk along a path on a winter day. How does her description of Phoenix Jackson bring to mind that experience?
2. Why does Phoenix put on her shoes when she gets to town? What does that act do to the narrative line of the story?
3. The reader is taken into the mind of the old woman, Phoenix, and brought to see and feel through her eyes and skin. What is the effect of that perspective? What do we learn about multiculturalism and diversity by being in her consciousness?

Writing Assignments

1. Consider a time when you have spent your money on something pretty or foolish rather than on something practical. Why did you do so, and what was the result?
2. Welty uses her stories to show rather than to tell. Write a description of something or some place that gives the kind of vivid detail that Welty presents. What is the difference between showing and telling?
3. What knowledge can be gained from very elderly members of your community? Interview at least one elderly person. Ask about that person's life experiences, and then write a paper bringing those experiences into some kind of connection with your own.